Oral history is already recognised as an important historical resource, and this study looks at how oral histories are constructed and how they should be interpreted. It also argues for a deeper understanding of their oral and social characteristics. Oral accounts of past events are also guides to the future, as well as being social activities in which tellers claim authority to speak to particular audiences. Like written history and literature, orality has its shaping genres and aesthetic conventions. It likewise has to be interpreted through them.

The argument is illustrated through a wide range of examples of memory, narration and oral tradition, including many from Europe and the Americas, and with a recurrent focus on oral histories from the Jlao Kru of Liberia, with whom Elizabeth Tonkin, an anthropologist, has carried out extensive research. She also draws on and integrates the insights of a range of other disciplines, such as literary criticism, linguistics, history, psychology, and communication and cultural studies. Her study points to the importance of crossing the disciplinary boundaries which close off oral productions as 'literary', 'historical', 'traditional' or 'popular'.

Cambridge Studies in Oral and Literate Culture 22

NARRATING OUR PASTS

Cambridge Studies in Oral and Literate Culture

Edited by PETER BURKE and RUTH FINNEGAN

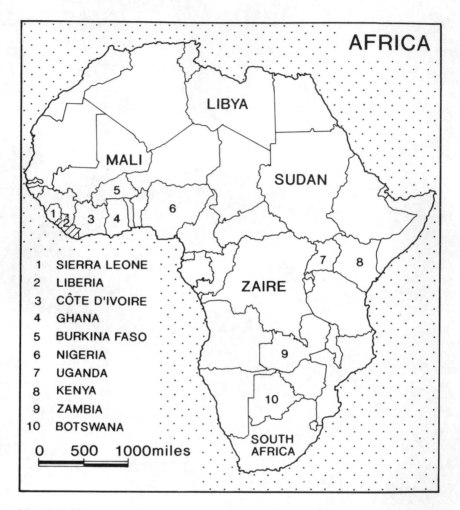

AFRICA

LIBYA

MALI

SUDAN

5

1
2 3 4

6

1   SIERRA LEONE
2   LIBERIA
3   CÔTE D'IVOIRE
4   GHANA
5   BURKINA FASO
6   NIGERIA
7   UGANDA
8   KENYA
9   ZAMBIA
10 BOTSWANA

7   8

ZAIRE

9

10

SOUTH
AFRICA

0   500   1000miles

Map 1. African countries referred to in the text.

NARRATING OUR PASTS

The social construction of oral history

ELIZABETH TONKIN

Professor of Social Anthropology, The Queen's University of Belfast

CAMBRIDGE
UNIVERSITY PRESS

Published by the Press Syndicate of the University of Cambridge
The Pitt Building, Trumpington Street, Cambridge CB2 1RP
40 West 20th Street, New York, NY 10011–4211, USA
10 Stamford Road, Oakleigh, Melbourne 3166, Australia

First published 1992
Reprinted 1994
First paperback edition 1995

Printed in Great Britain at the University Press, Cambridge

A catalogue record for this book is available from the British Library

Library of Congress cataloguing in publication data

Tonkin, Elizabeth.
Narrating our pasts: the social construction of oral history /
Elizabeth Tonkin.
        p.   cm. (Cambridge studies in oral and literate culture:)
Includes bibliographical references and index.
ISBN 0 521 40133 X (hardcover)
1. Oral history. I. Title II. Series.
D16.14.T66   1992
907'.2 – dc20   91–12506   CIP

ISBN 0 521 40133 X hardback
ISBN 0 521 48463 4 paperback

Remembering...
My parents Sylvia and Roy Tonkin, and the victims of
Liberian conflict

CONTENTS

xi

ILLUSTRATIONS

Maps

Plates

ACKNOWLEDGMENTS

Writing a book on the social construction of history and how others' lives shape our own consciousness makes one extremely aware of all the influences that have shaped the book itself. There are so many debts I would like to acknowledge. I should first thank the citizens of Sasstown who taught me about their culture and about the significance of oral history. Amongst the many Jlao historians and commentators – some sadly now dead – it feels invidious to choose names, but I remember with especial gratitude just some of them, who are rarely named in the text: Anna B. Nagbe, E. S. Togba, G. S. Jebo, General J. N. Blamo, S. B. Panti, Rev. E. M. Nagbe, Sergeant P. S. Broh, F. 'Marquis' Nagbe, Adolphus B. Kofa, Agatha T. Kofa, and Frank Nimene of Grand Cess.

As I complete this book, Liberians are suffering greatly through war, and many are refugees. The account of Liberia that I give is based on work completed before this unhappy time. It was facilitated by many government officials, and I have received over the years much help from officers and faculty members of the University of Liberia. Financial support came from the (then) Social Science Research Council, the Nuffield Foundation, and the University of Birmingham, where too Chris Wickham commented on all the chapters, Kim Davies, Sue Gilbert and Marlene Wray helped to lick the manuscript into shape, Jean Dowling drew the maps, and Geoff Dowling prepared the photographs for publication. Some passages of the book have already appeared in Tonkin 1988a and 1990a.

And then there are family, friends, teachers, students, colleagues and books: 'You have always been in others and you will remain in others. And what does it matter to you if later on it is called your memory? That will be you, the you that enters the future and becomes a part of it.'

A NOTE ON ORTHOGRAPHY

Words in languages other than English are italicised when first cited, unless they are being quoted at length. The conventions of authors' sources are followed. For Kru sources recorded by myself I have adapted the transcribers' orthography, which was developed in the Methodist Church of Liberia Literacy Program, except for most proper names where other versions are in use. Kru words often referred to are not italicised subsequently, and are given anglicised spelling. Kru consonants are given their nearest English form; l stands for a 'single flap' which may be heard as r or l. Kru vowels are open or nasalised: nasals are rendered here by n. The vowel system includes 'tight' or 'pharyngeal' vowels: ʌ represents 'pharyngeale' e (as opposed to 'open' e (ɛ) and 'acute' e); φ represents 'pharyngeal' o (as opposed to 'open' o (ɔ) and o as in 'oh').

INTRODUCTION

The argument

> The past is myself, my own history, the seed of my present thoughts,
> the mould of my present disposition.

The words are R. L. Stevenson's, and they were borrowed by Christabel
Bielenberg for the title of her autobiography, which describes her life in
Germany between 1934 and 1945. These for her were central and dramatic
years. She recalls a past which was 'another country' in more than one
sense. She experienced Nazi Germany at first hand and she can tell
outsiders what it was like from within, looking back on a world that has
thankfully gone.[1] But she was not formed by the same pasts that had
moulded the people she came to live amongst. Her own background
affected her perceptions and directed her actions, even as she also became
involved in events in Germany that in turn would change and develop her
too. Their effects would live on in her, the 'seed of present thoughts'.

We can look at the past in different ways. To historians, the past is
'another country' which we can try to reconstruct from the traces left
behind. If there are living survivors, they can be asked – or, as with
Christabel Bielenberg, they can ask themselves – what their memories will
yield about life in that different country. It is also possible to explore, in
Stevensonian vein, *how* the past is 'myself'; in what ways could it mould our
dispositions? Why is it that across the world, people seem to remember
different aspects of the past? These questions interest me as a social
anthropologist, and in this book I try to answer them.

I look at the interconnections between memory, cognition and history,
and show how they help to shape our individual selves. Individuals are also
social beings, formed in interaction, reproducing and also altering the
societies of which they are members. I argue that 'the past' is not only a
resource to deploy, to support a case or assert a social claim, it also enters
memory in different ways and helps to structure it. Literate or illiterate, we
are our memories. We also try to shape our futures in the light of past
experience – or what we understand to have been past experience – and,
representing how things were, we draw a social portrait, a model which is a
reference list of what to follow and what to avoid. The model is part of the
processes we live in and call 'group', 'family', 'institutions', 'society' and it

helps to reproduce or modify them. Sometimes these processes and structures from the past are overturned; then there is a social revolution.

In all this huge web of life, *representations* of the past have a significant and very varied part. In order to think about the past, one must represent aspects of it to oneself, or to others. The representations need not even be verbal, but as soon as a representation is communicated or interrogated, words enter in. And as 'the present' is a perpetually disappearing moment, so all languages allow their speakers to refer back. References to past events are continual, and judgments about them, explicit as well as assumed, occur in everyday conversation. They can be elaborated into lengthy discourses, but such discourses are not wholly distinct in either method or intent from briefer reference. Written accounts such as history books are, by the same token, shaping representations which operate through a second-order sign system, since the code of literacy represents the phonology and semiotics of language.

In more than one language, the same word – in English it is 'history' – has to stand both for 'the past', history-as-lived, and 'representation of pastness', history-as-recorded. It is easy to slip from one meaning to another because of the different ways that the past lives in the present and judgments about events which are themselves representations of pastness can also be a form of action. The ambiguity will be found in this book sometimes, because it is there in the sources, and also because the main focus is on the act of representing. I argue that one cannot detach the oral representation of pastness from the relationship of teller and audience in which it was occasioned.

Because history-as-recorded is a representation, it must be understood as such. Verbal representations are chains of words, either spoken or written, ordered in patterns of discourse that represent events. Arguments and opinions too are forms of words. When we grasp a historical fact or interpretation, we have ourselves made an extremely complex bunch of interpretations to do so. Facts and opinions do not exist as free-standing objects, but are produced through grammar and larger conventions of discourse which in turn are interpreted by hearer or reader in order to register as such. Meanings exist because people mean and others believe they understand what was meant.

The different conventions of discourse through which speakers tell history and listeners understand them can be called *genres*. A genre signals that a certain kind of interpretation is called for. To literates, for example, the layout of a sonnet suggests that one should not interpret the words as one would a mathematical equation. Genres provide a 'horizon of expectation' to a knowledgeable audience that cannot be derived from the semantic content of a discourse alone.[2] Since genres are the level of discourse through which interpretation is organised, any analyst seeking to understand a verbal message must learn the genre. Oracy has its genres just as literacy does, but their conditions include the circumstances of orality. Whereas literate genres are signalled by internal and external form, such as the sonnet's rules of scansion and its visual representation in fourteen lines, the oral genre can be signalled by the occasion, or the status of the teller.

When we consider that representations of pastness – a cumbersome phrase, but more exact here than 'history' – are made by persons in interaction, situated in real time and space, we can see that however modest the speaker's aim, they are purposeful social actions. This is so whether the past-oriented reference is a long, structured discourse, or just a brief comment or allusion. In either case, too, interlocutors must share knowledge of language rules and conventions of phrase to make sense to one another. So an outsider also needs to understand the mode or genre in which the temporal accounts occur in order to grasp the character of the interlocutors' social action and to evaluate the information that the account conveys. Such understanding has to be triadic:

> To grasp their historical intent we need to view [representations of pastness] as literature; to grasp their literary mode we need to view them as part of social action; to grasp their role as social action we need to see their historical intent.[3]

This book, therefore, connects the characteristics of tellers with those of their audiences, and both with the structure of their narrations. The representations of pastness that these interconnections involve include the occasion, when teller and listener intersect at a point in time and space, as well as the times recounted. So the temporalities in question include the tellers' own pasts, till that moment of telling, and the adjustments they make to their tales on account of their listeners' pasts. And, as Alessandro Portelli points out, 'to tell a story is to take arms against the threat of time ... the telling of a story preserves the teller from oblivion'. Told as it must be at a specific time and in a phase of irreversible time, the tale itself creates a special time, 'a time outside time'. 'Time is one of the essential things stories are about.'[4]

The representations of pastness discussed here are oral ones, because orality is the basic human mode of communication, and although peoples all over the world now use literate means to represent pastness, and written records have existed for many hundreds of years, the business of relating past and present for social ends has for most of the time been done orally; it still is so. The argument is the stronger when one understands how memory and cognition are interconnected in highly literate and non-literate peoples alike. Where there is little or no literacy, there can still be skilled historians, and part of the book is devoted to understanding how their representations of pastness are constructed. I argue that such 'oracy' – skilled orality – is found among literates as well, but literacy has far greater prestige, and so it is literate skills that receive study.

That genres are social products of particular temporal and economic conditions, realised in varying interpretations by different audiences, must be as true of literary examples as it is of oral ones. In this book, I concentrate the discussion on oracy. Actually, it is not as easy to distinguish literate from oral as some suppose; I return to this point later in the Introduction. 'Historioracy' is here treated as a counterpart of historiography, and I suggest it too can be studied, with varied traditions that can be analysed comparatively. An important point is that in oracy, as in literacy, genres, practices and traditions develop and change: the difficulty is to recover past states. But the very conditions of rapid change that cause oral recordists' struggles to collect material 'before it's too late' often give us the opportunity to see changes in the making – as they have always been.

In this book, the construction of 'oral history' is treated as a profoundly social process which is also bound up simultaneously with different temporalities. To some, a social perspective and a historical one are antithetical, the one looking at connections over time, the other to relationships at any moment and so in a sense timeless. In their practices, the direction of historians' and anthropologists' or sociologists' interests will certainly be different, but insofar as they are studying human beings in society, the theoretical premises of their enquiries ought to be consonant. To use one sort of analysis for the 'social' part of a practice and a contradictory analysis for its 'historical' aspects makes for very unsatisfactory conclusions when the practice is examined as a whole: this is not a case of opposed theories in obstinate co-existence, as with wave and particle theories. The model of social cognition and historical production presented here is intended as a unified model, with which to understand human beings situated in time and space, where societies, ideas and material conditions change.

A key question is the nature and status of the individual, and I consider it throughout: what is this self that the past 'is', and of what significance to others? When we consider that representations of pastness enter continually into different kinds of discourse and are produced in different kinds of society, any discussion leads inevitably to debates on *agency*, that is to the status of the 'I' who authors statements, and of the *subject*, a topic in literary and social analysis alike. Again, I argue for a model which takes into account both the material conditions whose importance can be recognised in social theory and the shaping power of language and form which is assumed in literary criticism, even though its character is debated through competing theories there, just as social theorists argue over the primacy of class and material factors of production.

The uses of illustration and case studies

I have tried to illustrate and develop my argument through examples from different times and places. Given careful thought to their conditions of production, and following the argument that accounts of pastness are socially constructed through the intervening power of genre, apparently diverse cases should be comparable, not taxonomically, whereby 'a genre' is identified according to its degree of fit, by form, into a universal classification, but by comparing social conditions of production and aesthetic practices. On this basis, it becomes possible to recognise oral genres, not just literary ones, and to compare the oral performances of literates and non-literates, as I discuss further below. Several of my sources are from Europe and America, other examples are from Africa. The choice of African material is due to my own background, and it is also the background of much debate on oral art. Students of oral history in Britain have looked to Africa for examples of what is presumed to be a live 'oral tradition' there. Ruth Finnegan and Jan Vansina, two leading writers on oracy, have worked in Africa and use African examples.

There are two sources from which I draw several examples. One is Yorubaland, whose millions of members live in South West Nigeria, and also across the border in Benin. Their rich oral arts are now being recorded in writing and have received skilled analysis, so it is possible to begin to see the range of Yoruba oral genres, and how they interconnect. For all the interest in African orality, 'it is sobering to reflect that after well over a century of collecting material, there is scarcely a single African society for which we have a comprehensive literary record'.[5]

The second source for examples is a small polity in Liberia, known in English as Sasstown, and in their own Kru language as Jlao. I have lived there and listened to people's histories, so I can exemplify from Jlao genres in their social context which I have studied myself. This is not a book about Jlao or its oral history, but an outline of Jlao history, its recent social organisation and the kinds of historians I found there in the 1970s is presented in Chapter 1. Jlao is focalised there, so that readers can get a rounder sense of what oral history accounts can be like in communities where literacy is still not omnipresent.

Some readers may prefer to use the Jlao case study for reference only; it contains after all, as any African case study must do, unfamiliar detail for many readers, and illustrations of genres whose contents are very different from those of industrial Europe or America. One reason for starting with this case study is that by later chapters, when I refer to Jlao examples among others, readers will hopefully share a little of that common context which all speakers and listeners in oral genres presuppose. One then begins, haltingly, to get some sense of how oral genres work in performance. The complexity and richness of some oral genres can only be asserted and exemplified in a general study like this one, but it's important to see that oral historians have powers which become clearer by detailed study, as in any work of art.

The details of content and construction that I give from my own findings, or from the publications of others, are intended to illustrate the skills and achievements of oral tellers. I recorded accounts by the outstanding historian Sieh Jeto which continued over several hours and were powerfully organised. When one considers that appreciation of such work comes, as when reading a book or attending a play, from an accumulating response to a long and substantially built whole, with many levels and dimensions, it's easy to see that to do justice to his art would take a book on its own. His art cannot be properly demonstrated here, the more frustratingly so since narratives of this scale and scope have been largely ignored or discounted in studies of oracy. Sieh's skills in organisation and plotting are discussed in the last part of Chapter 1, where I argue that it is through these means he directs interpretation; they are part of the meaning.[6]

Structuring conventions

It follows from the argument of this book that professional historians who use the recollections of others cannot just scan them for useful facts to pick out, like currants from a cake. Any such facts are so embedded in the representation that it directs an interpretation of them, and its very ordering, its plotting and its metaphors bear meaning too. However, if you share the author's conventions of interpretation, your own matching skills are deployed so automatically that no gap is recognised between yourself and the text. The meaning seems transparent.

One advantage of examining unfamiliar material is that this transparency vanishes. Having to translate, one finds words and phrases recalcitrant because they are embedded in different contexts from those presupposed in one's own language, and they segment and categorise the world in different ways. Thus, Jlao Kru *tú* means 'tree' and smaller species; it also refers to many objects made of wood, such as drums. English 'wood' refers to the substance too, but it labels many trees together, not on their own. More difficult are the very different ways in which languages code temporality, as I illustrate in Chapter 4. Here, apparent transparency can be very misleading, but, equally, a good knowledge of the language may reveal how people are using the resources of their language's tense and aspect systems to foreground attention or indicate the status of a report; the import of oral histories may obviously be affected by such means.

Although some language rules seem absolute, others can be flexible: people play on them. Since languages point to existing worlds, they have systems of address which work politically. Speakers may compete, not only for the right to hold the floor, but to have their own version of events accepted. I discuss in Chapter 2 how speakers must both authorise what they say as best they can and also orient themselves to their subject. They have to take a point of view on an event and on its relation to themselves and to their interlocutors. 'Bias', therefore, is an essential part of any communication, and not a flaw to which oral tellers are particularly prone.

Each language has its own system within which these claims and orientations have to be made. To the English, Indonesian languages with five distinct styles to use for different status relationships seem highly constricting, but to Indonesian speakers these styles can be a rich means of countering others' claims. Outsiders can find British language use exceedingly tricky. Ours is often a listener's game, marking a speaker up or down on some tiny nuance of accent or phrase. Most people don't recognise, consciously, that there are language-bound expectations about the placing of central and peripheral topics; they may then hear other placings as 'incompetent' or 'stupid'.[7]

Representations of pastness have no unique linguistic status. They work like any other discourse and are subject to the same constitutive conditions. They are composed of *mimesis* and *diegesis*, to use Aristotle's terms, that is the representation of direct speech, and the description of nonverbal events. A story is a mixture of 'a non-verbal matter which the narrative must represent as well as it can and a verbal matter which presents itself and which the narrative need simply quote'.[8] We can pause to note, however, that a narrator must re-present in time as well as through words, and that the direct speech is also a re-play of action. Any sustained speech, or writing, which includes more than one sentence is organisationally not reducible to the analyses of its component sentences. Listeners/readers make connections between the sentences and interpret them not wholly as isolates but in relation to one another. The successivity of sentences makes discourse because we simultaneously expect their connectivity. This cohesion of discourse depends on presuppositions which are not all deducible from the verbal surface.

If we are told 'The king died. His cousin was king', the 'his' of the second sentence must, by linguistic rule, refer 'cousin' to 'king' in the first sentence. Contextual evidence is required for us to evaluate whether the succession is normal or abnormal, but we must assume that the cousin succeeded and not the other way round because that is what the English sentence order tells us. This tiny example suggests the complexity of knowledge tucked away in any narrative, the possible linguistic opacity of the focus or direction of narrators to their subject matter, and the importance of understanding how the discourse is constructed if one wants to understand its presentation of time.

Jonathan Culler said, speaking as a structuralist, 'Discourse has the power to produce events: events of persuasion, understanding, revelation etc.'[9] A researcher and informant engage in discourse, but it is not the same type of discourse as the researcher's report. The discourse structures of conversation are also sometimes in sentences which are shared between speakers. 'You mean that' – 'Yes, that what one starts' 'Another can finish!' 'It's not even as simple as that. Conversation goes on even when presuppositions are not all shared.' Oral discourse can likewise be a lengthy monologue, itself varying in style and embedding in a maze of discursiveness riddles, proverbs, folk tales and myths – forms which are often studied on their own as examples of 'oral literature'. The narratives of Sieh Jeto are of this kind: their mode is historical, their means varied.

The conventions of discourse structure it at many levels. Historians have labelled as 'myth' what seem unrealistic ways of representing the past, but it can sometimes be shown that mythic structures encode history, that is they register actual happenings or significant changes. 'Realism', on the other hand, is an equally culture-bound judgment of likelihood. An audience always has expectations about the nature of reality, and judges whether the linguistic and genre patterns, as well as the content of the discourse, are appropriate for its representation. The qualifications of the teller must be scrutinised. 'Realism' includes criteria of intelligibility and rationality which are open to dispute, as for instance between those who believe in Divine intervention or in witchcraft and those who do not.

Truth, that elusive historical goal, can also lie in the intersection of narrator and discourse, where we have to see how accounts are authorised. The polysemy is significant, for the act of authoring is a claim to authority. How it is achieved varies generically and politically and culturally, as does the kind of truth claimed, expected or accepted. The historian who adjudges another only as an imperfect source of facts is probably using a different set of criteria from that other, but both sets derive from authorisations. There are, for instance, socio-political conditions determining the authority of the narrator, or which the narrator invokes as guarantees. Philosophers may look for truth conditions in the sentential structure of language itself: that is, discourse is the locus of logical consistency and therefore of authenticity. A genre of discourse can carry with it a claim to a particular kind of truth. How, asked Frank Kermode, do we know that the Gospels mean more than they say? He answers from the properties of the narratives and the necessity of their interpretation. Their authenticity is a claim embodied in the narrative.[10]

Truth conditions are different when Jlao Kru appear in court. It is accepted that they may 'deny' what actually happened; it is up to their opponents to prove them wrong. But this adversarial limitation of liability occurs under conditions which do not include, as they would in my society, the imposition of an oath. The question may then arise whether a particular description of the past is an adversarial narrative of this kind or not. The social context of delivery, its occasion, may be definitive, and not the narrative content.

There is another crucial connection between narrator and narrative. An apparently obvious but still often missed point follows from the condition that narration entails a relation to events described and the choices of relation – which can vary from sentence to sentence – *are* points of view. It is that these points of view need not be held personally and subjectively by their narrators. A first-person narrator in a fiction is created by the author. Indeed, the existence of a real me in a narration depends on your theories of self. Likewise, since not all literature shows the self-conscious split between narrating and authoring that is evident and played upon in fiction and drama today, there are obvious questions as to the conditions in which this sense of selfhood and indeed alienation occur. Oral narrators can also create complex selves, as we shall see.

Senses of history and its social structuring

People talk of 'the past' so as to distinguish 'now' from a different 'then'. At the same time, every 'now' is the consequence of many 'thens', of vastly different durations, in an amalgam unique to each person experiencing it. What goes on now is interpreted from previous knowledge, from memory. The present we live in is built from past events. Family, school, work skills: these are practices which may have a much longer life than anyone suspects, or, sometimes, be no sooner invented than they seem out of date. We live in other people's pasts whether we know it or not and whether or not we want to do so.

What history we actually know varies widely too. Appreciation of pastness may be a practical consciousness, people doing what they know how to do and realising that it has been done before. At the other extreme are the discursive accounts of academic historians. As schoolteachers wryly acknowledge, memory depends on interest, and pupils who seem to remember nothing may be able to list football results for years back in immense detail. I suspect that if one could reconstruct what numbers of people actually assume the past to be made up of,[11] the results would appear to be a muddle of sub-categories, and not at all a good match with professional world-histories. It is easy to be a university specialist in, say, nineteenth-century American political history and yet as hazy over the difference between Jurassic and Paleolithic as most fifteen-year-olds.

How people perceive the past varies too. An obvious example is historical painting: why is it that in the Middle Ages, 'Alexander the Great or Moses were represented ... as knights, in the armour of the day'? In medieval times evidences survived which could suggest that fashions and social patterns had changed, but Peter Burke and others have argued that it was not till Renaissance times that there was a slow acceptance that laws could change, that the Bible had not existed eternally but been written down by humans, in our world of time, and that the evidence of eyewitnesses and ancient 'authorities' was not of the same kind.[12]

Some think that ordinary Europeans and Americans only began to think of the past as qualitatively different from the present in the late eighteenth century.[13] Our interest in pastness can continue to change. There have been out-door museums, or even preserved birthplaces of well-known people, only in some countries and in recent times. In 1971, I looked at a hill covered with scrub, with occasional ruins barely visible, which we were told had been an important industrial site. Since then, Blists Hill has been cleared, many of the ruins restored and further houses and massive engineering transported there, to be testimonies, in the Ironbridge Gorge Museum, to the Industrial Revolution which we can say was born in this steep Shropshire valley of the River Severn where cast-iron was developed.

Blists Hill 'presents' what is at the same time a distant past to some and to others still part of their experience. Children are puzzled by 'old money' familiar to adults, charcoal irons are recalled by the very old and also by those who may be still using them where there is no electricity. The volunteers whose imagination, knowledge and hard labour have 'restored' the area had a very different consciousness of the past than the many, many others who just saw grubby desolation. 'Industrial archaeology' seemed an impertinent oxymoron, a contradiction in terms. Now, people have caught up with the fact that much industry is no longer modern but history. Nostalgia replaces distaste at a spoiled countryside, but it is part of a much wider enthusiasm for viewing the past in the present (a safely inaccessible past, conserved as jam is different from fruit).

The social structuration of recall

Such changes of interest and perception about pastness and its significances cannot be explained purely in individualist terms. We can see this in debates over what should be taught as history. The arguments on this question arise partly because our identities are both personal and social, as I show throughout this book. Individuals may therefore be supported or threatened by public representations of pastness that seem either to guarantee their identity or to deny its significance.[14]

Understandings of pastness vary immensely, as other examples in this book also show. Why did a 'sense of history' as that is now understood develop in the Europe of the Renaissance? The answers attempted by historians are social ones. A changing interest in the past is part of a present consciousness, and changes in social conditions appear to alter that consciousness. Comparative examples show how this can be. If I ask how many generations of your family you can name, the answers could be between two and thirty generations. Thirty generations take some memorising, which most people in most cultures are not required to do, but the fact that it can be done implies special interest or incentives, not some special memory IQ. People remember what they need to remember, and in some societies, genealogical knowledge is an important resource, used to support the legitimacy of a claim to political office or to land. The very organisation of social life may be expressed in terms of genealogical relationships (see pp. 110–11).

The differences between the kinds of account that people produce can be related to the different kinds of society of which they are members. Comparing the ways that some Libyan peoples who are organised in what anthropologists call lineages represent pastness with the recall of Spaniards, who were sharply contrasted by generation, John Davis found that the 'genealogically' structured history of lineage members

> emphasises the identity of people of different ages and the continuity of their mutual loyalties, the consistency of their mutual attitudes and actions. Genealogy provides a structure in which life and loyalty are mutually determining, and are granted by members of one generation to members of the next. Generation produces a structure of reactive reinterpretation in which the emphasis, at any rate in Belmonte, is on discontinuity: the fathers of the [present] controllers got involved in politics, sent their sons to war, and that shall never happen again.[15]

Davis argues that these differences in historical 'text' are produced by different social structuring and in turn contribute to a different history-as-lived. It is not accidental that the ideologies of Gaddafi's Libya remain 'genealogical'.

The connection between society and history is not so simple as this abbreviated example might perhaps imply; I suggest that we can identify a variety of significant mediations between the social practice and the content of the representation. To tell history is to act, but to act in a verbal mode. As the collection of evidences in a 'heritage museum' shows, there is also a difference between a relic and the recognition that it is a relic. To interpret it as such, and to represent 'our' past, according to whom we recognise as 'us', requires all the symbolising and cognitive activity of language, which shapes and constrains our concepts. The practice and act of recall, I further argue, is itself social and 'artful' and is mediated through the development of genre.

A further, crucial mediation occurs through memory. To understand how history-as-lived is connected to history-as-recorded, we have to look at the actors concerned, who are living and developing in times that also change. It's easy to see that explanations like 'That was before you were born' help to give a child a sense of finite intervention in the world (later, the thought will come 'that'll be after I'm dead'). In such ways too, a family identity is built up. A much more radical proposal is to see memory as the site of the social practices that make us, together with the cognitive practices through which we understand society.

It seems that infants are born with the ability to initiate and to organise, but they have to develop many basic cognitive skills through action which is largely inter-action. Nearly every child learns to talk, but has to learn to do so in a language – or languages – learned in interaction with other humans. Socialisation makes us social beings, that is, gendered, members of family groups, classes, ethnicities, speakers of certain languages, and though it is perfectly possible for people to change social affiliations and trajectories, they have to do so from given material–social conditions and with already existent cognitive abilities and social expectations.

The memories with which people interpret the present and go on to make the future are also social in that we recall social relationships, and scenes experienced along with other people; so that memories are less individual than is commonly supposed in a culture of individualism. These memories are means of social reproduction in the Marxist sense. The media of lived society and personal identity are thus also constitutive of them as well. It is from memory and stored schemata that one moves, when faced with new experiences to be interpreted and enacted.

Amongst such models, existing forms or genres are crucial when we seek to transmit our ideas verbally. It may not be helpful to call such genres history, in distinction to memory, for in fact one cannot always distinguish their operation. And, in these complex and very far from automatic or uncontradictory processes of social formation and identification, literacy, for all its enormous power and irreversible effect on the communication and preservation of knowledge, still plays only a small part. In this book, then, the construction of oral history is investigated as a profoundly social practice, but it is also argued that oracy implies skilled production, and its messages are transmitted through artistic means. An oral testimony cannot be treated only as the repository of facts and errors of fact.

Oracy and literacy

Can such artistic performances really be found outside 'traditional cultures'? Readers may still be wondering if it is proper to compare

'Western' oral representations of pastness with examples of oral history from Africa, New Guinea, Australia ... Can orality be the same in the heavily literate and industrialised countries of Europe and the USA and in 'traditional oral cultures'? Before considering the differences, we can note some similarities.

On the one hand, 'traditional oral cultures' are hard to find. All the world is now divided into nation states and their governments use literate means of communication to rule. Even predominantly oral people know about writing and have members of their community in school. At the same time there are actually millions of illiterates in western countries (many of whom completed school, to the incredulity of African friends to whom I explained this point).

Literacy is a label which covers many different skills and kinds of use. There are those who can read but not write, or are able to recognise road signs but not to read shop names; and those who can manage their literate needs quite well, but would be defeated by the lexicon and syntax of most academic books. The line is not so easy to draw between 'able to read' and 'able to understand' – it is increasingly being recognised that reading and writing are cognitively complex practices.[16] In 1980, official British sources in Britain calculated that one million citizens were 'functionally illiterate'. Contemporary figures for the US were between 50 and 60 million![17] Such enormous numbers are sad evidence of educational failure and wasted job potential. 'Functional illiterates' can testify to the difficulties of survival as well as to social shames; how to read a street name? Use a telephone book when a doctor is needed in a hurry? Find TV programmes or football results from the paper? Fill in a tax form or use a bank? What do they say when the children cry 'Read me a story!' or they have to pass on the contents of a memo from their trade union? (These are real examples, which I encountered in teaching on a Right to Read programme.)

Yet functional illiterates do survive, as their great number itself testifies. Like all humans everywhere they use speech much more than writing and reading. The similarities between book-centred persons – like myself – cross continents and in many ways divide us from literate fellow citizens, and family, who, as we say, 'don't read' – and certainly don't read history books. There are increasing differences between the aficionadoes of old literacy and those of new oracy, that is, the new media from radio and film to TV, audio and video cassettes.[18] These media are becoming rapidly more familiar in the Third World, and everywhere that literacy is limited, they are obviously a powerful alternative means of communication.

Historically, imperialism has operated without literacy, and there have been kingdoms in Africa which developed sophisticated craft technologies and arts and whose leaders also subordinated and kept control of satellite polities with no other media of long-distance communication than word-of-mouth. The media of literacy, Babylonian clay tablets, Egyptian papyrus, wood paper and more recently electronic media have in addition facilitated different kinds of organisation and hence of control. People have therefore struggled to possess them – contemporary coup leaders immediately try to seize the local radio and TV stations as well as the Presidential palace.[19]

When understood in its real complexity, literacy can be seen as having changed the world, since the invention of writing systems profoundly altered the means of conserving, transmitting and scrutinising knowledge. Today's technologies depend on literacy, which is one reason why Jlao Kru farmers, say, are not very interested in it. Literate tax-collectors can cheat them, they know, but it is presumed that one pursues schooling seriously so as to take up an occupation other than farming. Literacy therefore takes you to town. With only a few radios and no TV, oracy in such a milieu has hardly any competitors, and, as speech is the source of both political action and of entertainment, the arts and genres of oracy are recognised and highly valued. In 'the West', on the contrary, literacy has enormous prestige even when people are not skilled in its uses, and oral skills can be devalued – but there is plenty of evidence that people still have them, and I discuss on pp. 54–5 some of the forms they take.

Literacy and oracy have co-existed for hundreds of years. Mass literacy is a very recent aim; Ernest Gellner has tied it to the rise of the modern state, as a consequence of the needs of industrialism.[20] In the Balkans, for example, famous types of heroic poetry continued to be practised as oral arts apart from but alongside the world of books. Such patterns of co-existence were until recently widespread, but, before gramaphone recording was invented, oral performances had to be written down if they were to be preserved, so we not only have to base our conclusions about most oral art on written versions, it's often a matter of scholarly debate what sort of relation there was between oral performance and the early works of European literature transmitted in manuscript. There is also very early and widespread evidence of material from written sources entering 'oral tradition', and, of course, vice versa.[21] To distinguish oracy and literacy is thus in practice quite complicated.

Because of all these interconnections, it is appropriate to bring together the apparently very different examples of oral material evidenced in this book. This does not mean their differences, above all the social conditions of their production, are not important to delineate. The complexity of what we can mean when we talk of literacy is matched by the complexity of orality, and so, although one can argue that literacy's entry into the world altered the dimensions of human consciousness, I do not accept all the claims made for literacy as in itself causing cognitive change. According to some of the extreme proponents of this view, no non-literate could produce a narrative like those of the Kru oral historian Sieh Jeto. Hearing his stories indeed spurred me into writing this book.

'Oral literature' versus 'oral history': destructive boundary-making

One reason for the simplistic distinctions between literate and oral mentalities is reliance on very impoverished notions of oral arts. If your paradigm of oracy is 'drum talk' – the use of drumbeats to convey messages – then oral mentality must indeed look limited.[22] Much argument in recent years has cited work on oral formulae (with the citations repeated at ever greater distance from the original sources), as if all oral art was a kind of heroic poem. The evidence of this book is very different, and I consider examples of recall by both European literates and African non-literates which range from the heroic to the prosaic. In Chapters 3 and 4, I also show that heroic genres must be seen like any other as forms of social action. Generated within a specific set of socio-political conditions, which can occur in different regions and periods, we can see too that they celebrate certain values only, but this does not mean that such values govern everyday life. The aesthetic, emotional and intellectual resources of a community should never be judged on the basis of one genre alone.

Heroic genres are, nevertheless, an instance of how indigenous categories of oral art may not separate literature either from history or from politics. Even the term 'oral art' derives from the entrenched divisions between academic disciplines. Scholars have looked for 'oral history' or 'oral literature'. For Africa, oral literature has meant largely folk tales, praise poems, proverbs, and epics. Although historians have been exhorted to look for evidence in these genres, that advice simply repeats the methodological expectations of historians versus literary critics, who study, supposedly, style and form. Each side looks for its own material to appropriate and this means a division of labour which in no way fits oral performances since these lack an oral apparatus of critical specialism and the social, political and economic institutionalisation which underpins professionalised literate commentary.

Of course, African countries also produce distinguished writers, as they do literary critics, historians and professional investigators of oral culture and performance.[23] But it is doubly a mistake to impose academic disciplinary labels on such oral art, whether the teller is Nigerian or British: first because a mismatch of genres is likely – tellers do not set out historical monographs, for instance – and second because these labels derive from quite different socio-economic conditions of production.

African oral literature, for instance, had to gain recognition on literates' terms in a world dominated by literates and it was not till 1970 that Ruth Finnegan provided an indispensable base-line for doing so in her *Oral Literature in Africa*, reviewing the scattered evidence already available in print, contextualising and sorting it out to show something of its scope and scale. This endeavour was, like those of Africanist historians and of

anthropologists before them, partly designed to argue that Africans were
not lacking supposedly civilised abilities. This meant demonstrating the
range of literary achievements – not just wild untutor'd art – in literary
terms.

Finnegan bypassed a sterile definitional debate by simply arguing that
there *is* a domain of literature, irrespective of writing.[24] She stressed the
oral characteristics, the performance characteristics, which mean that its
transcription is necessarily reductionist, a skeleton standing for a live body.
This broadened sense of literature still depended on an opposition with
'history' and 'law', so that its subject matter also fell into 'literary genres'.
H. M. and N. K. Chadwick, who had earlier produced a great pioneer
survey, *The Growth of Literature*, had mainly to rely on evidence written
down without the benefit of sound recording, and had necessarily far less to
say of the oral as a performance. They still made many useful observations
about oral in relation to written literature, and they did not confine
literature to imaginative art. While they were interested in what they
thought of as the germs of fiction, they essentially took literature to be
sustained verbal expression of any kind – celebrating action, classifying
knowledge, speculating about origins as well as lyric effusion and stylistic
virtuosity.

The Chadwicks' evolutionary assumptions must be modified today, but
they did identify a historical process, through which the oral domain
became narrowed until its most noticeable European forms did indeed
appear 'literary' ones. History not only became a literate domain, as law
largely did,[25] it was identified with literacy – the preliterate world was called
prehistory – and for archaeologists. Some scholars still argue that there
cannot be *oral* history. Obviously I do not agree with them, but discussions
of differences between orality and literacy are unprofitable without a sense
of their historically shifting territories which have also affected our
assumptions about the character of politics, law, literature...

Because this book talks about 'oral history', it too may encourage
disciplinary divisions. But it is not intended to do so. I have focused on
representations of pastness as a crucial feature of the social, and I argue
that to see how this is so, one must also recognise the powers of patterns
and presuppositions in discourse – as literary analysis can help us to do. In
other words, I argue that different disciplines must together be brought to
bear on phenomena which are themselves multivocal and capable of being
used in different ways, if we are to understand some crucial features of
ourselves. This understanding in turn throws light on specific genres which
can be labelled 'oral history' as well as to topics like the status of
anthropological enquiry, the achievements of oral art, the construction of
identity, self-awareness, and the nature of socialisation – topics, that is,
which are of interest to workers other than historians.

The argument has required attention to a diverse literature, and ventures into disciplines where I am not at home. To make clear the links between issues that are commonly separated by disciplinary divisions, I have tried to retain a consistent level of explanation, which means that experts in any field will find simplified accounts of what they know already. But it's my experience that the working terminology of one discipline can be treated as incomprehensible jargon by another. That is one reason for simplification, though experts may point to ignorance as another. I can only argue that unless we try somehow to scramble over our own specialism's walls, our understanding of the world will remain a prisoner's distant view.

Any selection of perspectives also means that relevant themes have to be left out. Many more aspects of time could be considered, including the ways it is used politically to distance others. While discussing structuralists' views of history and agency, I have not illustrated the structuring of discourse as it is revealed by structuralist interpretations. Along with the power of symbolism and metaphor to constitute meanings, this is a relatively familiar and well-studied topic.[26] And, since I argue that verbal representations are forms of action, and that authors are responsible for what they say, I try to avoid impersonal constructions. This allows the use of active verbs, but requires that they be given a subject. You may consider that the consequent authorial 'I' is an intrusion of personality into the decent obscurity of learned language. But, if you consider the arguments of this book, the 'I' will become an ambiguous persona, and your narrating agent.

1

JLAO, AN INTRODUCTORY CASE STUDY

Introduction

I begin with an introductory case study. A historical portrait of Jlao, a small community in Liberia, sets the context for a discussion of the ways in which representations of pastness are produced there. I then look at the occasions on which past events are evoked, the qualifications of the tellers, and the genres in which they work. I conclude with an account of the histories of Sieh Jeto and his narrative art.[1]

Anyone who makes comparisons from different languages or cultures faces the difficulty that audiences may need a lot of background knowledge if they are to appreciate why an example is significant. Insiders have this knowledge; it's the outsiders who have to make explicit what insiders take for granted. And it's a common paradox that the more knowledge you bring to data the richer your interpretation, the more new information you can elicit. Just because Jlao was a foreign culture to me, I had to bring together as many sources as I could to understand it: contemporary social detail from observation and informants, historical information from oral historians and conventional documents.

I have therefore to begin by offering an interpretation of the Jlao past which has been formed by the very practices that I wish to identify and discuss later in the book. But, as I show in a sketch of one historian, Sieh Jeto, and his work, some of the social changes that had occurred in Jlao before the memories of those living had been pondered and recorded by local thinkers. It is obvious too that participants in the political processes of the last eighty years had varying knowledge of the pre-colonial, autonomous government and their actions resulted in the fusion or assimilation of earlier processes with new imposed systems.

In order to investigate the roles of Jlao historians, and to get some context for their 'representations of pastness', I have to make some reconstruction of this precedent, independent Jlao world and its structures. When I describe some key aspects of Jlao social organisation, I explain some of the features that existed at the beginning of this century as well as those which continue today.

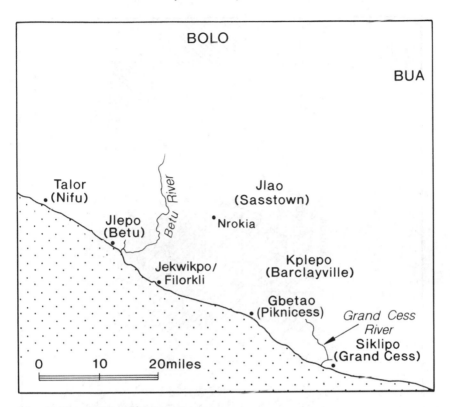

Map 2. Jlao and its neighbours.

Jlao/Sasstown: a portrait

(a) The polity's history

'Sasstown' and 'Jlao' – both terms are used. Sasstown is the official English name (English is Liberia's national language). Jlao names the people and their territory in their own language, a dialect of Kru (see Maps 2 and 3).[2] But the two labels are not quite synonymous. They have different referents and resonances which are part of the people's history. And as the sea brought most foreign influences and most internal movements came from the hinterland, so also has the polity been shaped both by indigenous competition and the contested assumption of control by the central government, still sometimes called 'Americans', the black settlers who set up the republic of Liberia in the nineteenth century.

If you fly down the coast of Liberia, you will see below a continuous band

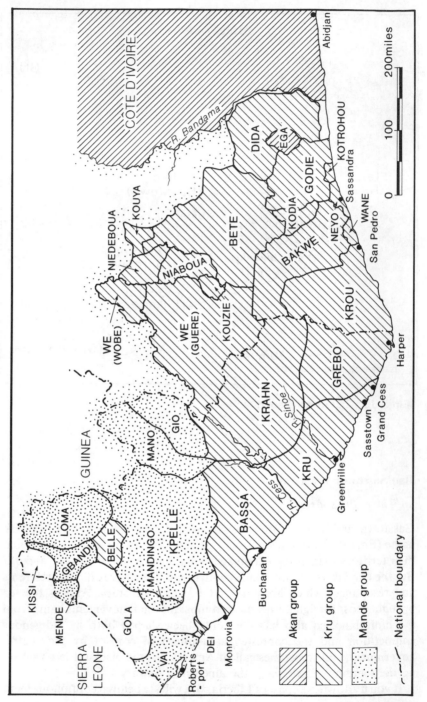

Map 3. Kru-group languages and their neighbours.

of surf, broken only by the mouths of rivers, themselves often marked by white. Offshore there are jagged rocks, and at intervals you may see up-turned canoes, looking like cigars, drawn up on the narrow beach bordered with coconut palms. The shore starts immediately: there are no cliffs, and it seems open and grassy. But there are also swamps, with mangroves, and inland stretches a heavy canopy of trees, uniform except for the round clearings which gradually present themselves as cultivated, and growing upland rice or cassava.   '

Buchanan, Greenville, Harper: these are the only obvious coastal towns east of Monrovia, with Robertsport to its west. Gradually, the stranger's eye takes in other houses, often zinc-roofed, some aligning the beach, and stretching, patchily, into the 'savannah mosaic' to form small, often very small settlements, some with a church visible, one or two larger buildings and a strip of red earth pointing inland, at which the plane may land.

Buchanan, Greenville and Harper are small places themselves but they have man-made harbours. It's hard to imagine that these other little settlements could have also been trading points, that European steamers anchored off them and that thousands of the local inhabitants travelled from this coast as contract labourers in every sort of job for the Europeans in Africa, from before the beginning of the nineteenth century to the beginning of World War II.

Sasstown is one of these former trading points. Since 1975, it has been possible to reach it by motor vehicle, and on that journey through the forests and rice clearings, diverging at a cluttered row of shops and houses from the single dirt road that links the country from end to end, onto a yet smaller one, and on through looming trees and small settlements, often of rectangular matted houses with thatched roofs, you reach Sasstown at the end of the road. You don't see the sea. That is out of sight, beyond the far houses of what prove to be a congeries of 'towns' (the word 'village' is not used in Liberia), contiguous, and, at first sight, hardly distinct.

These landward and seaward views of Sasstown reveal key features of the environment which have affected its social life and indeed continue to do so. The whole of what is today the Republic of Liberia is thinly populated (with less than 2 million people in the mid 1970s) and predominantly tropical rain-forest, now largely secondary, regenerated from rotating fallow cultivation of upland rice. Hundreds of miles are also planted with rubber trees, part (and sometimes relics) of a concession economy controlled by Firestone and some other American companies. At a distance inland from Jlao, iron-ore mining became another post-1945 foreign-owned interest. Iron had from much earlier had significance locally, but there was no gold,[3] or trade route bringing gold as the basis for local power, no massive output of slaves either; this area did not build up empires through trade, with or without Europeans. These found different goods, first the malagueta pepper which gave the coast its first European name, later water, rice and firewood to maintain the slaves on their ships, and some slaves too, but not many – the main exodus of people came later, was free, and largely temporary: the waged labour of 'kroomen', as they all came to be called.

It was presumably this 'emptiness' which led the European countries interested in Africa in the early nineteenth century to accept the attempts of Americans to settle it with colonies of black people. Britain was unwelcoming to the first ship-load, which was set down within the bounds of its Sierra Leone interests. The American colonisation societies put in their tiny groups of settlers along the coast from 1821, and treated them as citizens of an independent country from 1847. This was a paper independence. The settlers were surrounded by much more truly independent peoples, and those inland were stirred by the tremors of great continental changes, including more locally the conquests of Samori, while, along the shore, everybody competed to control trading points so as to buy and sell with Europeans.

From 1835, the settlers at Greenville, their colony on the Sinoe River amongst the Kru-speaking peoples, were struggling to survive, whilst the shoreline at a point equidistant from the next, rather more powerful settlement of Harper, at Cape Palmas (where there were also considerably organised indigenous Grebo settlements) was also being contested by different groups of Kru. One of these, the Jlao people (strictly 'Jla' as –o is a collectivising suffix) apparently secured rights to a trading point around 1840, when we begin to hear of 'Sasstown'. They were far from being absolute newcomers, for they had farmed and made towns in the area for some time. They started to assert themselves, however, by claiming and eventually holding a piece of territory of some 400 square miles, and stretching about 20 miles inland. In the 1880s, some of them settled closer to the shore than their head town Filorkli, which was situated on a bluff about a mile inland. These new settlements, now one town known as Jekwikpo, became a rival to Filorkli. The foreign members of a small Methodist mission set up at this time soon died, but Jlao Methodists remained, mostly converted on trips 'down coast' as kroomen, contract workers. Before World War I, Jlao kroomen also induced a Catholic mission of mainly Irish priests to come too.

World War I brought hardship to Sasstown as ships ceased to call for labour, but it also pressed hard on the fragile Liberian government, which was effectively living on German money. In 1917, the Allies forced Monrovia to declare war against Germany, and the traders, some of whom worked in Sasstown, had to go. The bankrupt government had earlier managed to get revenue by taxing kroomen and their employers, at a number of Ports of Entry which were set up in 1909, under the auspices of a British controller of Customs. Sasstown accepted to be one of these ports.

All along the Kru coast, during World War I, conflicts between local people and settlers grew. Prominent among the 'rebels' were Kabor Kru, mobile specialists in ferrying travellers and produce by boat along the coast and up the rivers – Liberia's lines of communication.[4] The war came to Sasstown. Government troops, led by black officers loaned from the US army and with American ammunition, patrolled the area, and started to put in their own officials. 'The government came in', as people say: the hitherto independent Jlao were conquered.

In 1931, they fought again. Along with neighbouring groups, they defied the government and a British League of Nations expert was sent to mediate – the League of Nations had been investigating forced labour in Liberia. Filorkli was burned, but Jekwikpo stood neutral and accommodated government troops. After waiting for guidance from the League, which eventually left Liberia to Firestone's investment, the Liberian authorities moved in, burnt crops, and so forced surrender. The region was under martial law from 1937 to 1944, when this was lifted by the incoming President, Tubman.

After World War II, Liberian out-migration steadily decreased, but increased internally. Not only Jlao and other Kru but people from all over Liberia went to work on the iron-ore concessions, continued to work on plantations, and in ever larger numbers moved to the capital. By the mid 1980s, one-quarter of the country's population lived in Greater Monrovia. The modest coastal-produce trade which had made Sasstown quite a lively centre in the 1920s has gone and the region is 'undeveloped' – actually it suffers from economic regression and depopulation.

Jlao expatriates retain a sense of their particular origins, and in Liberia such home territories continue to have political significance related to membership of one's wider ethnicity, here the Kru Tribe.[5] The experiences of work overseas, and education there and in the coastal mission schools, helped to give Kru a preliminary advantage in getting government and other jobs. Jlao have held many senior offices at national level.

In Jlao eyes, their identity is bounded precisely, territorially and by dialect. They are Jlao citizens by virtue of birth in one of the clans (*pàntɛn*) which constitute the polity (*dákɔ*). This membership also implies a contrapuntal identity, that is, Kru *dákiφ* identify themselves *vis-à-vis* one another, and *vis-à-vis* other neighbours who may be somewhat similar in language and culture. Jlao has such neighbours, for instance Kplepo (Barclayville) who speak a cognate Grebo language. At the same time, as all these communities came under the Republic's control, they were incorporated into a national system of local government. In the 1970s, Jlao was grouped with some of its neighbours into Sasstown Territory, a semi-autonomous section of Sinoe County, and Sasstown City was its headquarters. (The whole Territory had a population of about 10,000.) Later the Territory became part of Grand Kru County, with the 'county seat' in Barclayville.

Historically, as we see, Jlao's territorial integrity was still being fought over at the beginning of this century and Jlao identity must have evolved and continued to change, as it will go on doing. As mentioned above, imposed changes ran parallel with a superficially 'preserved' Tribal government, which actually included the modification or assimilation of precedent offices. The changes have been immense. Nevertheless, there are many ways in which the 'climate of assumption', the language and value world as well as the economic practices of daily life has, while continuing to change in some aspects, also continued in others; practices and beliefs thus worked so as to reproduce a Jlao people who were not so different from their predecessors a hundred years ago.

(b) Social organisation and agricultural economy

In the *dákɔ*, the territory, of Jlao there are about fifteen settlements each of which could be called *klɔ* or 'town' (although it may have ten houses or less). A town area will be divided up into 'quarters', one for each *pàntɔn* or major sub-section living there. Members of the same panton cannot marry one another; babies are affiliated to the clan of their fathers and males and females both keep this membership all their lives. Males' membership entitles them to farm land controlled by the town, which will clear one farm area per year. Each man 'brushes his part of farm': that is, he cuts down bush and trees, except for the oil palms whose nuts are gathered as a main food source. There is a plot for each of the women in his family, who will plant the upland rice and cultivate it along with cassava and plantain, plus pepper and vegetables. Children watch against birds; everyone harvests the rice.

In this system of rotational cropping, land may be fallow for ten or more years. Coastal land is poor, which encourages men of the coastal towns who have salaried jobs, or who fish, to exchange the profits of their labour with that of inland connections. Some of the inland towns may have been encouraged both as food producers and border or marcher settlements for the dako. The coastal towns Filorkli and Jekwikpo remained rivals when I was there in the 1970s; but by 1975 their conjoined Civilised areas formed Sasstown City, site too of the secondary schools, and the Administration office. Some inland towns were planning to get Civilised townships too; in these the land is allocated by deeded lot and not by panton and ruled by different Jlao laws.

By 1916, the key leaders of Jlao were the *klɸba*, chosen for his individual ability from any panton, and the *gbùdio*, provided by one panton only. Both offices included what to outsiders might be profane and sacred duties, but the budio (then known in English as 'king', now as 'high priest') embodied the dako's identity by living in a sacred house, *jiwɔn*, with his consort *tàpɛnyʌnɔ* who could settle disputes, as he cared for the sacred regalia. Neither were supposed to farm – the people fed them. It was Christian Jlao who effectively abolished their powers and destroyed the jiwon. The kloba became a government-appointed 'Paramount Chief' and new courts and magistrates took on many of the panton heads' disciplinary rights.

Leadership of the dako had been largely consensual. By a public initiation into the *bɸ̂* or army, Jlao males became adult citizens. Suppressed after the Sasstown War, the bo had been divided into eight sections which cross-cut panton membership. All male citizens could be called by the drums to their central meeting place *tùgbɛdia*, and each panton was led by its oldest male, the *nyɔfùɛ* (big man): these also met privately at the jiwon. Different panten also provided office holders for tasks which varied in symbolic and pragmatic importance.

Some Jlao problems were also taken to an oracle, Ku Jlople, in the interior, but in about 1914, Jlao were persuaded to cease their delegations by some of their own Christian converts, who as I've said also attacked the jiwon and threw the 'idols' into the sea. These 'civilised' people, whose experience abroad had set them to working for the European trading houses, the churches and later the Liberian government, were still Jlao although they opposed much of its indigenous order. They set up their own town. Later 'Civilised towns' would come under government law; and there the land was divided into individually owned lots instead of being divided into quarters for each panton. By the 1970s, these divisions between Civilised and Tribal were still very important but their span and scope had also changed and would change further. Literacy and command of English no longer simply made one 'civilised' when so many boys and girls went to school, but the two terms had still important political and legal implications, with certain powers allocated to the Paramount Chief/kloba and other, greater powers over the whole Territory to the Superintendent, who was and had been for many years a person of local origin, if not from Sasstown then from another polity in the Territory, as were all his administration.

Jlao historical practices

I first recorded historical material in Jlao and neighbouring dakio in 1972, spent a year there in 1975–6 and have returned for several shorter visits since, including three months in Monrovia, working on Jlao texts, in 1980, shortly after Liberia's military coup. These details are necessary because oral records are made to particular people on particular occasions, and these were I believe significant years for Jlao historical consciousness.

In 1971 President Tolbert succeeded Tubman's long rule with promises of new openness to indigenous cultures and offered expectations of real political participation to what by now were large numbers of indigenous educated men and women with good jobs in the capital. These new hopes reached Sasstown, with its memories of suffering, coercion and defeat. Through the 1970s, the hopes turned sour and the economy declined. But the populace became conscientised and politicised. Rice riots in Monrovia in 1979 were commemorated in 1980 by the coup which broke 'Congo' (Settler) hegemony and brought young, little-educated 'tribal' soldiers to power.

The people who told me of Jlao's past ranged from literates with government salaries, some but not all of whom at first felt they had to tread warily, to Tribal men from 'the interior' who had little to lose by frankness. In 1972, I was recommended to meet Sieh Jeto, the major historian whose work I discuss below, by the then President of the University, a compatriate who had heard him talk on a recent visit to Monrovia. Sasstown Territory's Singer, Nimine Gbei, had made enough money from performances to Jlao in the capital to build her own house at home in Nrokia in 1976. In other words, there was an incipient 'cultural nationalism' spreading from the urban centre, which I encountered and perhaps encouraged because I took seriously a Jlao past whose very existence was officially ignored – Liberian history as taught in schools mostly portrayed indigenous peoples as 'savages' who fought the 'pioneers' who brought civilisation to the country.

'History' was nevertheless quite often used as a loan word in Kru. This suggests it was felt to capture a meaning not available in the existing Jlao Kru terms *fànpo nli, fànpo tʌ*, 'old time' tale or matter. School 'history' might be an anti-model of what to tell, but it was also a model for setting accounts of the past apart from the practices in which they could otherwise be embedded. Kru culture generally is highly rhetorical, in that speaking skills are valued and many issues are, and are supposed to be, publicly debated. The past here can get recalled as a function of *tʌbotinanʌ* the 'talking of the matter', which carries a sense of 'bearing witness'. This could include participation (by anyone present) in the settlement of a case, or in a Territorial Inquiry called by a government representative, somewhat in the style of a British Commission of Enquiry. When I visited places and asked about them, a common response was for the old men to mobilise themselves into a collective (but argumentative) information session. I had triggered a standard response to outside investigators.

Sieh Jeto was a respected speaker on tribal matters, and said that he had learned his material from a relative who was often consulted for advice. After he went blind in his fifties, he seems to have consciously rethought what had previously been 'active' information which could be used to advise and to support judgments, realising that much of it was now a record of history in our sense, of times that have disappeared. Others had talked and consulted with Sieh Jeto; G. T. Wojroh, a former Territorial representative who had had a stroke before I arrived in 1972 and died soon after, and Police Sergeant Broh were two fellow Jekwikpo men who wanted Jlao history recorded in writing, and had made a start by setting out a list of Jlao offices on the model of the Liberian Senate and House of Representatives (institutions themselves of course modelled on USA ones).

Of all the places where I tried to learn about a dako, Jlao was the richest in content of recall. This was partly because I spent most time there and developed relationships of trust where mutual interest and discussion developed. But I think that Jlao's long fight for territory and against government rule also promoted a historically directed consciousness of identity. The long fight was an ethnicising process which could be supported and indeed defined by developing accounts of Jlao's heroic past.

It was locally recognised that individuals might have special interest in and knowledge of the past, and this, in an essentially oral community, meant simultaneously that such men (rarely women) were known as good tellers, skilled artists. In my experience there were Kru women who knew a lot of local history and I several times heard them correct a male teller. In another dako, Grand Cess, I was directed to record an elderly woman historian. As lead singers and praise singers (like Nimine Gbei) women seemed supreme. (I discuss her work and Kru heroic praising in Chapters 2 and 3.) Kru society is patriarchal in that public authority and therefore the public voice is male; it follows that skilled speechmakers would be male too.

It was not impossible for women to be historians or men to be singers, since this is structurally a relatively unspecialised and unhierarchised society, in which women have been fairly free agents (note for instance that they do not lose panton membership on marriage, bridewealth is rarely paid for them and there is a high turnover of marriages). By the same token, older people know a lot about the past not because this is a gerontocratic preserve but because such knowledge is picked up bit by bit over time by individuals who, if male, can become more experienced as they grow older in delivering it as part of a coherent argument or narrative. This is presumably why when I asked a neighbour, Jua Sieh, in 1976 if he would like to say something I could record, he was able to respond immediately with a very skilful and complexly ordered historical account. Jua Sieh was in his sixties, a purely Tribal farmer who had been chief of the town (population c. 400). I discuss aspects of his account in Chapter 2.

I have been given exciting performances of history, full of declamation and gesture, on a windy hillside outside a rice farm's temporary house with the family and their chickens for audience. As with Jua Sieh, the locale does not here seem criterial, but the speaker was nevertheless operating in a public mode or genre. His delivery was self-contained; he was not conducting a conversation – or answering a researcher's questions as he went along. This mode could be distinguished from the contributions to a collective statement, though here too there are rules for gaining the floor and being permitted a hearing.

Speakers were quite willing to answer questions on what they had said after they had delivered their piece, or for an interpreter to take over, whenever they paused, to give a free translation – for that was standard practice in courts of record, Territorial Inquiries and sermons by non-Jlao clerics. It has been claimed that oral set-pieces, when the teller appears to resist outside interrogation, reveal the non-literate's inability to make detached argument, but I wonder if the literate critics would themselves take kindly to interruptions when they are trying to formulate an argument in writing? I think the claim can only be made by underrating the intellectual effort which oral artists like the Jlao historians continually make – theirs are neither 'traditions' learned by heart nor casual recollections.

All the people recommended to me as tellers said they had learned about the past by choice. They had no formal apprenticeship, though often they had become interested by listening to an older relative. It's part of Jlao openness that children wander freely and learn to listen quietly on all adult occasions. All the sessions I attended drew passers-by and family in; tellers were in fact anxious not to look 'private'; because that registered as (malignly) secretive. It would not have been surprising to find that the Jlao's own previous government offices included a specialist historian except that, as we see, history was deployed as part of debates in which many people had the right to put their word. Court historians seem to have supported supreme rulers in societies more elaborately hierarchised than Kru communities ever became. Jlao citizens needed to know the boundaries of farm and dako, and a walk anywhere with knowledgeable people would prompt brief resumés of past events including the settlement of boundary disputes – I was given such information as I'm sure any young person accompanying the speakers would have been. This too was part of the 'bit by bit' process to which I've referred.

The 'open' structure which also supported this attitude to knowledge becomes clearer by comparison with other communities in Liberia organised through membership in so-called 'secret societies'. For the Vai of Western Liberia, 'secrecy,' not 'openness', is a prime value, and different knowledges are channelled through different routes (including Vai, Arabic and English scripts), which give only restricted access to specifically learned adepts.[6] Jlao did not have such closed inner societies. Historical knowledge therefore became a resource which people could work to get if they wanted; it was not a limited good which a few controlled by keeping it to themselves.

Sieh Jeto's narrative arts

Sieh Jeto (c. 1899–1975) was one of the first Kru historians I heard, in 1972, and he proved to be the richest teller I recorded. Over several hours, on different days, he delivered two main accounts, of his own choice, and expatiated on many aspects of Jlao life in answer to my questions. His house was in Jekwikpo near the Methodist Church, of which he was a member. He and his wife Togba Mna had three children, all of whom had left Sasstown. The sons had completed high school and had good jobs, but their parents were not literate. Sieh Jeto had travelled as a Kru labourer, especially in the 1930s, and knew some English, but he had not chosen the Civilised way. In his fifties he went blind, but when I met him he was still a valued member of the Paramount Chief's Tribal Court.

I have analysed Sieh Jeto's narratives in some detail elsewhere.[7] Here, I select from this account to show how he organised and plotted them, so as to give some idea of the range and scale an oral historian can achieve. They are very different from the chanted epics or praise singing which are sometimes taken to epitomise oral achievement, or the folk tales which also have received critical attention. Sieh Jeto's narratives are much more complexly ordered than these, and he set tales within tales as part of his story.

How we came to the sea

Sieh Jeto's first narrative is structured as an answer to an implicit question: how did Jlao come to be where they are now? He must have accepted the many recollections and tales of earlier Jlao movements as a key issue, and he organised an account of their emergence as Jlao, the dako of today, through describing these movements. Setting their origins in the hinterland of today's Côte d'Ivoire, he told of their disputed passage over the years, stage by stage till they had achieved the trading point on the shore where they are today.

Sieh Jeto may have repeated the ordering principle of histories that he had heard from others, but of course he had to appreciate their force in order to assemble his own version, and its clarity and pace depended on his own abilities. He also answers implicitly the question 'how did we become who we are?' and he makes 'reaching the sea' part of the answer: the people I call proto-Jlao, the forerunners of today's 'us', decided they must try to reach the sea. His narrative therefore becomes plotted, in that a plot implies a problem which needs to be resolved. And he forwards his tale by delayed resolutions: that is, every new solution brings a new problem, sometimes through Jlao's bungling, sometimes because their actions arouse conflict with other peoples who bar their way.

The narrative proceeds, over more than twenty 'stages', that is, elaborated turning points, often with subplots, to bring its subjects from Ivory Coast till they win their settlement at Filorkli, which is the point at which their rivals are forced to admit that Jlao are there to stay – and the story continues with several twists and turns after that. Narratologists use terms like obstacle and movement metaphorically, but in this history they are metaphorical and literal, because every action Sieh Jeto describes is a twist of the plot that either advances Jlao one point nearer the sea, or leaves them static, or causes them to deviate from their true destination.

The stages of the story, then, are likewise an itinerary, which may act as a checklist for its recall[8] that also provides a spatial framework for duration and change, in contrast to the chronology which structures Western historical accounts (I discuss this point again when considering temporality in Chapter 4). Plots have to start, and so do societies: Sieh Jeto's history has a means of achieving both these aims at once. He describes how a group called Pahn (which means people in plenty, and is a term used to categorise Jlao along with some peoples inland of them today) emerging from named places, said to be in the Ivory Coast interior, meet with another group called Kwia (Upper) Pahn. After fights, they settle in amity and share out the fruit of the *pùnplùn* tree between them according to the divisions of their bo/armies. But 'we', who want to go to the sea, secretly pick alone from the tree at night, and, the news getting out, steal secretly away...

This is the same plot motor as Milton's:

> Of Mans First Disobedience, and the Fruit
> Of that Forbidd'n Tree, whose mortal tast
> Brought Death into the World, and all our woe,
> With loss of *Eden*, till one greater Man
> Restore us, and regain the blissful Seat,
> Sing Heav'nly Muse.

So *Paradise Lost* begins; and whereas Milton attests that the Fall is revelatory of God's design, Sieh Jeto guarantees his story by stating that it is Jlao's destiny to seek the sea; I return to this point below. The incident at the punplun tree also allows Sieh to address and elaborate the social puzzle, how does a polity emerge? He understands the processes which anthropologists call 'fission and fusion' in so-called segmentary societies. By picking and sharing out the punplun fruits on their own, the proto-Jlao did not learn good and evil – and we know they already practised peace and war – but they showed that fission from an earlier group is the price of a new fusion and of collective purpose. Many African communities tell of their origins in mythic terms. Here, a mythic event sets the plot moving by expressing a central social paradox.

Once the story and people are in motion, the early succession of movements is recounted with little elaboration. This succession can itself always act teleologically; that is to say, if the declared aim is to get to the sea, the audience will assume any movement is purposeful. As they move, from time to time a section of Pahn stays behind, thus explaining their location today. 'We' therefore is a changing unit, with Jlao the outcome after these 'peelings off' and also some accretions. But as he goes on, Sieh Jeto increasingly describes lengthy incidents, which are often full-blown stories in themselves, and full of drama. Sometimes one can compare his version with those of other Jlao historians: his choices notably work to make the incident serve the grand design. He is also a strictly narrative historian. Episodes which others might treat as aetiological anecdotes (like the 'staying behind' of other groups) are dovetailed in to make a connected account; he chooses one version, he doesn't discuss the existence of competing explanations, although he might know of them, as I came to do, since they were given by other Jlao historians.

As the story develops, listeners begin to hear about an oracle, who, it becomes clear, is Ku Jlople, the oracle which Jlao and others really did consult before 1914, and who is presented as the automatic recourse when Jlao are in an insoluble jam. An example of Jlople's help comes in the tale of the leopard. Jlao have struggled against Tuaon, who are said to have occupied what is now part of Jlao's seaside territory, a long time in the story before they finally achieved this land. Tuaon first beat them off, and demanded as indemnity a huge length of punplun seeds. The day is saved by a Jlao woman who gives up her store of seeds. Jlao settle nearby until Tuaon pick another quarrel; this time they beat Tuaon and demand as their indemnity 'a male dog who lays eggs'. Tuaon's attempted solution, a dog with unripe palm nuts stuffed up its anus, is rejected. But they barricade themselves successfully against Jlao: what to do?

Jlao send a delegate to 'one-who-knows' (probably Ku Jlople). He says that if they throw a female child on the barricade, they can get in while she is being cut up. The delegate offers his own daughter. Toborpo (literally Tobor's people, proto-Jlao's then social incarnation) sack the town, but some Tuaon escape in their canoes to an offshore island. Jlao, an inland people, do not have canoes. Tuaon come raiding and harrying them. Delegates from Jlao go to Ku Jlople: he says that he can destroy Tuaon, but at a price. He will give them the magic materials to make a leopard, which will destroy Tuaon, but when his work is done, he must be compensated by the gift of a young girl.

The delegates agree to this price, their leader pledging his own daughter.

The magic works: an unripe core of a palm-nut cluster, a 'want leaf' and 'magic dust' are set on the sea to 'make it angry': the magic leopard on the island destroys Tuaon, who have never had a town since. The tapenyeno, the consort of the budio, had however overheard the delegate's report made in the jiwon, including the leader's promise of his daughter. She tips off the mother, who escapes with her child, leaving no one willing to make the sacrifice. The leopard starts to kill Jlao, starting with the budio, until the people flee from the town, scattering inland.

A woman married to a Jlao man returns from a visit to her people in Kplepo to find the place empty. Puzzled, she lights the fire, and climbs into the roof-store for her axe-head. But the leopard arrives as she does so:

> she fitted it, it (the) leopard looked all around, he looks for her,
> ɔ kɔwo ɛ,   ɛ mɸji   mɸ nʌ   wati,   ɔ pɸn ɔ ti,

> he senses her scent, he turned up his eyes,
> ɔ wɔn   ɔa nuɔ   ɔ wlăwa jijie,

> he climbed on the ladder, he was climbing to her,
> ɔ jawo gbogbɸ nakpɔ,   ɔ jâ   woɔ   bɔ̀,

> he climbed up there, (the) time he climbed there
> ɔ ja le jiɛ,   tini ɔ ja ɛ na,

> (the) woman said "ha, if I do not put this thing there,
> nyʌnɔ nanʌ   "ha!   sepa dɛ na ponʌ,

> he catches me here (in) the attic, then he will eat me!"
> ɔ kpɔnwo mɸ kla sla na,   nʌ ɔ diwo mɸ!"

The woman fits the axe on its shaft and brings it down on the leopard's skull. It falls off the ladder. But she remembers that 'while the leopard's tail lifts, it lives', and she throws down palm nuts from her store till the tail is still. Then she runs off to look for her people. They do not believe her when she says she's killed the leopard, and beat her, but she shows them the evidence. Then, it's back, shamefaced, to Ku Jlople, who eventually relents and gives the delegates instructions which will (a further story later) enable a man called Kupla to beat a magic drum which all Jlao, wherever they be, must hurry to join. Jlao are together again.

To many people, this story sequence would hardly be called history. It does indeed have features which anthropologists can interpret in symbolic or structuralist terms, though they can also make such interpretations for accounts that look more obviously realistic. It is no more or less historical, I suppose, than the story of Alfred and the cakes, which I was taught as history when a child. Moreover, Sieh Jeto presented it as part of a history that includes lots of 'realistic' data, and indeed weaves it into the sequence particularly carefully so as to reconcile it with known topography. As I mentioned, Tuaon are described as living on part of Jlao's current territory, but it is later explained that Jlao did not stay in their town, inland from today's capital, after the magic drum called them together. Sieh Jeto had to make careful and quite complicated explanations as to how they got in conflict with Tuaon at this site, when they appeared to be moving in another, different direction. Either he or a predecessor had noted a discrepancy between his sources – and the stories of the 'male dog that lays eggs' and the leopard are well known, and enjoyed by children – or the oddities of the Jlao itinerary, which include more than one abortive settlement on the coast, at different places, followed by retreats inland, have been repeated for a long time and tellers scrupulously repeat them. They may be true, or pointers to truths about the early history of the Kru coast.[9]

On these grounds, a conventional, literate historian would be wrong to skip this material, but I think it would also be wrong within the terms I've been approaching it here. One can see the more possibilities of interpretation the more closely one looks at different features together, including the perspective of the narrative's own form. I can illustrate this point by looking at Seih Jeto's second long history, 'the chiefs'.

'Shall we come to the chiefs now?'

Thus Sieh Jeto to our interpreter, Emmanuel S. Togba, who would give a free translation between longish passages of telling, after he had brought the story of Jlao's quest for the sea to what they, as Jekwikpo men, believed was its final conclusion, the founding of Jekwikpo itself in the 1880s and the end of the physical opposition that this continued to provoke, both within and from outside Jlao, into the early years of this century. The story of the chiefs (using *chiefi* as a loan word in Kru) is ordered by the sequence of named leaders, and is related to the geochronology of 'how we came to the sea'; it gives accounts of their rule and the means of their succession to office. Such a framework is much more familiar to Western readers than a geochronology. Its existence also suggests that Sieh Jeto felt he needed more than one frame of explanation; his data could not be handled fittingly in terms of one type of story alone.

In distinguishing the quest of a people from the more personally oriented account of successive reigns, Sieh Jeto also recognised that the processes which culminated in Jlao's securing a seaside territory could not be explained only in personal terms. He therefore used two types of narrative to encompass this complexity. Jlao's drive to the sea fulfils its Manifest Destiny, carried out through imperfect individuals, some of whose actions actually tended to thwart instead of further Jlao's success.

Manifest Destiny is an agency which has been favoured by literate Western historians as well. If it is attacked by those who prefer socio-economic destiny, blind chance, or a complex and changing combination of pressures, well, these explanations are usually equally unprovable and are certainly disputed as alternatives. Manifest Destiny is the counterpart historical theory to certain propositions of religious belief, and Sieh Jeto may have been encouraged to favour it because of his Bible knowledge as a long-standing Methodist. However, it appears in very many narratives across the world in the guise of prophecies, oracles and the like. Logically, if one is to envisage a number of events as linked, not fortuitous, then Manifest Destiny – or some reason – must be seen as propelling cause and effect, and the representation of this plot must include Destiny's manifest-ing itself from time to time, as here in the oracular voice of Ku Jlople.

If a geochronology 'mimes' duration and time in terms of sequential movement over space, a dynastic account mimes social successivity as a sequence of rulers. A continuity of status is implied, whereas institutional, economic and power changes in reality tend to transform the real nature of particular offices, let alone make their incumbents less or more relevant to the lives of their subjects. In fact, Sieh Jeto does describe changes in the nature and scope of his offices. Referring back to his first narrative, he argues that Popo who led us from Ivory Coast was called 'father'. Next came collective discussion with nyefues. Each panton is still formally headed by a nyefue, so Sieh is showing a change from the model of a family to that of a collocation of clans, from undifferentiated humanness to differential social organisation. The first *lida* (Sieh Jeto used this loan word) is Boi Tobor, who held the office of *jugbadio* (who, formerly, directed wars, but did not fight in them, although he would have been a warrior). Thus the direction of warfare precedes civil society. In the first narrative, as we've seen, the punplun story models the process of dako and panton fission and identification.

By the time the Liberian government conquered the Jlao Kru in 1916/17, the polity was made up of panten, which actually continued and continue to change their scale and number through fission and fusion, a process which is not investigated by Sieh at panton level, except perhaps through some stories of disputes over panton offices. The very emphasis on the office of kloba – 'chief' – is actually historical in that there is some comparative evidence of its late and limited appearance in Kru groups.[10] Its emergence is shown here more obliquely, through a story that carries over generations. After the death of his wives, Kupla (who might be the magic-drum player, though Sieh does not say so) marries the widow of his friend. Wane is a Gbeta (Pikniness) woman. Dying, he asks his own two sons to take a 'thing' from his mouth. Both refuse in fear, and Wane calls her own son, Jeple, who does what is asked. Kupla tells him to return to live in his own father's panton, and, as he is born of a stranger woman, his own first wife should be a stranger too. Then, Jlao will submit to his authority, and not as office holder or nyefue but as an overriding kloba.

This prophecy comes to pass, but there are many incidents on the way. The 'thing' may have been iron. It was in the kloba's belt, which therefore embodied his power, as Sieh's account of its theft, which I describe below, makes clear. But this did not mean that the klobaship was wholly sacred, any more than the office of the high priest, budio, in that both could be deposed. The priestship, however, was a – very important – office whose holders are not recalled by name.

The story of the klobaship's origins also represents in an exaggerated way the rule of succession as it was understood by Jlao informants: that is, by selection of outstanding individuals from any panton, except Suapo, the panton which had to provide the priest, budio. Sieh Jeto's story is not, therefore, underpinned by a dynastic principle of succession. Rather, he has to explain why each kloba's reign was terminated, thus also graphically exemplifying Jack Goody's contention that this is the crucial problem of all systems of succession to high office.[11] Instead of having a dynastic principle to recapitulate in order to mark out the plotting (compare Manifest Destiny) we have prophecies made at point of death, oracular direction, and genealogical relationships given to explain the sequence of competition. The affinal connections of Wane are a simple example of the latter. The story of Ble Boi is more complicated.

It is difficult to show ability to command a long and complex narrative by fleeting examples. I look a little more deeply, therefore, at the Ble Boi story, which depends on this command for its effects, including a strong moral evaluation, which is embodied through the structure of the narrative itself. Ble Boi was also named by other historians, and described as an oppressive ruler who in one interesting version sold his own people into slavery. (Sasstown Kru repeated the claim, which has been widely reported for Kru generally, that they did not sell slaves. It is known that kroomen worked for slavers.) Sieh Jeto again selects information which can be described as actions within the plot, and the plot in turn is very distinctly organised so as to contrast loyalty and betrayal, and to make a series of dramatic ironies which are part of Jlao's history as well as informing Ble Boi's own story.

To accomplish these effects, Sieh Jeto has to handle futurity and retrospection and clarify for us the connections between a number of events over an impliedly considerable span of years in Ble Boi's lifetime. The story starts not with Ble Boi, but the preceding kloba, Bete Kle, and by specifying the Jlao relationship of *nanɛbi-nanɛju* which is crucial to his moral. Translated into Liberian English as 'godfather' and 'godson', these reciprocal terms, literally 'walking with' (*nanɛ*) 'father' (*bi*) 'son' (*ju*), name a Jlao relationship of patron and close follower, analogous to the father–child relation but freely chosen and characterised by mutual loyalty and respect. Ble Boi is the 'godson' of Bete Kle, but uses one of his own godsons, who is also a fellow panton member, to steal away his godfather's constitutive regalia, knowing that he cannot unseat him through public disapprobation. We are told how Bete Kle is forced to resign himself, and travels to a 'country doctor' in a neighbouring dako for help in his revenge. In Jlao terms, he would not have been kloba without having (supernatural) 'medicine' powers of his own, but he does not seek to reinstate himself. He needs help to create a surrogate – this is the nearest translation I can find to the Kru *slɔn*: to use as executor of one's intentions, do in one's stead. Jlople's leopard was also compensated, given back a person, for carrying out its duty in this way.

It is not until Bete Kle has gone through the scenario predicted by the doctor – You will meet a man, he will say ... you will give him the bananas ... that Sieh Jeto tells us that this man is Bligbo Wle, who he had named earlier as another godson of Ble Boi. We now see a pattern of retribution in train; but it is not immediate. Bligbo Wle forms an opposition to Boi, but does not oust him, and their factions' outright fighting is eventually stopped by their respective sons. Bete Kle prophesies at death that the third kloba after him will reach the sea. Boi opposes Wle's plans to go there, but he fears Wle's faction will seize him, and he himself flees inland with an interior client, or 'slave', Blee. Their hiding place is betrayed both by the wife who brings them food and his own brother, but they are impregnable until the attack is taken over by Sompon. Sompon is the son of a man who was caught by Blei Boi quarrelling with his wife: he interfered in this domestic quarrel by having the man smoked over the household fire. Sompon, the man's young son, defied Boi, to the latter's admiration, and took his father down. Other men told me this story, but without Sieh Jeto's moral intensity, gained as usual through the sequencing and balancing of significant actions, not direct comment as others' 'Ble Boi ruled with an iron hand.' Wle's ironic agency is matched by Sompon's; and the repetition intensifies; one immoral act of betrayals touches off a sequence of 'moral' ones, till the loyal son, Sompon, is the agent of the disloyal Boi's end, knocking him down with a cutlass so that the people can finish him off.

These narratives put forward moral and other *arguments* through their ordering and plotting, in other words, the shape of a narrative is not neutral, and – as with genre in general – adds to implications of the story. In his insightful book *The Emergence of the Past*, Dale Porter first takes this point and then argues further that narrative history is a proper form of interpretation, a means of proposing plausible connections which is different from scientific-experimental method and for which the truth criteria proposed by some philosophers of history may be irrelevant. He believes that narrative may be the most powerful way of understanding events that occur complexly through time. It is a 'self-justifying mode of explanation' which can actually be scientific, in ways comparable with scientific method as it is now understood.

The quality of Sieh Jeto's narrative history, in a community with a strong interest in aspects of the past, and with such a number of competent practioners[12] testifies to a tradition, a long-developed practice of historical telling, which as I show, diversified into more than one genre. Thus, although the uses of history have been pragmatic, and the choice of interest directed and reproduced by the social organisation of the community, one cannot say that recall is a simple function of the social structure, and likewise it does not only serve the present-day interests of the tellers. As with any art, performers of past-oriented discourses in Jlao, and their audiences, have a developed intellectual and aesthetic enjoyment of what they do, and their performances can be enjoyed, and understood, at different levels.

2

THE TELLER OF THE TALE: AUTHORS AND THEIR AUTHORISATIONS

Every tale has to have a teller. In this chapter, I consider this obvious point from different directions. I discuss some of the consequences of authorship – that tales are told by tellers, and of authorisation – that they are intended to be listened to. I examine more closely the status of this narrating 'I': as eyewitness; as implicit subject in an impersonal account which nevertheless may be structured by reference to the teller's life; and as explicit hero, the subject of boasting and praise. All these perspectives include assumptions about the audience to which performance is directed, so that narrations always exist through a web of social relationships.

Orientation and claim: the necessity of authorship and authorisation

The study of oral representations of pastness involves the study of their narrators and audiences as well, because they will affect the content and direction of the narrative. A narrative in print may be read centuries later, but it still was produced under specific social and economic conditions by authors whose attitudes to a perceived potential audience would have affected the way they presented their material. The social contexts of oral histories include the additional condition that their tellers must intersect with a palpable audience at a particular moment in time and space. What they choose to say is affected by these conditions, which also mean that they can get immediate feedback. Just as narrators may monitor the audience's reactions, and take account of them to adjust their tone and presentation, so the audience may play an energetic part in the proceedings, ask questions, answer back, or perhaps just walk away.

There is also a sense in which no historian can avoid taking a stance to audience and subject matter, in that everyone who speaks, or writes, has to take a point of view. Is one asking a question, or making a statement? Who was the doer of an action? Were the events described long past or repeated? Language itself demands that we choose a particular noun or pronoun as subject and an appropriate verb-form, and the rules of different languages are not the same. They also carry inescapable connotations: 'We are not amused' may refer to one person only, and it now makes ironic reference to the usage known in Britain as the 'royal we'. When Mrs Thatcher the Prime Minister said 'We are a grandmother', people laughed at the presumption rather than the grammar.

I look further at the constraining and constitutive characteristics of language in the next chapters, and focus now on the point that using language not only involves a choice of *orientation* to a topic and to the person or persons with whom one is in communcation: it also involves a *claim* that one should be listened to. To speak at all makes this claim, as can be seen when people ask if they may 'say a word', or test if they will be allowed a hearing by giving an interrogative look or modest attention-calling cough. Speaking on a topic implies a claim over it, so one can challenge another's claim to authority by challenging their orientation to one's topic. Many British conversations are actually small contests of this kind. 'With respect, I don't think the government really intends . . .' or, 'Oh! You poor thing! Fortunately, I don't feel the cold . . .'

Status claims are necessary for writers too. The words 'author' and 'authority' have a common origin. The state of being an originator or author itself authorises, gives one authority. However, as we know, it may not give authority enough. A bigger name may be asked to write a preface to a smaller one's book, and endorse the product. Authors' names may be followed by qualifications or job-description as a guarantee. Much authority-claiming is done through the form of the product itself, so that the sober format of an academic book, its hopefully witty punning title (legitimated by a realistically pedantic and more limited sub-title) and the apparatus of citation and footnote are all reassuring to fellow academics that this is serious stuff. It will not impress some other potential readers who can be put off before they even look inside. Their topic-orientation is different, and status for them might be successfully claimed if the cover shouts 'AS SEEN ON TV!' with photographs of the star actors.

Academic historians must test the authority of oral tellers, but of course oral tellers are putting forward their own claims as well, fitted to the audience they know. Likewise, their claims may be made by the way they use a genre by right, as their orientation to the subject matter will also be evaluated by listeners. Samuel Schrager said, generalising from his experiences of story telling in an Idaho community,

> What we are telling seldom can be verified in a strict sense, even when we can produce supporting evidence. Ultimately, its validity rests less in its content than in social relationships. We agree to regard each other – at least some others – as bearers of truth. We accept what we are hearing even though it is not and never can be a literal transcription of events. Our expectation is that it will be faithful to the teller's knowledge, interpretation, and imagination, a realisation of his or her perceptions of what is significant and worth repeating to us at the time.[1]

Eyewitnesses and truth

Schrager makes the important point that knowledge of other members of a
shared community is one basis for judging the status of what they say.
Anyone who has lived and worked as an outsider in a community with an
unfamiliar language and culture – or even just a different dialect of the same
language and a different body language – will know how difficult it could be
to evaluate speakers' remarks. Gesture, intonation, bodily stance and facial
expression are all cues, in the *oral* ambience, to topic orientation as well as
to the speakers' claim to authority. Yet as Schrager also shows, we often
cannot go beyond a teller's claim to *experience*. If people say they've
experienced something, and the personal quality of that experience is
asserted, one cannot prove or disprove what was felt by the other.

This bedrock of the human condition has been frustrating to many,
leading behaviourist social scientists to try to make a virtue out of the
inaccessibility of others' inner selves by privileging the accessible as the
only proper evidence. Yet since these selves as well as their inaccessibility
seem a reality, other analysts have tried to take them into account. Schrager
is an example. Like him, I argue that human selves are partly social
creations and am interested in the implications for the ways that they
present the past. An obvious point of departure is to ask what is the nature
of the 'I' when narrators claim to tell their own story. This is also a matter
of importance to oral historians, who often concentrate their attention on
life histories and personal reminiscence.[2]

The most obvious historical use of the 'I', then, is when people claim to
give an eyewitness account. Whether or not a historian specialises in using
oral evidence, the importance of eyewitnesses is indisputable. Historians
have therefore worked out many ways of testing if what they say is likely to
be true, and have discovered that people may sincerely say they have seen
what they could not have done.[3] But this should not be just a negative
exercise, learning how to sort out bad apples from good apples, because one
can further ask what sort of 'error' is being made, and why.

A first point to sort out is what eyewitnesses are doing. In an acute study
of 'narrative conventions of truth in the Middle Ages', Jeanette Beer points
out that history was defined as different from fable because it was the true
narration of events that really happened, whereas fable describes impossible and invented actions.

> Isidore of Seville's definition of history also contained the bold
> and influential *non-sequitur* that the eye-witnessing of events was
> the best guarantee not only of the accuracy of the historical
> information but also of its presentation. *Quae enim videntur, sine
> mendacio proferentur.*[4]

Two kinds of truth are conflated in this medieval claim, as well as at least two kinds of experience. There is the truth that is, because it is existent, and there is the truthful, therefore falsifiable account. There is also the experience and a discourse about it. For experiences must be put forward (*proferentur*) in discourse, and quite apart from providing the possibility of lying, discourse is also a translation (mimesis and diegesis) of experiences. Putting an experience into words is an inevitable alteration of that experience. But as with observation and understanding, these two kinds of experience are often hard to untwine.

> Because the individual, narrowly restricted by his senses and power of concentration, never perceives more than a tiny patch of the vast tapestry of events, deeds, and words which form the destinies of the group, and because, moreover, he possesses an immediate awareness of only his own mental state, all knowledge of mankind, to whatever time it applies, will always derive a large part of its evidence from others. In this respect, the student of the present is scarcely any better off than the historian of the past.[5]

Two immediate points can be made. The first has been well put by Schrager, urging attention to a teller's 'point of view' (compare 'orientation and claim') to other participants in the events described. 'It shows that far from dealing only with ourselves when we tell about the past, we incorporate the experience of a multitude of others along with our own; they appear in what we say through our marvellous capacity to express other perspectives.'

The second point, Marc Bloch's, is that there is nothing direct and simple about observation, even when, perhaps especially when, one is a participator. Anthropologists have been very aware though very unanalytical about this particular knot, and that is why they have become so fond of the term 'participant observation', an oxymoron whose interpretations have also been quite contradictory. Understanding is a process which in turn modifies perceptions, and it is very difficult to recover later the sources 'put in' from memory or current reading or conversation which alter the significance of what you see. Which stage and what kind of reporting is then most truthful?[6]

Answers to these questions will require us to move from the narrator to the narrative itself; to the different and complementary accounts that could be made of a complex set of events, to the different genres available for such renditions, and to the different truth claims embedded in the genres themselves. Remaining for the time being with the narrators, here is an apparently contrary case, where there is no 'I' for most of the time, yet it transpires that the narrator was in part an eyewitness. How does this affect his telling?

Subliminal life stories? The example of Jua Sieh

After I had been living in Nrokia, Sasstown, for some months, I invited a neighbour, Jua Sieh, to speak into my tape-recorder. Nrokia was then (1976) a community of about forty houses – not small in local terms – divided up territorially in quarters belonging to the patriclans and their subsections, and with mostly male houseowners. I saw Jua Sieh every day, but had talked little with him. He knew I was interested in history but I did not specify any topic for him to talk about.[7]

Much of Jua Sieh's narrative describes phases in the Sasstown war of 1931–7. This was a far from neutral topic, as is explained in Chapter 1. The people of Nrokia fought and suffered in it, as he pointed out. As farmers who aligned themselves with the Tribal–Filorkli fight, very few had sided with the government, as a lot of Jekwikpo people and most of the 'civilised' persons of Jlao had done, albeit passively.

Sieh's story is opened by a brief statement translating as:

> we (are) the Jlao, who came from the high forest, who always made Jite angry, who today occupy this land, [and who] from when our ancestors struggled to reach the sea, never suffered privation except in the war between Major Grant and the Sasstown people.

Clearly, Sieh's opening claims authority for the narrator by (i) subsuming himself into 'we Jlao', and (ii) by emphasising in an allusive way, which is clear to insiders informed about their past, that Jlao's quest for the sea was sponsored by oracular spirits (*kui*). The characteristically Kru positioning of the topic sentence in final position allows him neatly to lead up to, and to stress, the word which will also be his next topic: war. Jua Sieh situates contemporary Jlao as a people with a sequential, differentiated history of virtuous struggle. This claim implicitly legitimates their struggle with the government too, and gives it moreover a climatic status in Jlao history. Jite was angry because – as other Kru historical narratives make clear – Jlao did not always obey their oracles. This is also a characteristic self-ascription of Sasstown's 'sassyness' which can be taken as a legitimating, even ironic reference to Jlao's decision to fight back against the government.

Jua Sieh's compactly efficient opening is succeeded by a long, equally carefully composed and variously dramatised narrative. He continues by briefly describing how the Paramount Chief Jua Senyon Nimene summons all male Jlao to an assembly after his first confrontation with Major Grant of the Liberian Frontier Force. When Sieh uses 'we' this time, he means the males from the interior towns of Jlao, and himself as actually present, as I later learned he was. Although he tells in a later episode how some Jlao warriors literally 'tested the water' – because the government officers had forbidden them to get their water from the stream – he does not say in his account that he was one of the boys sent to draw water, covered by Jlao guns. I only learned this when discussing some points of translation with him. Yet this was a key moment, which each side agreed was when the first shots were fired.

Jua Sieh then explains that, after a day in which 'we', now meaning all male Jlao, fight in Filorkli until at last driven out, 'we' divide into groups, one for each town. Thereafter, 'we' becomes according to context, either Jlao as a whole, or the people of Nrokia, or the fighting males of either entity. Actually Jua Sieh was too young to be made bo (the Kru adult male fighting citizenry), he was a *kafa* – one of the youths acting as runners and messenger.

A burnt-earth policy finally beat Jlao, and Jua Sieh describes the scene of their capitulation, and the limping return of Nrokia people, by then also forced out of town, to camp in the church, until they were permitted to build temporary houses. Gradually they got better food, but also had to act as carriers for the occupying soldiers. He then describes the so-called Peace Conference, after which it was decided that Sasstown's reparation would be to build a road – the road that was finally extended in the mid-1970s so as to link the towns of Sasstown to the main motorable road that spans Liberia. Finally, Sieh identifies himself. He describes how he was chief of Nrokia, instrumental in the final phase of road building, when President Tolbert parked outside his house and asked for him, but he was in Filorkli, how Tolbert asked for him again the next day, wrote down his name, and as chief, not overseer (the newer minor official title), but, after his departure, Jua Sieh was deprived of office. He ends by saying this is the story of how he has suffered for his land.

Jua Sieh's main narrative is implicitly autobiographical. At the beginning of most narratives I recorded, the tellers introduced themselves by name and panton. They often go on to give a history of their town, so that their self-introduction simply shows that they have authority as sons of the soil. Jua Sieh does not do this. He focuses on events which were important for him, and claims that they are crucial to his people too. He does not dwell on his personal sufferings and this was true of the many participants I talked to; they describe 'suffering' briefly as a general state. When asked later, he said that he had had to be a carrier for the soldiers, and joked that his head was bald still from toting the loads! He was perfectly aware of his own individual experiences, and could talk of them, but his formal narration is never individualised until he identifies his own role as chief, and his praises from the then President of Liberia.[8]

Jua Sieh, as I've said, does not refer to himself at all when describing what must have been an important moment for him personally, and a portentous and frightening time for all his people, beside himself, as they watched the Liberian Frontier Force troops with their guns ready on the other side of the narrow river. Instead, his style remains impersonal but becomes weighty and heroic: he names in turn the Jlao warriors, describing how each 'swears to' a dead relative or friend before he makes ready to shoot. This could have been an episode in one of Sieh Jeto's histories, and it is stylistically comparable with the heroic boasting of Blamo Kofa, which is described later in this chapter. I have argued elsewhere that Jua Sieh here moves into a 'high style' precisely to stress the event's wider significance.[9] We have no means of telling whether the warriors did act as described, but we can see that Jua Sieh stressed their heroism as part of Jlao's warrior tradition, and left out his individual experience.

Jua Sieh's narrative is not overtly an autobiography – a life history – but it is a history which is also a story. Like Sieh Jeto's histories, it is plotted. The selection of events and their ordering help to create a moral order, which redeems the sufferings of Sasstown from senseless chaos. This ordering is also oriented by reference to his life experience, but the self which is either overtly presented, or which implicitly structures the story by the choice of events described, is less an individual personality than a social being, one of 'we Jlao' and Jlao itself takes on a personality, tough, cocky to the point of self-destruction, but enduring in creative purpose.

This 'social personality' does not replace a sense of individual personality, as we can see from the last part of the narrative. Jua Sieh is not subsumed into some 'tribal' collective consciousness, and his narrative interestingly suggests rather how his making of history had been a means of creating a social personality for himself, a sustaining and positive identity indeed.

If there is a *self* who directs Jua Sieh's narrative, then, it appears obliquely, and partly through changing orientations to the people he describes, with whom his identification alters in span. He also shifts styles in ways that could evoke the emotional identification of knowledgeable listeners, with experience of Kru 'heroic praising' genres. An outsider who wanted to know 'what really happened' could make better judgments by understanding these modulations. It would be equally limiting to classify Jua Sieh's performance as either 'testimony' or 'life story' and then to treat it as a source of evidence which is all-of-a-kind. The performance must be considered as a whole, not least so as to understand its plot and drive, but it is a complex and nuanced whole.

Heroic personae

The old man is in the doorway of his mud-rendered house, behind him a corridor. He begins by identifying himself and his origins.

I am Blamo Kofa: my mother is Jugba, my father is Blamo Suen Blamo and so I become Blamo Kofa, and my mother is Gbla Jugba so I become Gbla Jugba Kofa.

When the main part of the war begins, they look for us heroes. I am here among Weapo, [with] Jugbe Wea of Weapo who loves me. He said 'your heart is hard!' I said 'Say what you are speaking about . . .'

Plunging *in medias res*, Kofa went on to tell us how his 'godfather' Jugbe Wea took him to a fearful place where the waters rushed over the rocks.

"If your heart is truly grown, the thing that will come from inside me, will you hold it?' I said 'Ho!' Fiim, there I was, it came from the interior, it travelled t a u m – I stretched my left arm, I caught it. It stays in my hand, it stays in my hand.

This was the first stage of his magical protection as a warrior, followed (as usual) by a medicated meal. Kofa went on to give a brief account of the fighting, and then told us how he had bought[10] further protection from an interior man who sent him to the grave sites of his mother Jugba's people. Here Kofa plucked a white plate from his grandfather's grave (such as would be one of the prestige goods that formerly were piled up there at a burial).

Blamo Kofa fetched out this plate and fixed it on his back as it had been when it was his powerful wartime protection. He ran up and down, calling his own praises, and his individual 'horn name' – 'I am leopard firm!' etc. and as his declamation grew in rhythmical urgency, an old woman in the knot of onlookers began to 'call' him, so that he could respond and shout his praises: 'Nʌ je bê! Nʌ je bê! Nʌ je bê! Nʌ je bê! Nʌ je bê! Nʌ je bê! – I see bravery! I'm very brave!

Kofa turned his rhetorical questions to the old lady, in shared memory:

Wele-o! We're the people who made this noise [fight] – Isn't it Senyo who is there? Isn't it Ton Kle Sakor and Wle Sakor who are there at Dayakpo?

He told more of his own part in the war, and then he recalled Nrokia's other hero, Kle, with whom he could laugh over the old days, but Kle is dead. Finally, he asked me for 'something' to 'take the plate off his back'.

Blamo Kofa was performing in a known genre. To the young, he was just a turn, but for older people this was one of the ways in which their great fighters could boast or savour – the Kru word used, *bɛ*, means to drink or lick – the times of their glorious deeds. The old lady's interventions were part of the genre. Such a singer is a *dabɛ*, she calls, *da*, *bɛ*. The Singer of Sasstown Territory, Nimine Gbei, often called by her title Blenyeno,

Songwoman, also lived in Nrokia. Unusually, she headed her household, but a previous husband had been one of Sasstown's leaders in the 1931–7 war against the Liberian government. Many people had told me of her powers, but it took a long time for her to be free to record a performance, and when she did so, she missed the stimulus of a convivial occasion, and also of sufficient appropriate people to 'call' since, as for some other praise singers and bards,[11] part of her art is to target representatives of different *panten* in the audience, so that the recipients will acknowledge her calling with a gift, in order not to 'shame their names'.

Nevertheless Blenyeno called the names of men and women in this way when she chanted for me and also introduced herself genealogically:

Tàgbe Wìàka Ti nʌ blé –	Tagbe Wiaka Ti then sing –
Nʌ Niminɛ Wlⲫn Gbeɛ̆ Nagbe wlu –	Ne Nimin Wlon Gbee Nagbe then talk –
Nʌ i-a tʌ nʌ kantií –	It is their matter I open up –
Blĕ dí Niminɛ Wlⲫn Gbɛ̆ɛ̆ Nagbe wlu –	Ble's mother, Nimine … talk –
Dɛgbè Wlɛ Dumú Wìàka Niminɛ Gbɛ̆ɛ̆ Nagbe wlu wà –	Degbe Wle… Nimine … talk now –
Nʌ nyli Nlⲫkwìà-o- Mɔ́ Nlⲫkwia jugbé –	I reach Nrokia-o- I am Nrokia's child.

We separated the Singer's words into lines since the dashes mark clear pauses, and they can rise into climaxes delivered with a thrilling virtuosity, chanted with amazing control and rapidity. The words are sometimes hard even for locals to catch, but the message partly comes over by the repetitions, allusive variations and ideophones.

I jé lé wlɛ nyʌnɔ boa wlu-o	As they were talking to songwoman-o
I na lé wlɛ nyʌnɔ a mu tⲫ na fⲫn	They said – song woman, we will fight the war –
Ná lé à po wà ie bⲫ bí-o	I said stand firm-o
À nʌ sela lé mɛ nyɔ ii síe	You will not leave dead person there

With herself as inspirer – and she has a reputation for prophecy, the dead speaking through her[12] – Blenyeno also described magical preparations. Her means of doing so simultaneously 'presents' this past and exhorts her audience to a shared, active Jlao identity.

...Kru war men-o! the horn blower is dead-o!
Something is happening: look for one another-o!
Close ranks there, close ranks there – war has arrived
   now-o!
Jlao people-o – close ranks there – look for one another-o!
Look for your father-o – look for your son-o!

Genre as social practices

These two performances, of which I try to give a flavour, obviously share a
stance to the past that is more widely found. Heroic boasts, praising
sessions and the celebration of warfare are known in many literatures. To
judge by published commentaries, they are the meat of 'oral tradition',
along with folk tales, and, therefore, oral tradition appears to be sharply
distinct from contemporary oral reminiscence in Europe or America. There
is also a large body of commentary on epic, epic and culture heroes, and the
formulae with which bards construct their narratives, which again do not
seem immediately relevant to students of industrial and post-industrial
society.

I am arguing in this book that oral histories are much more diverse than
this perception of oral tradition leads people to expect. I also think that
there are other, important ways of looking at heroic accounts, which see
them as social practices in social contexts, and comparison within this
perspective helps us to see the particularities of different kinds of oral
history more clearly. Here for instances are two Jlao genres which are past-
directed. What processes of individuation do they reveal? In what social
conditions do they flourish? What kind of past do they portray and with
what rhetorical means?

A first point to make is that in these genres we can catch changes in the
making which can be connected to wider social processes. It is possible that
what were presented to me as quite separate performances could earlier
have been part of celebratory occasions on which leading singers orches-
trated several heroes' interventions. Since there had been no warfare
since 1937, Blamo Kofa, who died in 1987, outliving many of his
contemporaries, attested in 1976 as a survivor of what is probably a dying
practice. Blenyeno, however, noted as an outstanding practitioner, had
built up her art into a solo performance attractive to urban armchair
audiences who in the 1970s were conscious of being educated professionals
and yet excluded from ultimate political control by the ruling Americo-
Liberian families. She gave value by her virtuoso art to what had been
despised – the history of the 'uncivilised' country people from whom the
Civilised Monrovian Kru derived – and she also made glorious the seven

long years in which they had managed to withstand the Liberian government.

Blamo Kofa and Blenyeno are in different ways permitted by the conventions of their genre to celebrate themselves explicitly. Jua Sieh could not do so because he had not qualified as a warrior. He had also simply been asked if he wanted to talk, unlike the others, whose reputations in Nrokia meant I was urged to record them as 'performances'. His use of heroic motifs celebrated the historical significance of an event; while thus giving 'name' to the adult warriors, he effaced his own personality and participation. Kofa's self-assertion as a hero includes his own 'name', which is gained metaphorically, as honour, when one is actually named as here in a genealogical framework which of course is also reproduced, along with its values, partly by repetition in these circumstances. All such celebrations of lineage are tied to patterns of social structuration that are not often reproduced in the capitalist culture and economy of Western Europe and North America.

Here, the meaning of 'individual' is very different. Our ideology of the individual versus society sets up the ideal of individual uniqueness as a counterpart to the mass, in which, too, individuals appear as atoms, aggregated to form the mass. Not surprisingly, then, recollection is privatised and seen as personal, unique – the webs of sociality in which capitalist, Western classes, too, are reproduced, are not celebrated by public, past-directed oral genres, and it follows that in a capitalist society, successful tellers seem to be a fluke of nature, 'gifted individuals', while the unsuccessful ones are inarticulate. For those of us whose culture is consumed as mass, commercial output (though even here, many are not passive, nor without their own cultural networks and creativity), popular, mass genres have to be a route to self-celebration, hence, partly, the popularity of pop groups and TV soaps.

Significances of the self

The genre of Nimine Gbei, which praises others, can clearly be connected to that of Blamo Kofa, who praises himself. This is hardly surprising, since the 'I' of any text must be a construction just as much as that of the hes and shes. Writers of fiction very commonly construct 'I's as narrators whose characteristics are entirely different from their own. There is no reason why artists of oracy should not do the same. A student of Mende story telling in Sierra Leone observed that tellers, who often worked with well-known materials, 'argued with the narrative' and briefly but ironically counterposed their own 'self' to the narrating 'self'.[13]

It is open to any teller to construct a self, but because the telling is 'in person' it may be risky to create a persona which deviates too much from what others think is one's personality. Sometimes, of course, such discrepancies are intentional jokes. The artful practices (in both senses of the words) of Texan tellers of tall tales have been subtly studied by Richard Bauman.[14] Writers today often manipulate and render ambiguous the distance between themselves and their narrators – Proust was the great exemplar. They recognise that texts are constructions, and show this by using a perceived tension between the constructor and the construct.

Because it is possible to argue that theories about the nature of the person and practices of constituting its boundaries are culturally variable, oral texts can be important evidence.[15] One can look, in this evidence, for both implicit and explicit presentations of the individual, but, as the example of Jua Sieh shows, a teller's self can be differently presented even in one performance, let alone in different contexts. Besides the tension between constructor and construct, an oral performance is also by definition a tension between bridging and separating, the tension which is inherent in relating the distinct comprehensions of teller and members of the audience. A successful artist everywhere plays to the audience, but audiences vary – and performers vary in their power to hold their attention. Tension may also exist between author and material, since different performers can take the same basic forms, or contents, and organise them in different ways, as storytellers seem to do everywhere.

Analytically, the difference between the narrator and the person who narrates is clearly complex. It cannot be addressed without a closer look at the nature of genre. Already in this chapter every discussion of specific tellers has had perforce to move into the *form* and *occasion* of what they tell. In the case of Nimine Gbei and Blamo Kofa, the occasion and expectation of audience is obviously part of the genre; for Blamo Kofa, there were also real-life qualifications which permitted him the heroic boast. For Jua Sieh, I made the point that his life story directed the selection of episodes and their interconnection, and also that a sense of self-identification was projected partly by his alignment with different 'wes'. Since oral historians very often assume 'the life story' is a generally found or even universal genre, it's important to note that a life story may not be so visibly a form. But we can also ask if it is really universal. How culturally specific is autobiography, or the presentation of one's life as a sequence, in speech or in writing? And how far does an active sense of individual identity develop with the aid of genres, whose existence gives people a model of how to represent themselves, and which later, others in turn will develop so that a tradition emerges? I return later to these questions (p. 56). In the next chapter, the focus turns from narrators to their narrations.

3

STRUCTURING AN ACCOUNT: THE WORK OF GENRE

Narrators are, in more than one sense, formed by their own narrations. Their reputations, and thus their self-identities, can be made by the skill of their performances. If they describe themselves, that description is part of the narration, and so, as we have seen, may be their claims to authority, their topic orientation and the stance they take to listeners. They may also be performing in a mode which encourages – or denies – certain presentations of self; again, that became clear when scrutinising different Jlao performances. It is possible to argue that it is the rules of that mode or genre which shape the self-presentation. There are also members of oral societies who would agree with certain literary critics that the teller is irrelevant to the tale.[1]

Questions of subjective determination and levels of agency are difficult to resolve and I shall come back to them. In written literatures, such arguments assume or turn on the predefined structures with which artists work as novelists or essayists, poets or playwrights. The rules of form in these genres may themselves construct the presence of narrators, or require that they are absented, though it is acknowledged that creative authors play with the rules, and also extend boundaries of possibility for successors.

I argue that there are also oral genres, but some of their constitutive features are necessarily different from literary ones. Here too artists can innovate, with features that surprise the listeners' expectations, and do so by oblique means as well as by explicit direction. It is easy to 'misread' such creativity or subversion as spontaneous originality if one is not part of a knowing audience. Genres depend on shared rules of interpretation: they are not explicable by form alone, even in written literature. I illustrate and justify the category of 'oral genre' by further reference to life stories, moving between written and oral examples, and return to heroic accounts to discuss generic choice and the different kinds of sequencing possible in oral narrations.

Genre and mode

Arguments about classifications are frequently confused because a classification can be made for different purposes. So it is with genre, which is a term used in several different senses. I am not here attempting to make taxonomies or typologies which seek to classify universal types of form, or to discuss their validity.[2] Insofar as I consider classifications, they are indigenous ones by participants, not researchers. Genre in the perspective of this book could be called 'patterned expectancy'. Genre in this sense labels an agreement between writer or speaker and reader or listener on what sort of interpretation is to be made. It is a dynamic process and also a situational one. We can say that the sonnet is a genre of poetry although poetry itself is also a genre; novelists may 'mix genres' and move into what is recognised as a poetic mode as part of a narrative fiction.

The cues which signal to knowing recipients how they are to interpret a text can come from its format and layout, its properties as form, its orientations and authorisation, and from other features embodied in its content. The process of interpretation is not necessarily conscious, but interpretations there must be.

> If a text means what it says, then it means nothing in particular. Its saying has no determinate existence but must be the saying of the author or a reader. The text does not exist ... till it is construed; until then it is merely a sequence of signs.[3]

E. D. Hirsch made this point as part of an argument to demonstrate how literary texts are always interpreted, and he gives detailed examples of conflicting interpretations, from student literary analyses, so as to see how they could be made. Linguists also increasingly work from the presumption that linguistic signs (e.g. 'words') are not wholly interpretable by their grammatical ordering plus lexical knowledge, but depend on complex presuppositions. This is true of any language exchange, but with genre one is also looking at a higher-order concatenation of whole sequences of words, or 'discourse', and the means by which such phases of discourse are interpreted as a whole. For Hirsch, the over-all expectancies about a genre with which readers approach any particular work are crucial to its step-by-step interpretation. He treats genre as a purely literary phenomenon, and it is as such that genre is ordinarily a matter for critical discussion.

Hirsch's arguments are equally applicable to orality, although I would argue that one needs to take into account an important difference between the constituents of literate and oral genres. Whereas with written genres the setting in which one reads a text is often irrelevant to its interpretation, in oral genres the occasion of performance is clearly important and may be definitive of the audience's expectation. Features of delivery – voice quality, chanting or singing, accompanying music or dancing, the type of occasion on which a performance occurs and the place, the status of the performer and the nature of the audience itself – all these can be criterial features of an oral genre, as they prepare the audience to respond in certain ways. The oral conditions of performance mean too that oral genres are actively 'dialogic': they are social activities in real time.

The term 'dialogic' evokes the usage of M. Bakhtin, who pointed out that meanings are not singular givens but contestable; interpretation is a movement of interaction, as every use of words brings with it the contexts and conditions of previous uses. Bakhtin also argued that the genres of literacy transmit and elaborate 'speech genres', which he treated as the elementary formative constraints of speech. What linguists today might distinguish as discourse and a component register (the style of a particular occasion or purpose), are for Bakhtin equally dialogic, because of this active social history which is immanent at every utterance. For him the subject is 'specular', 'derived from the other', and the 'word is a drama in which three characters participate (it is not a duet but a trio)'.[4]

In criticism working from this perspective, it can be said that 'the division that has opened in academic discourse between oral literature as performance and written literature as object is thus closed. All texts are seen as an aspect of social action, and as cultural production, indivisibly interrelated with other forms of symbolic process'.[5] Oral genres may have importantly repeatable and stereotypic features which can be classified and compared, and these are important to recognise, but they will be misunderstood if they are treated solely as texts-in-themselves, detached from these conditions of production. This is so even when the genre is regarded as more important than the performer, since the performers are then 'licensed to speak' material which otherwise they might not be socially or politically able to say.[6]

A problem for the investigator of oral performances is that not all of them can be neatly divided into different genres, nor do they always have indigenous names or categorisations, such as Jlao use for heroic praising and boasting. Once genres are seen as practices, that is human actions for particular purposes (and these though intended are not always realised in full-blown achievement), the apparently fuzzy boundaries of some of them are less problematic. But of course one may want to point to a genre clearly marked by form, or the kind of fully achieved performances which, as with Sieh Jeto's histories, bear witness to a developed tradition of representing the past which has demanded intelligence and reflection by successive historians improving on one another – so that Sieh Jeto's powers are better understood when they are compared with the more limited accounts of other men and women. And how should one distinguish a well-formed historical narrative from the teller's brief answer to a question about it, given in a much more conversational style?

It is often possible to shift into genre, meaning a recognised performance or a special mode of talk, with minimal cues. A single phrase cues the

Liberian Kpelle listener to expect a move into (secret) 'society business'. A child can nominate a kitchen chair as a spaceship and the players immediately act to one another in space-voyager roles.[7] In the Jlao case, I have taken the teller's unwillingness to be interrupted in his narrative as a sign of being 'in genre', but obviously it would be silly to separate such formal accounts from much more informal and conversational recollections so as to make them incomparable in historical terms (and see pp. 27–8).

As the term *tradition* can indicate a large-scale, long-term and cumulative practice, which includes the conscious development of aesthetically satisfying forms in more than one genre, so the term *mode* might be used in contrast to 'genre' if one wants to stress that there is a focus on a topic such as 'past events' for which more than one genre can be employed. But this is really a matter of convenience for an outside analyst. 'Mode' like 'genre' will then indicate a practice and intention. In the Jlao case, for instance, a speaker in historical mode may be able to modulate stylistically from one generic form to another so as to evoke interpretations from the audience which in turn depend on knowledge of different genres. All the tellers I've described did this. Jua Sieh evoked the emotional intensity of heroic genres, Sieh Jeto incorporated etiological stories, with their 'Just So' explanations, and probably all the performers I heard used, or just alluded to, what I would call proverbs, but which were called in Liberian English 'parables'. This word translates a single term which in Kru, as in some other African languages, refers to short fables of different form but common moral pedagogy, an example of how oral genres can be identified by purpose or use rather than form.

I have suggested that as in literary genres cues of form and style are much more important than cues of occasion, so in oral ones occasion is much more likely to be significant than form and style. These modulations of 'mode' suggest how stylistic references can play their part too. There are of course also many oral genres world-wide which work within close and elaborate constraints of form. They testify to aesthetic elaboration and, sometimes, to a demand for accurate transmission as memorable art and message.[8]

I include purpose and use in 'occasion'; the word is intended to label all the social characteristics of performance. It is noticeable that there are plenty of such performance-centred identifications of genre in ordinary English speech, as when people say 'he's only joking' or 'she gave me a sob-story'. The professionally produced performances of neo-oracy are ordinarily categorised into genres, such as TV's 'sitcom' or drama-documentary. Yet while we notice these types, which are obviously relatable to the dramatic genres which are already elaborately defined in critical analyses, the prestige of such public and elaborately presented

forms, and indeed the prestige of written language itself, mutes the oral achievements of everyday. In a literate, largely urban and mass culture like Britain's, formerly respected performance genres like folk tale and folk song have a consciously preserved look, though actually there are plenty of practitioners who have updated songs into 'folk' and – as some modern folklorists point out – folk tales live on in new contemporary guises too. Good storytellers are admired, and their genre gets critical and informed support in the pub. But little academic attention is paid to the rhetorical skills of ordinary speakers. They never seem to rate study by literary critics, though psychologists and political scientists may be interested in them for their own disciplinary ends.

Historians and anthropologists class some informants as better than others, and textbook writers on oral history methodology direct attention to the possible effects of a choice of venue and of a non-participating audience, such as a husband's presence when a wife is being interviewed, whether one is interviewed on one's home ground or in an alien office. The triggering effects of venue and audience are noted as affecting orientation and content. Since the social relationship between such tellers and listeners almost always includes power inequalities, sometimes represented as moral ones, these may make a story appear condescending or an attempt to curry favour, or to be reckoned as unsuitable for certain ears. Thus the choice of a genre will itself send a meta-message. Inappropriate choices show social 'misreading' (which of course could be deliberate, or an attempt to make a genre 'license' the performer). The outside researcher is socially 'read' or 'misread' too and is not, therefore, a neutral recorder of 'data' but a factor in a social event.

Though these points are well understood in certain sociological and social anthropological perspectives, some of their significance can still be missed if one does not also take into account the existence of oral genre as I have tried to define it here, because of the ways in which genre *mediates* narrator and audiences, as well as narrators and narrations. Thus researchers often assume that their work is 'doing an interview' *with* interviewees. They have not been taught to consider that interviews are oral genres, so it is not in these terms that they could recognise interviewing as a genre which the tellers may not feel qualified to talk in, although they have command of other genres in which they would speak differently. It could be more fruitful to tap into tellers' expertise and not to insist on their confirming to the interviewer's genre.

It is unfortunately easier to give this advice than to show in detail how a particular British oral past-oriented genre might work. There is even a lack of examples to examine, because the material has not been recorded so that it can be looked at in this way. Although oral historians transcribe their data as best they can, I've found that elements of text as well as paralingual features are often missing when I've listened to excerpts from tapes, played at seminar or conference for illustrations. That is because the analyst, who in looking for significant information is clearly alert to nuance or pause or phrase, still may discard features of oral rhetoric as the repetitiveness they would indeed convey in writing, and there is no training in the 'choreography' of oral rhetorics.[9] The transcript is thus a translation into the literate text which is still required as evidence by professional historians. Researchers without a 'lit. crit.' background indeed are led to treat oral arts of delivery as part of the decorations of 'style', in which words are the envelope of content. Why anthropologists and historians should make this assumption is discussed further in Chapter 5.

The orientations and claims of autobiography as a genre

In the last chapter, I treated the narrators' presentations of self as a matter of orientation and of underlying structure. Blamo Kofa even had to be his subject if he was to perform the genre of heroic boasting. Academic authors are not supposed to boast in this way, though, as I pointed out, the very format of their books will include claims to authority. Impersonal authorisation is a hallmark of their genre; the use of passive, or, more properly, nominal constructions for which no subject can be deduced. 'It is thought that' allows the writer to escape responsibility and at the same time to imply the support of even higher authorities, which is why this construction is so much favoured by bureaucrats. The construction is also authoritative in its implication of a timeless present. Such usages as a style become generic, that is, they cue the reader or listener to expect a certain status and point of view. Since speakers and writers must also, simultaneously, orient themselves temporally to topics and audiences, temporality is an aspect of narrations which may also indicate genre, or be directed by genre. Temporality is therefore discussed at length in the next chapter.

Life stories may also form a genre, as with their written counterpart autobiography, a term which has a broader reference than life story or life history, and implies 'a literary form of representation' as Raphael Samuel pointed out.[10] When one considers how religious and political leaders have also presented parts of their lives as examples to others, thus making them 'exemplary autobiographies', one can see that the term may even be appropriate for actions as well as verbal description.[11] Verbal description is the focus here, however, or rather verbal representation, which requires the most artless and unselfconscious narrator to select, order and relate, and to describe events from assumptions that they are somehow connected, even if this assumption is simply that they are worth mentioning because the teller heard of them or was involved tangentially in their production – in that case, ego is the link and the stories are 'cards of identity'.[12]

As Samuel points out, 'autobiography, whether the author recognises it or not, inhabits a social as well as a personal space'. Autobiographers literary or oral are communicating with an audience, and justifying themselves. These needs direct their subject orientation; so that even when the view ostensibly is that events matter more than the personality of the author, who just cares about 'setting the record straight', it is only certain events, in which the author has a particular interest, that will be dissected.

A narrative presentation of self is a social action because it anticipates and therefore adjusts to particular social responses – it is 'specular' in Bakhtin's sense – in print as well as in the oral conditions explored in the last chapter. The public figure in Britain today who gives an autobiography 'tells all', or deliberately refuses to do so, because there is hunger for privileged intimacy (an audience/reader becomes an equal, knows more than the public face) and because there is, as yet, a climate of permissiveness which encourages and protects some kinds of personal revelation. Other times, other manners.

Written autobiographies are nevertheless not inevitable social products. They do not appear in all literatures. Their emergence can be charted. Would-be autobiographers have modelled themselves on precedent examples. In other words, written autobiographies have developed as a literary genre with subgenres, whose conventions guide the reader to recognise what they are (as when looking for something to read in the public library!) and to expect certain features.[13] The emergence of autobiography as a literary genre indicated changes in social conventions as to the events which are proper to describe and worthy of notice, as well as to self-description and analysis. We should expect the same conditionality for an oral genre; I discuss such conditions later (pp. 132–4).

Oral presentations of one's life are, no less than literary ones, the product of canons of appropriateness and rhetorical stereotypes. Samuel's examples from published writers would apply as well to humble talkers. 'The comedian goes in for whimsical anecdotes; the statesman cultivates an air of discretion; the rolling stone or traveller effervesces'. The social occasions for personal reminiscence are also highly ordered, as one can see on occasions when they are out of place – or when they have to be tolerated because of the speaker's influence and standing. On British private and public occasions they can also be used manipulatively, and like jokes, make rhetorical devices of political force.[14] It is wrong to assume that oral societies are specially constrained in the format, timing and functionality of recall.

All these characteristics imply that life stories and autobiographies create personae, not transparent self-portraits, and they may encourage reflective self-consciousness too, since the genre itself contributes to the development of self-presentation by providing models to follow or modify. Literary critics note that truth and falsity prove not to be useful yardsticks of analysis, because the relation between 'the self' and the self which is presented varies. Sometimes, 'the author says to me "my life was as the tale I am telling" . . . an extended, epic simile'. To Stephen Spender, himself an autobiographer, 'The autobiographical . . . is no longer the writer's own experience: it becomes everyone's. He is no longer writing about himself: he is writing about life.'[15] Yet other narrators appear uninterested in their own, and sometimes in other people's personalities. They may argue for instance that they are simply bearing witness, impersonally. Such variations are equally possible in an oral genre, as the previous chapter illustrates.

James Cox suggests that Thomas Jefferson was an autobiographer of the impersonally biographical kind. For Jefferson, says Cox,

> Beginnings are more important than endings; statements are more important than narration; recollections are more important than memory; dates and facts are more important than emotion and consciousness . . . The present from which he writes is not so much a point from which to renew the past as it is a point of vantage from which to stabilize it, to reinforce it as the fixed source and foundation of the present.[16]

Cox makes these claims on the basis of explicit statements by Jefferson which are matched by inference from the style and structure of his Memoir. He also argues that the literary style matches the political style, it is architectural, setting out checks and balances. Such matching might reveal more than a cast of thought: Jefferson is also making a history-as-recorded of the history he has made. A comparable process can be seen in Jua Sieh's narrative.

Autobiographers in writing and orally may nevertheless reveal their personal interests through the structuring of genre, which comparison can reveal. This is a major argument in Samuel's valuable paper. He points out that:

> In Methodist autobiography – as in that of other religious and political sectarians – stories, while retaining the appearance of fact, also take on the character of fables, and are used as homilectic devices to exemplify moral truths: 'remarkable conversions'

illustrate the possibilities of redemption, while renegades and backsliders encounter an invariably melancholy fate.

We can add that such persuasive testimonies presuppose a persuadable audience and a shared ideology of the person as being only the instrument of God. The minutiae of one's career can then, paradoxically, become evidential of Providential design; so is the humble exalted. A dissident outsider interprets these evidences as ideological and cosmological constructions. The co-believer perceives deeper meanings which can be taken to demonstrate a super-rational Truth.

These examples suggest there are complex connections between genre and the construction of self, a point to which I return (p. 134). For the time being, I note that a generic perspective on autobiographical accounts indicates recognisable and therefore repeated features of organisational structuring and content. Their selection is directed by rules on appropriate topics and their order, and personal choices between them can be self-revelatory. Writers may choose for instance to start before their own life: 'On the father's side, I am descended from a long line of Welsh squires...' or to look backwards from the present: 'As I sit in the window seat and look out on the bright sails of the pleasure craft, I often think back to those very different views of the sea I had from the lower deck...'

The familiarity of such somewhat parodied openings itself shows that autobiographies are patterned, and that would-be autobiographers have models to follow. As Samuel points out, the patterns of autobiographies can also convey meta-messages. My parodies exemplify orientation and status claim; the moral fables noted by Samuel were constitutive models as well. They not only showed that the writer's life was exemplary in such and such a way, they also made it so. By following the model, the representation of one's own life was inevitably shaped morally: it took on that appearance retrospectively, even if it was not so experienced at the time.

Clearly, spoken life stories may equally be patterned, expectable, even stereotypic. The tellers may choose a pattern which will construct a satisfying sense of self, and which may even re-order events so as to overcome otherwise uncomfortable discrepancies.[17] The ordering as well as the orientation to audience may convey meta-messages – as Jua Sieh's account illustrated. The occasion of any oral autobiography is extremely important. Personal anecdotes can be appropriate or out of place and sanctified or made ribald by social context.

Heroic genres and their social conditions

I now return to heroic genres, which in the last chapter I considered from the tellers' perspective. Here they are foci, first in a brief comment on performance effects, next in discussing the implications of genre choice, and finally to investigate the variety of sequencing possible in oral performances.

Although many African oral performances have been targets for academic description and analysis, their efforts have very often been directed at *texts*, for which the words of a performance have been literally reduced to writing. Their specific kinds of orality have so far been only partially addressed, which suggests how powerfully the researchers are constrained by their own literacy.[18] Yet if we look at the Jlao Kru heroic praises which were illustrated in the previous chapter we see that even their ordering of components has to do with the actions of the tellers and their delivery.

It's a well-known defect of transcriptions that they read flatly on the page. The reader misses the occasion, the delivery, and also, very often, the allusions, and so is unable to share in the genre. The fast and soaring chant of Nimine Gbei is exciting to listen to even without understanding Kru. Actually, Kru listeners also find it hard to hear all the words. But her repetition of allusive phrases and their tempo has a drive which is itself creating part of the excitement, besides offering a redundancy which means that even the not very knowledgeable, young Kru listener can get the gist. Others will respond to deeper, metaphorical meanings. If they have heard similar performances over the years, they will get more out of this one, like any experienced theatre- or concert-goer or poetry reader; oral artists like literate ones can produce 'deep' work which will appeal to different members of the audience in different ways. Moreover, a singer like Nimine Gbei had through her voice to be accompanist and MC as well as solo performer, controlling and modulating a many-figured performance in which others could also come forward as the centre of attention, and always having not just to hold and play on the audience but to persuade different members of it to applaud and reward her.[19]

The 'literary' effects of such performances therefore depend partly on purely oral means, including co-presence. We can also investigate the social conditions of a heroic genre by looking at a European example where it was considered, but not chosen, as a written literary form. The historian F. W. D. Deakin was sent, during World War II, to liaïse with an unknown Yugoslav guerilla leader, and found later that he had been air dropped into Tito's retreat. What sort of account of Yugoslavia's war would be most faithful? He published two in his book: first a personal narrative of his experiences, then a more historically conventional overview, which modifies some of his understandings in the light of later knowledge, but which itself could not have been written without eyewitness evidence. He says that at one stage he thought an epic poem would best express his sense of those events. The region of course has long been famous for such performances of heroic tales.[20]

To the question 'What happened in Yugoslavia?' Deakin could give many answers. There was a political dimension which meant that *realpolitik* for World War II leaders included choices of which Yugoslav guerilla leaders to back. The partisans' internal political differences were often lethal. Ordinary people experienced, voluntarily and involuntarily, extremely harsh conditions which Deakin partly shared. No single representation in writing could accommodate all these features. His thoughts of epic poetry show that he felt no single form or genre of writing could convey them all, either.

A literate historian who tried to set up a chronologically based cause-and-effect account could give only a limited explanation of partisan life and conflict if confined to official documents. Partisans' eyewitness accounts would not be fully explanatory, since they did not know how much their lives were affected by decisions taken far away. We should also note that while the still active local epic tradition offered a means of evoking genuine emotions, it would use an existing rhetoric to reformulate Deakin's unique, subjective responses. These traditions go back hundreds of years, and it is well attested that apparently new representations there are often old ones – the teller 'codes' memories or reports of remembered events into existent stereotopic forms.[21]

Deakin's problems also show the limitations of eyewitness, discussed in the last chapter. As Tolstoy rightly imagined in his portrayal of battle in *War and Peace*, the eyewitness not only sees fragmentarily, but may not know enough of the background to understand what is going on, though his experience is none the less vivid! And Deakin's problems of rendering his early ignorances and later, cumulative additions of knowledge into one account, which I have just looked at as a problem of historical evidence, point to the fact that different genres will render and amplify different aspects of the 'same' events, including the intense emotional experience of participation, a reality quite irrespective of a participator's ignorance or knowledge of wider causes.

Deakin's thought of writing an 'epic' was presumably encouraged by knowledge of Balkan epic traditions. In other words, he felt he could have realised aspects of his own wartime experience more truthfully by working through a well-standardised genre – and one that in many ways seems formulaic, and inimical to individual autobiography. Such is the power of genre – but it requires the consent of one's intended audience to succeed. The academic historical community and more general readers were not participators in such a heroic genre, nor could we have learned from it all the information conveyed through his actual narratives.

In their survey of oral literature, H. Munro and Nora Chadwick recognised repeated patterns of plot, form and characterisation which H. M. Chadwick had earlier decided was part of the 'Heroic Age'.[22]

Although this conception included notions of evolutionary stages which now seem dated, it is surely correct in linking kinds of society and forms of literature. It is therefore not surprising that the social conditions of wartime resistance can produce heroic tales. And heroic genres can be adapted: there are new versions of Zulu *izibongo*, praise songs, which 'define the corporate identity of the unions through their struggles with management, police, informers, and they inspire individual workers in much the same way as royal praise poetry once inspired individuals, and to some extent still does'.[23]

For all its glory, a heroic tradition is of course ideological, and it glorifies some at the expense of others. Women have little place, non-fighters likewise, and violence is made desirable. There may, of course, simultaneously be other genres in a culture which extol different values. The Jlao dabe praises herself as well as men by giving her own genealogy, and, as men and women commonly do in this community, she and Kofa both give matronyms as well as patronyms. Blamo Kofa was normally called by his patronym, so I have done so too. Sieh Jeto is given his patronym, and as a surname, because when I interviewed him he explicitly requested it; he was normally called by his matronymic, as Tipla Sieh.

Nomenclature can also mislead: Kru talked to me in English of their 'war dance', in Kru *gbela*, which on the occasion that I saw it performed in Sasstown did indeed feature men in war or pseudo war garb, but it was being danced for a respected woman's funeral, and this was clearly not an out of the way example. Some virtues of heroes belong to the special needs of war, and they need not be otherwise likeable. In 1972, I visited Harper, which had been President Tubman's favoured home town, and when I wondered how the inhabitants would survive the loss of his patronage, Emmanuel S. Togba drily quoted a proverb, '*Biɔ mɛ, ní à jé biɔ!*' 'When a hero dies, you find another hero!' He explained *biɔ* as a man who doesn't fear, whether in war or town, 'anyone who confronts boldness', who makes 'fearful things fearless'.[24] Some of the antics of heroes in Sieh Jeto's history gave rise to a sort of wry pride, 'aren't we awful!' in my assistants. One of these, Frank Nimene, had to consult an older man, N. Wiah, to get the meaning of the word I've translated as 'hard heart' in Kofa's story: it could also mean doing bad things, being 'too mean', ruthless.

Kru life is not so heroic in practice, nor do its citizens intend it to be. As agriculturists and migrant labourers, they did not live like nomadic Bedouin camel owners, whose segmented political organisation was accompanied by 'uncertain, agonistic, political adventurism'. In the Rwala Bedu oral literature of Northern Arabia investigated by Michael Meeker, male identity turned on political skills, of persuasion by speech and violence. Words are action and order most especially where technology is not; so that rhetorical skills, including heroic genres, are important parts of such political cultures. Rwala poems also commonly evoked battles without giving details of when and where, 'but this is just the point. The necessity of knowing the narrative tradition in order to place the scenes in context only emphasises how discontinuous, fragmentary and unstorylike the poem is.'[25]

Narrative and non-narrative forms in oral genres

Meeker's explanation calls in question the term 'narrative history' for the Rwala Bedu heroic poetry he analyses, because he claims that its evocatory power depends on an audience's 'intertextual' knowledge of another historical narrative, or of other accounts of specific historical events. There is a sense nevertheless in which all the examples so far presented can be called 'narrative history', given that this term seems often used simply to mean any account of the succession of events which has no overt editorial qualification. Dale Porter's defence of narrative history as a theoretically satisfying and genuinely revelatory mode of representation has already been referred to when discussing Sieh Jeto's work. Other analyses suggest a variety of assumed definitions. In the sense defined by Morton White, the emphasis is on explanation. 'A narrative consists primarily of singular explanatory statements, implies singular factual statements that are not explanatory in form and rests to some extent on value judgements made by the Historian.' This definition is very different from those of text-centred analyses which consider the means by which such statements cohere in a discourse.[26]

In my first chapter, I showed an oral historian plotting narratives which both describe and place past events. Sieh Jeto's means and ends were largely the same as literate historians'. He accounted for the emergence of a social unit, Jlao, as a destined struggle, and while Jlao listeners could take pride in the story of their becoming, the occasion, aspects of delivery and the scale of argument all differentiate his performance from the local heroic genres. We can also see, from the very constitution of the narrative, that the historian had been reflective, had grasped an order and had contrasted accounts of past events with social conditions known to him; he had evaluated the characters' actions morally. The shaping intelligence of the historian has operated even if he followed precedent models, because he needed to understand if he was to follow them.

It's possible for anyone to be a historian in this sense, and several Jlao people explained past events to me informally as well as presenting longer, more complexly organised accounts, both in Kru and in English. Blamo Kofa and Blenyeno also used sequencing in narrative as an organising principle, but they employed other means as well. Kofa raised the emotional temperature by interposing shouted praise names, '*Mɸjikpan!*

Mɸjìkpan!' (roughly, 'I'm leopard hard!') and personal horn slogans, 'One person doesn't fight a whole town's war!' His aural and visual effects helped to carry the audience with him. Delivery characteristics were even more important in Gbei's performance, with its repetitions building up the importance of otherwise small incidents.

Jesse Jackson, surprisingly successful in the run-up before the Democrat nomination for the 1988 US Presidential campaign, clearly owed much to his oratory, which evoked both recognition and involvement in his audience: 'I know it's hot. It's been hot in Chattanooga for a long time. It used to be hot when we picked cotton. Now it's hot and we're picking presidents!' As in Rwala Bedu songs, a concatenation of images here works – punningly – together; accumulating, apparently discrete examples resonate with one another and with the previous knowledge of the knowing listener, who does not experience them as 'discontinuous' and 'fragmentary', as they may seem to outsiders.

It is therefore possible to convey the accumulative power of narrative through purely oral means, which build up delayed climaxes by the pitch, pause and tempo of vocal delivery, and also by clustering evocative suggestions whose implications the knowing audience themselves link together as powerfully conclusive. It's not surprising to see these two means working together on an oral occasion, with speaker and knowing audience co-present.

As Karin Barber has shown, comparably evocative effects can also be made by the accumulative delivery of 'heroic epithets' which are not otherwise cohesive in the ordinary senses of 'narrative history'. She has given a very rich analysis of the powers and effects of Nigerian Yoruba *oríkì*, brief but condensed, attributive 'praises' which a person can accumulate over a lifetime, and a town for much longer. Again, they may individually be oblique to those who don't know the background – 'Cock o' the North' is said to be an evocative praise name to knowledgeable Scots, but it's not so to me! In Yoruba terms, the background story of an oríkì is its *itàn* (discussed also on p. 92), and ìtàn also are hung on oríkì in intricate symbiosis. 'One could see oriki as a mnemonic aid for the oral historian; but one could with equal justice see the oral history as an amplification of an essentially non-linear, disjunctive form ... they represent the symbolic capital of specific sub-groups – lineages or families – within the town.'

A 'big man' is 'built up by an intensive bestowal of fragments from the past' – and this is in an African culture where 'bigness' includes body-weight as well as maturity, the accumulation of material possessions and of others' good opinions (like a British business's 'goodwill'). Oríkì are, separately, brief, and they are intended to be condensed, cryptic and 'heavy'; by concatenating them, the praiser intensifies her desired impression that there is no end to them. Barber notes that if they are treated as 'texts', they are 'peculiarly resistant to the mainstream techniques of literary criticism'; one can see also how they are inimical to conventional historiographical techniques. Unlike Blenyeno's performance, oríkì are not intended to give a single review of a past, rather, many pasts are held to be immanent in them. They are therefore multiply past-oriented, and their ambiguity of actor-reference is a feature that I have already referred to as a feature in other oral accounts (pp. 42–4, see also p. 82).

For the Yoruba audience, these are powers literally animated by the singer in each new performance.

> When a performer utters oríkì, she addresses herself intensely and exclusively to the subject of the oríkì she is currently uttering, whether this subject is living or dead, human or spiritual being. If the subject is a living human, present at the performance, she can be seen leaning towards him, almost visibly bestowing her words on him, creating and maintaining a powerful dyadic bond. The subject is visibly affected: he seems to expand, to take on afflatus, and to be profoundly moved.

Oríkì can even call back the dead, and 'uttering oríkì to an *egúngún* (ancestral masquerade) is what empowers it'.[27]

Blenyeno's pre-eminence and title was due to her special power, too: 'whenever she is singing there must be a dwelling of spirit among the people'; 'during the time of the war she was the only woman to stand and sing and called the warriors' Name [and] then the spirit dwell in them to perform their Africalist [supernatural 'science'] to kill as many people as they can'. Agatha Kofa, who gave me this explanation, got it from her uncle, son of Blamo Kofa. He also reported to her that, in 1987, Blamo Kofa had lain in a coma for three weeks, but could not die; people therefore suggested that 'the great singer Gbei' should sing over him. 'She begin to sing calling his Name and explaining how he fought the war and how he kill people in the war, to everyone's surprising he stood up' and he shouted out seven times how he fought the war, then storm and heavy wind came and 'tree fell' and he was dead.[28]

'Heroic' tellers certainly have power through their mastery of genre. When they tell stories of 'how we became what we are' their evocative identifications are compelling (as we say), that is, they persuade listeners to see themselves differently. Such re-presentations can be called emotive, persuading people to reject counter-presentations that seem to attack their own social identity. Yet emotionality is not intrinsically resistant to objectivity, or, to put it in another way, rhetoric and veracity are not incompatible. The presentations of the past that I have just described were not merely rhetorical in the sense that I have argued all good accounts must be, that is persuasive to their intended recipients, they were also as it were meta-rhetorical, strongly intentional actions, some of which are believed to have especial powers in their performing.

The means and effects of these rhetorics exploit the features of orality, which are so often forgotten by literates and resistant to their analytical assumptions. Women animate words, as they bring life into the world; the past is purposefully deployed so as to change the future and people are honoured and individualised by specifying their names and the past of these names. No wonder, then, that the language structures in which they speak can carry such oblique and complex placings of persons and of time, as the next chapter illustrates.

4

TEMPORALITY: NARRATORS AND THEIR TIMES

Telling in time

There is a truly enormous literature on time, which continues to engage the attention of philosophers, scientists, linguists, novelists, anthropologists ... – and all of these approaches may be relevant to the analysis of a historical account. In any discussion of temporality looms the weight of the possible approaches not discussed, of massed reference and theoretical complexity, including the complexity of 'time' as one English label for many characteristics which peoples all over the world and in different past times have understood very differently.

In this chapter, then, the illustration is actually very limited even when the detail seems dense, and discussion moves from the consequences of temporal contingency to the constraints of verbal representation. Time as 'contingency', because every narration is prompted by the intersection in real time of a narrator and listener(s); and the narration itself occupies a phase of irreversible time. The narrators and listeners connected by this contingency are thereby caught at a certain stage of their lives; they have also been formed inescapably by their own personal pasts to date. These factors influence the narration whether or not it is autobiographical; tellers are constructing retrospective accounts for audiences with different time scales, and they may adjust their own narrations to the memories and understanding of their listeners.

The narrators are also influenced by prevailing cosmologies and cultural expectations or theories as to how duration and successivity occur. These not only direct narrators' framing and explanation of events, they enter into the collective representations of genre, and, as we know, by choice of genre telling is constrained, shaped in a particular way. The inescapable rules of language, through which temporality is expressed, also interact with the rules which shape and differentiate genre. Once seen comparatively, across languages, the structures of temporal references in which we think and express ourselves, which therefore are the texture of our thought, cease to seem transparent and are shown to be conventions, patterned in ways that can make other peoples' representations of time look eerily unfamiliar.

All tellers have to use collective representations so as to make sense to others, and to represent the organisation of events to themselves. These representations must include accepted ways of indicating duration and the punctuation of time: the syntax of language, its allocation of aspect and tense forms are social facts which no-one can bypass except at the price of non-communication (and that is often characterised as insanity). Orientation and claim must include temporal orientation and claim. Is the teller stating that events described took place in times remote to all present, or to the audience but not the teller? ('Things were different when I was young.')

When they want to collect examples of oral data, researchers commonly set off instances of narrative production by asking for interviews or to learn about the past. They thus intervene in their subjects' lives, asking them to crystallise themselves at this chance moment in time. Even the apparently un-autobiographical narrator sets out a narrative from the perspective of that moment. 'The remembering and the telling are themselves *events*, not only descriptions of events... "An event lived is finished, bound within experience. But an event remembered is boundless, because it is the key to all that happened before and after it."'[1] Of all the *time* that the historian considers, not the least important in an oral context is the timing of a particular incarnation of the oral text itself – an incarnation because it fuses the narrator, narrative and audience at this moment of time in a perspective on all those other moments.

A narrator who is asked to narrate must consider the occasion, above all the perceived character, intentions and possible power of the audience – even when giving a monologue which bears all the marks of a familiar rendition. Strictly even then the narrative is a kind of dialogue – and one whose structure is not reducible to the separate component contributions of different speakers. On these formal grounds alone the structure also contributes to the meaning. 'When the researcher's voice is cut out, the informant's voice is distorted.'[2] All this means that the times in the narration are affected by times outside it; even the audiences' interventions may direct and alter these times and the choice of representation through which they are effected.

Alessandro Portelli, in an article neatly entitled 'The Time of My Life', elegantly sorts out some of the many times used by his Italian narrators. These include the appropriate times for reminiscing, whether 'the old men's empty afternoon on the park bench' or the diffused time of intermittent interchange between a mother and daughter. The story itself may be set going from a point in special time, 'before-the war', 'before-Fascism', which is really a time out of ordinary time, like 'once upon a time' (so that the story thereby enters our experience, in the time of everyday). He discusses the oral narrative's character of time unfinished, ready to be reworked by subsequent living, as I have exemplified in Jua Sieh's tale. He comments on how the variable velocity of speech is meaningful – we could add the speaker's arts of *timing*, which make Kru stories, for instance, most calculatedly dramatic.

Portelli also very interestingly analyses the ways in which tellers 'place time in the text'. As he points out, time is a continuum, but humans periodise it: 'time is divided horizontally into periods and eras, and "hung" on key events which operate as partitions and as interpreters of the meaning of each period'.[3] Every narrator must also make a choice of which sort of event to describe in a unit of time, since we simultaneously experience life in different aspects, such as family, work, and the effect of national or international events. Portelli found that tellers tended to choose either an 'institutional', 'collective' or 'personal mode' of selection of events to recount. (Mode in his sense is rather different from mine as set out in the last chapter.) Mode and periodisation will change, even in the same narrative, and may be hard to distinguish, but he could sort out the dating of events by attending to tellers' modes. For instance, though many tellers referred to the death of a young factory worker, Luigi Trastulli, in a demonstration in 1949, half of them, including some eyewitnesses, dated this in 1953, when three days of non-fatal street fighting followed the sacking of 2700 steelworkers in the town of Terni.

Portelli found that Trastulli's death was recalled with shame and he noticed that it was correctly dated by users of the 'personal mode' ('I was standing right beside him', 'We didn't have a car yet...') who could therefore set the event in a context where they felt self worth, and by users of the 'institutional mode', who dealt with it as part of a leadership crisis in the party and the unions. Speakers in the 'collective mode', where the shame occurred – 'Nothing! We did nothing!' – shifted the date to an occasion when 'the workers can affirm that they retaliated and can feel that, though there was heavy loss of jobs, at least there was no loss of face, pride, identity'.[4]

Making sense of time

(a) Collective visions: cosmologies and chronologies

To evoke past events is to respond to what G. M. Trevelyan called

> the most familiar and certain fact about life ... the quasi-miraculous fact that once, on this earth, once on this familiar spot of ground, walked other men and women, as actual as we are today, thinking their own thoughts, swayed by their own passions, but now all gone, one generation vanishing after another, gone as utterly as we ourselves shall shortly be gone like ghost at cockcrow.[5]

To Trevelyan this paradox was 'poetry' and its recording part of the aesthetic satisfactions of being a historian. Yet, as Portelli's work reminds us, the paradox can be a painful one and evoke memories which tellers with different experiences may construe in contradictory temporal modes.

When people talk of Time they are very often interested in grand questions like What is Time? Death's inevitability and attempts to arrest or reverse death and time are major themes in the literatures and the religions of the world. But theories about time's nature and people's part in it vary widely. Trevelyan's perspective on the past is a product of the times he lived in. At some periods of Europe's history, the focus is on personal dissolution, as in Trevelyan's humanist vision; today many people's imaginations are caught by truly cosmic visions, of many universes and therefore of alternative societies: the world of science fiction and its time warps, which does not have a God-centred cosmology, rather one that asks if humanness can be altered by humans.

Cosmology may seem, for historical narratives, to be a matter of content and not of structuring form, but, as Jua Sieh's opening gambit showed, a personal orientation and claim can be asserted by reference to cosmological authority. Cosmologies, after all, can answer many questions, including Where have we come from? How is the world constituted? What is my place in it?

Answering such questions may be the main purpose of a 'mythic' or a 'historical' account, or of substantial sections of it. Such a myth is not necessarily authoritative, even though proposed by authoritative persons: Vansina argues that such accounts/myths are proffered by Kuba speakers in a speculative spirit, as one version against another.[6] Very often the cosmology informs a teller's account, guiding the choice and interpretation of events. Then, as Africanist historians have found, one needs to understand the cosmology if one is to understand the history which is being proffered.[7]

British or American histories are just as much predicated on cosmological presuppositions. One cosmology indeed validates the temporal grid which structures *all* Western temporality, and is taken by many historians to be the *sine qua non* of their craft: this is our annual Christian chronology, the classification of succeeding years as 1990, 1991 and so on. Very many peoples have recognised the year as a minimal unit of natural or agricultural seasons, and frequently have related these recurrent changes to astronomical features too. But this knowledge does not itself make our chronology, which is a classification system assigning a number in sequence, from 1 onwards, to years of the same length. By this means, all years can be treated as identical, unique, and serial.

In classical antiquity, there was no very efficient system of chronology available to historians, who tended to place events within rulers' reigns – a very widely used categorisation. Our chronology came about as part of the effort to calculate the correct timing of Easter. Competition between a number of calendrical computations was resolved at the Synod of Whitby in 664, which chose the Roman solar calendar. Calculations of the dates of holy days could be made by following Easter tables set out in years, and 'great churches and great houses ... found it natural to record important events on them, with a brevity determined by the space between lines and the width of the margin'. Early recensions of the Anglo-Saxon Chronicle list events in this way, and Eastern Tables became sources for narrative histories like Bede's Ecclesiastical History.[8]

Today's most universal chronology is therefore validated according to Christian cosmology, and charts the progression of the Christian Era beginning with the 'Year of Grace', Anno Domini, the Year of Our Lord, AD. Islam also times itself from a unique temporal occurrence, AH, Anno Hegirae, the year God's Prophet, Mahomed, fled from Mecca to Medina.[9] Both these systems mark the incursion of sequential time into Eternity, and permit a sense of linear progression which could, ideologically, become identified with progressivism, that is with evolutionary development and Progress.[10]

(b) Tools for timing, tools for thought

The Muslim and Christian chronologies are also tools, like watches – or computers. Once invented, they can be used by people who do not understand how they are made, but they will alter the users' perceptions, nonetheless. To use a chronology, clock, watch, seems to shape my sense of reality more fundamentally than to use a pocket calculator, at least for commonplace arithmetical operations, but that is partly because such operations were already encoded for me in multiplication and mathematical tables. What cognitive expansion these could make is brought home when one reads Samuel Pepys's diary for 4 July 1662. 'By and by comes Mr. Cooper, Mate of the *Royal Charles*, of whom I intend to learn *Mathematiques*; and so begin with him today, he being a very able man ... After an hour's being with him at Arithmetique, my first attempt being to learn the Multiplication table.' At that time, apparently, children rarely learned this beyond five times five.[11]

Nowadays, it is argued that computers can extend, change or even replace human cognition.[12] The modelling used in computers is very influential as well, as it offers so many disciplines new representations of action, which are also haloed with the prestige and power accorded to computing developments. I do not think these modellings yet form truly popular collective representations, as do the segmentations of clock times, but this should soon come.

Measurements of time, from years to minute divisions of seconds, are made by scientific calculation in relation to movements of the earth in the universe. Their representation through watches, timetables, negotiated hours of work and the like means that for much of the world there is now a collective representation of time as our allotment of repeated apparently identical units and sub-units: years divided into months, months into weeks, weeks into days, days into hours, hours into minutes. This system has had to be fitted onto previous systems which used different categories. Jlao Kru, for instance, could adjust their farming cycle into a year quite easily. Since each year a town makes a farm on a named area, they had already the practice of differentiating events in previous years according to which farm was then being made. (I found, however, that this recall only lasted for a few years.) The rise of each new moon was ritually marked. The week was a new category. Other West African peoples had – and sometimes have still – to adjust the cycle of the seven-day week to their 'market week', a system where a group of markets would be held in regular sequence, each marking a day.[13]

To most literate historians, our annual chronology is the very ground of history and even defines it. Historians of non-literate peoples have come to realise that they too have ways of periodising time. Mostly this information has been used so as to try to fit such periods into a datable framework. Obviously the use of a time-line on which we can fit a sequence of events is a powerful tool for connecting and comparing, just as the existence of written items, 'documents', which can be tied to points on the time-line reveals sequences over time which the continual recreation of oracy is very likely to elide. Pepys in his diary relates his new mathematical knowledge; it is also dated. Some Catholic missionaries at Sasstown kept diaries: these day by day accounts of what was happening in 1913–21 have helped me to chart formally the steps by which the dako became incorporated into the Republic of Liberia.

Much of what the mission archive diaries tell was also recounted to me by oral historians, often using dates. It's noticeable that Sieh Jeto moves quite smoothly into annual chronology starting at the end of the nineteenth century when it 'came in' with the complex of literacy, Christianity, English and waged migrant labour. Such is the power of literacy, however, that dates validated by documents are considered more authoritative than oral record, partly because of the ways that documents can be tested. I return to this point in the next chapter.

While it is easily understood that events on the same or contiguous dates are not necessarily connected by this coincidence, it may be less realised that the annual chronology has its own teleological drive, not least when it is recounted through the automatic serialisation of narrative sequences. Not merely a tool, it can also direct thought. We have seen how Sieh Jeto 'drove' one narrative by sequencing events tied to places and motivating them as Manifest Destiny; the other was sequenced according to another well-known model of time succession, the reign, which is very often in turn premised upon another selective representation of temporal connections, the genealogy (see p. 125). Literate historians have used both genealogical and regnal classification; both systems segment time in meaningful ways that are humanly, not 'scientifically' defined, and both are ideological in their very structures. As with narrative itself, this is because the structure's own order regularises and relates the segments of time it has itself created so as to suggest they are causally connected.

(c) Co-existent times

Perhaps the main illusion purveyed by all chronologised accounts is that there is only one stream of time. Its speed may vary; oral tellers like literate ones can suggest that nothing happens in a segment of time/event (notice how the two categories become fused through the structure). Sieh Jeto sometimes explained that the people stayed in a place for a long time: the structure of the geochronology means that 'staying in one place' when no events are recorded also implies 'no change'.

Despite the structuring of 'clock and watch time' which I've described, people also accept that many durational units seem to conflict with the evidence of their watches. Time 'stands still' or 'flashes by', one finds that at fifty, a year feels very different than when one was fifteen. We actually work with language uses and visceral expectations that can be monitored by a watch though it does not record them itself: 'dinnertime', 'afternoon', 'teabreak'. We use such categories instead of calendar references when we say 'when I was young', 'that was the honeymoon period' or 'since he was made redundant'. These different times are felt to be referable to the formal chronology, even though they can seem incompatible with its measures.[14] We can laugh at the story of my friend's mother, who would not use the kitchen clock to time her eggs, because the minutes were too big.

Any 'periodising' schema which is tied to a chronology implies there is a fit between duration and time, so that there is a fixed rate of change. Our individual perceptions are different. We know too that personally crucial events may be over in a moment and we can further set against this fact the apparent timelessness of the environment in which they take place: 'the rocks remain' – though geologists tell us that this stasis, too, is illusory. Historians learning from the social sciences have tried to work out *trends*, shifts in economic conditions, say, or in social attitudes and practices, which become apparent when a mass of minor details are aggregated and analysed though they may not be recognisable as such in individuals' perceptions of events. It is nevertheless very common for historians and social scientists to illustrate their statistics with details of events of personal encounters and life histories, with the claim that these sum up or encapsulate larger histories. They are therefore treated as symbols, metonyms or epiphanies – to borrow the term James Joyce used for his short stories,[15] and they are in different 'time-rates' from statistical trends.

The French historian Ferdinand Braudel and his school of contributors to the journal *Annales* are currently the most cited exponents of the idea that historians should distinguish rates of change, and be able to delineate the appropriate 'life-scale' for each. Their set of terms and their criteria have been conveniently summarised by Jan Vansina, and adapted for his reconstruction of Kuba history, *The Children of Woot*:

> the flow of events (*histoire événementielle*) is but one of the features of change with which the historian must deal. It occurs at a level of time in which each unit is short. Beyond this, trends (*conjonctures*) appear, which may take half a century or more to run their course. Beyond even these trends, one senses structural changes, which may develop over very long periods and alter the identity of societies and cultures. But there is nothing rigid about the time perspective. The main characteristics of historical time are its variability and the possibility of very long units. There is no single wave-length of time necessarily associated with each structure or institution or culture pattern. Some shifts may take a very long time to reach completion, and hence may be extremely difficult to discern.

Vansina was pointing out that these distinctions can be used as guides in the reconstruction of African history, for which few documents exist, and oral sources, as he points out in his book, may incorporate records of different sorts of change in different ways. The Zairean Kuba mode of production did not change fast:

> 'nothing' seems to have happened for perhaps a millennium to the basic pattern of Kuba food crop production, before a new pattern, based on American crops, began to be introduced in the seventeenth century. This in turn became dominant before the late nineteenth century. The second system took at most two full centuries to develop; the first may have taken much longer or much shorter ...
>
> As is true for so much of precolonial African history, an analysis of the sources available for Kuba history allows us to perceive trends and even structural change much more readily than events, since so many events have either never been selected for transmission in oral tradition or have been forgotten ... As for structural

change, what appears is what happened. No major structural change has remained undetected because these phenomena are of such magnitude that traces always seem to remain.[16]

These distinctions are valuable, even if some points may be disputed for other areas: it's been claimed, for instance, that 'structural change' can be at least simplified in recall, and may be only indirectly inferable.[17] The dismissal of *events* would be surprising to some commentators, for whom 'oral tradition' seems to be the epitome of *l'histoire événementielle* – but that is partly because it is supposed to be both innocent of *conjonctoral* and *longue durée* perceptions: the surface of political history. 'L'histoire guerrière et l'histoire événementielle sont solidaires' remarks Paul Ricoeur briskly, but he uses a definition of 'event' so ideal in its emphasis on contingency, uniqueness and individuality that one starts to notice the actual social and cosmological authorisations of a medieval war-chronicler like Froissart![18]

Portelli's narrators clearly did not just give *histoires événementielles*. He comments:

> There is no such thing as a duration-less event or an event-less duration. Whether the duration or the event is stressed depends on the speaker's pattern of perception, on the needs of the situation in which the story is told. The traditional distinction between 'événement' and 'longue durée' seems more a matter of how we look at time than an opposition inscribed into 'objective' reality.[19]

It is perfectly proper to use theories external to the tellers so as to scrutinise their work, and that work may be appropriated and applied in different ways, like any expression of ideas. Vansina has applied the *Annales* distinctions so as to enhance understanding of the African past, and he also shows how important it is to ask what an oral teller leaves out. But if you are simply looking at an oral account as a resource, for data, it is easy to assume, as Portelli infers, that a reminiscence must consist of a string of contents and thus be a descriptive recital: hence it will appear to be 'merely' *histoire événementielle*. In Africa there has been a comparable tendency to treat reminiscence as a pragmatic resource which is especially useful for political scientists and anthropologists, whereas non-eyewitness accounts in contrast have been labelled 'oral tradition', a more arcane construction which has to be cracked open for useful data. I discuss this dichotomy in the next chapter.

My argument here is that, just as historians have developed careful and successful methods of scrutiny which start from regarding an oral account as a data base, so it is equally profitable to scrutinise with just as much skill and care the ways in which aspects of time have to be incorporated into oral accounts, since this examination will show how the structuring of any account has necessarily structured and ordered duration and change in it, while the 'times of the telling' have also helped contribute to the teller's interpretative and explanatory framework. That these necessities include the very usages and rules of the language in which the narration is delivered is the argument of the final section of this chapter.

Language and temporality

We inhabit language and language inhabits us. A main means of communication, we can't think without it, and while it has many rules that can't be broken if we are to communicate at all, there are also rules that can be bent, so that skills in playing with language are everywhere recognised as artistry. Languages always change and this means individual innovators and their copyists change languages without knowing it.

Debates on language and cognition have included explorations of 'primitive logic' which usually centre on the intellectually liberating effects of literacy. Very little attention has been paid in these debates to the intellectual calibre of language systems themselves, though of course some linguists and philosophers of language are concerned with language and logic. Yet all languages organise quite fine and complex discriminations of persons, actions, and their relationship in time and space. It's a fascinating paradox (again little discussed) that nearly all members of the human species learn to talk, and can choose these discriminations correctly, even if they are 'educationally sub-normal', but most people find it hard to analyse how this is done. In England, pressures for teaching formal grammar have rarely been off the political stage, showing clearly that people grasp that language is powerful, but how and why is only confusedly realised.

Difficulties arise because grammars are only models and not in themselves generators of well-formed language, and because literates can represent speech to themselves as if it were written, with distinct words shaped in linear succession, modulated by capital letters, punctuation and paragraph spacing. Many solecisms in writing are just attempts to render actual speech, with its pauses, stresses and intonation, and all the sounds which in English at least are so different from spellings. Transcription of oral accounts, therefore, is not just a problem, it is, properly speaking, impossible. Some scholars agree with Dennis Tedlock that spacing and different types must be used to render the pace and pause effects of oral art, so that he sets out the work in lines, like poetry.[20] But even this visually suggestive transposition does not of itself render pronunciation features, such as the 'accent' which in Britain is such a socially significant part of speech performance. Few linguists have treated paralinguistic features like facial movements and bodily gestures as cues to genre, though there is increasing attention to the linguistic uses of pitch and tempo.[21]

An interesting linguist's account of how paralinguistic or 'expressive' features of languages can be used to structure narrative and genre is Joan Russell's analysis of Swahili women's stories in Mombasa, Kenya.[22] Whereas a genre like Swahili poetry, (which is also male-composed, prestigious and can be printed) is signalled by 'strict syllabic measure and rhyming conventions', *hekara*, a type of story told by women, uses a paralinguistic means, in controlled and skilful ways which include the achievement of what would be normally done by 'grammar'. Thus temporal *aspect* (which I define and discuss below) is usually conveyed syntactically, but here by 'lexical repetition', 'vowel lengthening' and 'pitch raising'.

Such skills of oracy are, as I have already suggested, surely much more used than they have been analysed. We lack especially a careful study of chanting, which has been mentioned already as both genre cue and emotive medium of heroic praise; it is a widespread and probably diversely complex feature of oral art. Lacking such data, we can still ask in what ways are pastness represented in the language as linguists have analysed them? What cognitive distinctions and temporal orientations simply appear through the grammar?

I will spend little time here on one very important feature of language, its mutability. Knowledge of diachronic changes means that earlier documents and monumental inscriptions can often be placed in a chronology, and a location, as evidences in spite of themselves. The means of dating include the use of models of language change over time. Well-attested patterns of phonological shift show how an anterior language, now no longer spoken, diverged and differentiated through time into separate varieties, like the current dialects of English, or even into mutually incomprehensible and in many ways quite different languages, like English and Hindi.

The base-line rules about the nature and direction of language change are not in themselves durational, because they say nothing about the social conditions in which a phonological shift may occur, or how long it takes, nor of the complicated ways in which language is modified by the needs of intercommunication by peoples of different language. They only specify the larger phonological environment in which particular changes occur, and their likely sequence. The model of Indo-European cognation which relates English and Hindi can be supported by many temporally intervening documentary evidences, so that we can see the stages through which the varieties of language spoken in England in 1066 became the way they are today, for instance. They hardly exist for Africa, where few orthographies were set up till very recently. Instead, the comparative linguist has to scan mostly inadequate records of some, by no means all, the language varieties to be found.[23]

Since these are contemporary evidences, the models of change that can be drawn from them have no datable time reference. Still, they are very tempting for historians. Considering Sasstown, for instance, we have the opinion of local historians like Sieh Jeto that the forerunners of Jlao came from the interior of what is now Côte d'Ivoire. Is there any linguistic support for this view? We know that closely comparable languages are spoken today in an unbroken belt through the eastern half of Liberia and the western part of Ivory Coast. Neighbouring languages are all in what linguists consider are separate groupings. It is not yet decided into what larger-order classification the so-called Kru-group languages can be put. Currently, Gur or Voltaic connections are hypothesised: that is, there are languages possibly cognate with Kru-group ones in today's Burkina Faso.[24] So far as I know, no recent oral historians in Liberia have recalled such a linkage.

Another tempting hope was that oral historians might preserve earlier usages in memorised speech. That was essentially part of the talking-book syndrome, which I look at in the next chapter. Vansina has set out the likely conditions for retaining anachronisms of form and content in oral accounts.[25] If tellers want to be understood, they may insensibly update their language: except in deliberately esoteric formulations, it does not seem that many African historians use unfamiliar language; they have other resources for marking occasion, like special voice effects, repetition, metaphor and gnomic allusion. Perhaps these are always specially appropriate to orality: and students of orality in other cultures would find comparable effects if they looked, even in what appear prosaic, everyday accounts when they are transposed into writing.

What of the language's own expressions of time, particularly in the grammatical system itself, where presumably temporality must always be expressed? Memories of language-learning send us, if we are not professional linguists, to 'tense', expecting the form of the verb will convey past, present or future temporality. But Yoruba, it appears, has no tenses! Contemporary linguists distinguish both tense and aspect.

To Comrie, tense is 'the grammaticalisation of location in time', and tense can relate 'the time of the situation referred to and some other time', which is usually the moment of speaking. He defines aspect as 'the internal temporal contour of a situation'. 'Thus the difference between "John was singing" and "John is singing" in English is one of tense, namely a location before the present moment versus a location including the present moment; while the difference between "John was singing" and "John sang" is one of aspect.'

Non-specialists may concentrate on grasping that this distinction (i) can be used to differentiate languages (such that for instance in German 'there is no grammaticalisation of aspectual distinctions'), and (ii) that aspect and tense can be distinguished without using formal grammatical means – 'grammaticalised' doesn't mean 'correct' but is a formal term. If our first broad point is that the rendering of temporality is a complex linguistic phenomenon, it follows that these renderings will be made by several linguistic means. Absence of tense or aspectual forms does not mean that Yoruba or German speakers can't distinguish past from present, or make aspectual distinctions. However, while it is possible to say that such distinctions can be made in all languages, they may in the one case be hard to make, and in another obligatory. Many other language categories share these characteristics: for person, there is no exact English equivalent of French *on*, for example, while Kru ɔ identifies third-person singular without gender distinction, and refers to 'he' or 'she'.

If we concentrate on language's communicative character, we can see it in the perspective of interlocutors locating their messages in respect of the topic and of each other. A teller pivots, as it were, to select the span of time involved, and also an orientation to this span of time. This focus may be as much on the speakers as on the location of what is being described.

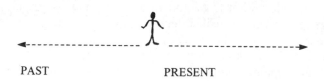

PAST   PRESENT

Comrie points out that tense in human language assumes the same 'diectic centre' (the language points equally) for speaker and receiver, though the inventions first of writing and now of sound recording permit a temporal distance between them. He claims that his version of the diagram here is an adequate account of tense in all human languages. He thinks that it is irrelevant linguistically, though not philosophically, to consider bounding its end-points, and his schema does not distinguish future from present. Some linguists, indeed, argue against the category of future tense. Just consider the acceptability in English of saying 'I'm here/for the next hour/all day/for the rest of my life.' Linguists are very leery of connecting language systems to world-features, but Comrie remarks both that languages as a whole grammaticalise and segment past time much more richly than present or future, and that the metaphor of location is not specific to English: space and time very commonly interfuse linguistically. Space can equally evoke temporal associations.[26]

The sense of a pivotal interlocutor was a guiding image for me when I was trying to puzzle out temporality in Kru. Having – as I thought – learned how to say that something happened 'yesterday', *poblaka*, I was surprised to find that, apparently, the same word meant 'tomorrow'. Actually it means rather 'the next day', one-day-away. The verb suffix *ka* can similarly point backwards or forwards one day; *Do jika klɔ*, Doe came to town; *Doa jika klɔ̀*, Doe will come to town. The difference is signalled by the *–a* which marks incompletive aspect.[27] Kru dialects, therefore, discriminate finely – and grammaticalise – the spaces immediately before and behind the diectic centre. Their speakers can actually specify 'two days away' also. We can compare English 'the day after tomorrow' and 'the day before yesterday' – after this, like Kru, British English moves to broader categories in the lexicon, a week, a fortnight, a month ...

As in many languages outside Europe, Kru has verbal forms which linguists characterise as Recent and Remote. But this distinction, which at first sight is an important one for historians, is actually

> discourse sensitive. Although the REM[ote] suffix is usually tied to actions in the distant past, it can be used to describe an action which occurred as recently as two days ago when the speaker wishes to express temporal distance from the action. Similarly, while the REC[ent] suffix ordinarily is attached to actions which occurred 'earlier today', it can be used to refer to actions another day when the speaker wishes to minimize the time which has elapsed between the moment of speaking and the action.[28]

'Discourse sensitive' usage is crucially important for all students of orality, and indeed in historical documents too. In French, famously, the *passé simple* is a signal of pastness which is confined to writing. It is 'for the French speaker the single most striking mark of literature'. It is not used in spoken language. But it may not only be an index; its use also conveys that each action described through it is separate and distinct, 'nettement determinée dans son commencement ou dans son terme'. It's been noted that French narratologists assume this characteristic when they write as though literary events always speak themselves.[29]

In some languages, there are conventional expressions of pastness which signal the beginning of a genre, and so, also, an attitude towards the past: examples are in English 'once upon a time' and in Swahili '*zamani*'. In order to grasp the nuances of speaker or writer, one has to know the convention, which in the English example implies 'this is a fairy tale'. When speakers of Syuwa, a Nepalese language, start a story, they begin it in 'the completive unwitnessed second-hand mode'; the ensuing narrative will itself use the set of finely discriminated grammaticalisations of which this mode is one. Others indicate (i) narrator = observer throughout, or, narrator deduces this is what must have occurred, (ii) this information came from an eyewitness, (iii) the source was not an eyewitness, so that its temporal origin is uncertain. A man who told the foreign researcher of this system about a fire he had gone to see in Kathmandu used the forms 'completive unwitnessed but not secondhand' to show that he had not personally seen how the fire started.

Not all languages are so circumspectively informative to an oral historian! Other languages can demand equally fine discriminations from their speakers but in strikingly different ways. In Kham, also a Nepalese language, there are two modes which in one sense mean the same, yet they also distinguish quite different connotations grammatically. The 'orientation mode' is neutral, as in '*kana n bazyao*?' 'where are you going?' (merely for information), but '*kana n bazya*?' means 'where are you going?' (and you'll have to explain yourself) and this is the 'response elicitation mode'. As the reporting linguist points out, these modes also imply quite different relations between speaker and hearer. When telling stories, either mode may be used for the dialogue and event description, but commentary and situating will be in the orientation mode only.[30]

These are just two examples of the ways in which linguistic means of specification and entailment are also extended to organise discourse, where they may be an aspect of a particular register, signal a genre, or be played on more freely as a stylistic effect. So long as phrases and sentences remained the level of linguistic analysis, such practices could not be really understood. The organisation of larger units of discourse proceeds by many means, including syntactic patterning of the kinds I've just hinted at. The needs of pivotal speakers combine with available organising conventions so that expressions of temporality (for instance) cannot be understood within the paradigms set out in beginners' textbooks to be learned off as *j'aime*, *j'aimerai*, *j'aimerais* etc.

As a common example of deceptive temporality with quite different possible meanings, consider what linguists call the Conversational Historic Present (CHP). If you listen carefully to many varieties of British and American English, you can often hear the speaker switch into the present even though the past is being discussed. To Nessa Wolfson, who studied a recorded corpus of US autobiographical tales, the effect of switching is itself crucial, in that one cannot explain the incidence of present tense simply on the grounds that its use makes events 'present' and therefore more vivid and important. She looks at the patterns of alternation, and how they relate to speakers' characteristics such as age, gender and occupation. She concludes that 'CHP alternation may be seen as an index of professed commonality between speakers, and its use may provide insight into the way speakers view themselves and their relation to others.'[31]

This is an important point, showing how deeply social relations enter into the linguistic forms of discourse. Researchers investigating reminiscences can learn from Wolfson's findings so as to check the significance of CHP uses in their accounts. But I believe much more remains to be done in understanding the quite distinct purposes and effects of CHP alternation in oral genres, which of course include perceived occasions as well as speaker–hearer relations, which will also be likely to vary by class as well as by region.

When I read John Fowles' *The Ebony Tower* I was struck by the uses of the present in Marie de France's Breton *lai* of Eliduc which Fowles presents in epilogue as a kind of literary theme on which he has woven the novel as variations. (I have used his translation of this twelfth-century manuscript because he specifically notes that he has retained the original present tense usage.) A closer look shows how artfully Marie deploys alternation, in what is a versified story written for a sung performance to music, in a world where literacy was not yet divorced from oracy as it is now.

After beginning 'I am going to give you the full story of a very old Celtic tale',[32] Marie first moves into the present from the past when her hero Eliduc takes a decision – to go to England: 'So now he says he's sick of Brittany...' Later, she foregrounds that Eliduc has supporters, when he leaves the walled city of Exeter to ambush their attackers. Their triumphal return is momentarily shifted to the present, switching back to the past to describe the king, who was fearful of Eliduc's motives. The lai is a love story with double-takes. Marie always moves into the present to describe the lovers' feelings; she brings us, by a shift to the present, to the princess's room, to which she has summoned Eliduc for a first tête-à-tête.

At successive later points in the tale, CHP alternation always marks a shift of angle and briefly focalises. 'As she sat by the deathbed ... a weasel darts out... The servant struck at it', and as a final surprise: 'Eliduc had a church built... When all was ready ... he surrenders himself with his servants to omnipotent God. And Guillardun [the princess] whom he loved so much, he sent to join his first wife [who had voluntarily become a nun so that Eliduc could remarry].'

These then are different ways of using a linguistic possibility, as a feature of spoken art in different places and at different times in the past.[33] The effects produced by its use in the lai of Eliduc are not the only ones; Wolfson's material, for instance, shows different patternings. CHP couldn't be a universal, given the very diverse grammaticalisations and lexicalisations of temporality that exist. Since there are many possible constituents of narrator–hearer–discourse relationships, any genre may permit, emphasise or insist on deviation from normal practice so as to mark one of them, as the brief examples from Kham and Syuwa reveal. And all the examples underline the need to grasp these rules of discourse and signals of genre if we are to grasp different cultural perceptions of temporality.

Comparable points can be made about the persons of a discourse. Marie pivots with her story as well as in it, turning, as it were, to involve her listeners. In oral art, the participants are perhaps especially conscious of the magical power of mimesis and diegesis, which both represent and re-present the past. Our words 'present' and 'presence' still significantly unite time and place in their range of meanings: it is in art – in the broadest sense – that we explore the domination of time and place by escaping from it. Samuel Schrager has also pointed out, here exemplifying from one case – that 'insofar as the experience of others is seen to be representative of others, she can be speaking about specific persons directly and about others symbolically at the same time'.[34]

I suggested in Chapter 4 how different may be the spans of 'we' in successive stages of Jua Sieh's narrative, and also how a sense of Jua Sieh's self-identification – an 'I' – is projected through it, often implicitly through reference and inference. It is not a fixed and finite presentation, but that openness itself tells us something about Kru peoples' characterisations of identity. Understanding how temporality works in language thus tells us more about the narrators too. For all these reasons, we will only begin to grasp the full dimensions of meaning in oral representations of pastness if we can understand the rules of temporality in the speakers' languages, and their techniques of exploiting and bending the rules in genre.

Plate 1. Jlao historians: Gabriel S. Jebo, retired journalist

Plate 2. Jlao historians: Nimine Gbei, Singer of Sasstown Territory

Plate 3. Jlao historians: Emmanuel S. Togba and Anna B. Nagbe

Plate 4. Jlao historians: General Joseph N. Blamo (retired)

Plate 5. Kru fishing canoes, Sasstown

Plate 6. Crossing the river:
Kru raft

Plate 7. Planting rice: Jlao work party with drummer

Plate 8. Jlao funeral: beginning a war dance for the dead

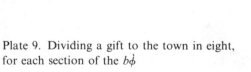

Plate 9. Dividing a gift to the town in eight, for each section of the $b\phi$

5

SUBJECTIVE OR OBJECTIVE? DEBATES ON THE NATURE OF ORAL HISTORY

Witnesses in spite of themselves

I remember my fascinated delight when, as a schoolchild, I was first shown aerial photographs revealing barrows, hutcircles and tracks which were invisible at ground level to the naked eye. The photographs conjured these evidences from what I knew as uniform cornfields as mysteriously as the magnet above a mass of iron filings pulls them into patterns. Looking back, I realise that the mysteriousness was the richer because I already responded romantically to prehistoric forts and camps on neighbouring hills. It did not I think occur to me that all the rural landscape had been worked over and remade: that farms were as historical as the ruins of Roman lead mines, that the Enclosure Acts of 'History' might be deciphered around me, and I did not know that hedgerows could be examined like churches to determine their age. Nor did I realise that oral history can recover the techniques, technologies and social details of labour organisation which made the more recent alterations to the landscape.

Apart from that last, very important input, this sort of historical approach, of which the historian W. G. Hoskins[1] has been the great progenitor, seems entirely different from the interrelated focus I've been advocating on narrators, audiences and genre. I make it an example for two reasons. First, there are important ways in which material evidences are cues to recall and themselves living records of social activity. I shall return to this point, which has also to do with social reproduction, history-as-lived. Second? I need to discuss an apparent opposition between these two sorts of history-as-recorded, the one registering as objective – and indeed using objects as evidence – the other subjective, in that it is provided by fallible human subjects. The reality or otherwise of this opposition is central to debate about the status of oral history, a considerable debate, which I now confront. I will comment on it largely by reference to historians of Africa. The thinking behind their works originated in the European or Western scholarly tradition and is active there too.

To historians, said Marc Bloch, 'the past is their tyrant. It forbids them to know anything which it has not itself, consciously or otherwise, yielded to them.' Even in a landscape, many changes lose their traces in time, while others become 'traces' through independent developments – as with aerial photographs – or are literally revealed by chance discovery. Traces which yield the past 'in spite of themselves', in Bloch's well-known phrase, are believed to be the very best kind of documentation; they are historically reliable. Bloch urged that 'a linguistic characteristic, a point of view embodied in a text, a rite, as defined by a book of ceremonial or represented on a stele, are realities just as much as the flint, hewn of yore by the artisan of the stone age – realities which we ourselves apprehend by a strictly personal effort of intelligence'.[2]

Is such history absolutely different from the forms of autobiographically organised recall? The one is subjective testimony by definition, the description of oneself. 'Traces', on the other hand, have occurred without any intervention by the teller. In an academic culture of objectivity, this is their moral charm. They are purely impersonal. Their survival into contemporaneity with the historian is fortuitous. They are small lighted windows in the darkness of time, and the glances they permit seem miraculously to override the natural law by which we cannot re-play the past.

The moral impersonality of traces distinguishes them from the 'eyewitness' character of the main historical resource, documents. These letters, laws, intelligence reports and other forms of sometime action have also survived to be read long after the writers' deaths by persons with other interests, but to Bloch they are, insofar as they are intentional productions, 'full of prejudices, false inhibitions, and myopias'.[3] But they can even then be made to yield information which their authors could not be aware of at the time they wrote, since they lacked the ability to foretell: we can correct their delusions by comparing one document to another, or translate their self-importance into mere instances of significant trends by using technology unknown to the writers and assemble statistical information, some of which would have been inaccessible to them. It is through the collocation of data, both traces and intentional records, that a historian can plot change and assess its significance. As a chronologist, the historian needs evidences successively through time.

During the last forty years, professional historians working largely within this paradigm have been trying to recover the African past by the use of oral accounts. Whereas the history of imperial and colonial relations with Africa could be studied in the conventional way with documents, African peoples' own history seemed inaccessible by these means because so much of the continent did not use writing – although there has in fact proved to be quite a lot of usable documentation too. That within living memory, huge changes have occurred in Africa which, as everywhere else, included social and technological transformations such as are currently studied in British oral history, has been until recently neglected by historians and left as the work of social scientists. Historians were particularly seeking memories of time earlier than the tellers' lives, which they hoped could have been conserved as 'oral tradition'.

The main exponent of methods by which oral historical accounts can be evaluated has been Jan Vansina. He makes a sharp distinction between oral reminiscence and oral tradition, which he has defined (in a universalist manner, not just for Africa) as the transmission of oral messages, at least a generation old.[4] Although this distinction looks commonsensical, there are theoretical and empirical objections to it, and in trying, myself, to understand oral representations of pastness, my perspective has come to be very different from that of the seekers after 'oral tradition'. Largely the difference is pragmatic, the consequence of different interests, but it is also in some cases fundamental. To explain why, and as part of setting up an alternative argument, I return to Marc Bloch's 'witnesses in spite of themselves' and the origins of their reliability.

For Bloch, traces still had to be interpreted. They were 'realities which we ourselves apprehend by a strictly personal effort of intelligence'. To him history's intellectual mode is understanding, its subject matter people in time, and its starting point is the historian's critical questioning, not those phenomena which have 'no other common character than that of being contemporary with us'. Replace the element of time by society and you have the working creed of many social anthropologists. It's not surprising that some of these have also praised and recommended Marc Bloch! In this type of perspective, interpretation is quite compatible with objectivity. For the historian of this kind, thoughts can be preserved through time like flies in amber and it is that very artefactuality which guarantees them. Similarly anthropologists trust a ritual for embodying social relations, or trust their own modelling of a social imperative because in their fieldwork experience they 'have come up against it' like a moral obstacle on which you can stub your toe.

The authenticity of experience simultaneously appears to guarantee the interpretation, for the anthropologists because they themselves are the subjects and loci of translation from random phenomena in a society to anthropology, for Bloch because 'a strictly personal effort of intelligence' is the necessary condition of history. His emphasis on 'personal' seems an attempt to stress the necessity of subjective agency.

This is, in one sense, a defensible argument, but it is easy to see that the absence of reference to theory and ideology allows Bloch to free the interpreter from the prejudices and errors of those whose actions and artefacts he seeks to interpret. Exactly the same inhuman omniscience has been tacitly claimed by ethnographers. As Edmund Leach pointed out of Malinowski, 'empiricism could hardly be carried further [when] culture consists in what the fieldworker himself observes'.[5]

Most anthropologists would argue that their observations are never value-free, but they still want to stand by the reality of experience. Instead of treating the results of their reflections on their experiences as if they are purely thing-like facts, which would be verifiable, truer, only if compared statistically with others as instances of a trend,[6] they are trying to come to terms with their status as reflective representations of social encounters – often unequal ones – with informants. They are also beginning to ask how to construct narrative forms which will represent this reality.[7]

Vansina might not be sympathetic to this anthropological movement. He was himself trained by anthropologists who could accept their findings as 'social facts' because they worked within the paradigm of structural-functionalism. Here one aims to abstract information from events so as to model a set of interactive 'institutions' which reproduces 'society'. Competing theories choose different bases, e.g. modes of production, which also take into account the practice of society. The structural-functional model can only accommodate society's members as occupants of roles. It fails to illuminate the choices and conflicts of actors, on which historians, for example, have generally concentrated.

Vansina in his first works argued from a structural-functionalist perspective that informants (the translators' word for *témoins*) were better or worse channels of transmission. In *Oral Tradition as History* he treats them as performers, with their own interests and social place, but he still looks for the core of knowledge which they may be dressing up differently through different genres. For 'as historians, we deal with stable texts, permanent messages'. The problem is to find stability in the flux of oral performances.[8]

In this book, I argue that the conditions of transmitting memory and the nature of past-oriented discourses are different from those posited by Vansina. Recapitulating his arguments, let me take first his distinction between reminiscence and oral tradition, since he says his methodology applies only to the latter. Yet it does not seem empirically tenable if one goes by the form of the discourse. Examples such as Jua Sieh's account show a movement from olden times to the present in one coherently connected performance. Tellers, therefore, might not distinguish, generically, eyewitness from hearsay or olden times from the present.[9]

As my earlier discussions of eyewitness have shown (pp. 41 and 60), this 'impurity' in presentation has many reasons. Vansina has himself discussed the inherent limitations of eyewitness, as when he found that only one out of one thousand eyewitnesses had been able to observe the whole of even a small battle in Libya. He was keenly looking for his requisitioned camel, but he could not recall all that happened.[10] Bloch's criticisms add to this defect the point that there will be an inevitable accretion of material not witnessed. This is because the witnesses are social beings who *must* bring previous understandings to their lived experience in order to interpret it.

And, when they try to proffer this experience in words, they will turn to known formulations, modes and genres to do so. This may mean that deeply felt experiences appear cliché-ridden, but even the most 'original' experience has to be represented through accepted rules of language and of narrative production.

Vansina's methods, therefore, depend on distinguishing two types of data, each of which have different rules of evaluation, whereas it can be argued that his terms of distinction do not hold good. One can also wonder whether the difference between information transmitted in one generation and that transmitted across the generations is criterial; might not any important difference really derive from the number of transmitters, even in the same generation, rather than be due to time-lapse alone? Claims for the efficacy of his method depend further on arguing that (i) conserved communications can pass through successive generations of tellers because (ii) even if the language of the communication is reformulated by them, language is essentially the carrier of content. These points in turn depend on (iii) treating social conditions of transmission as essentially extraneous to their contents. What the historian looking at oral tradition has to do is to discern the stability in the flux of performances, and, stripping away the effects of language and transmission conditions, find the 'stable texts, permanent messages'.

Versus historical speech acts

Yet, as Barber's study of oríkì has already shown us,

> no stripping-away process such as Vansina advocates is possible. It is a theoretical as well as a practical impossibility. The whole point of an oríkì text lies in what the performer is *doing* (as Speech Act theory would put it) – and what generations of the performer's predecessors were doing before that; this is what shapes the form, structure, style, imagery, relations with the audience, and every-thing else that Vansina agrees we need to look at before we discount it. It is only from this standpoint that some oríkì texts become visible at all: seen from any other angle, they collapse, dissolving into a jumble of obscure fragments. What the performer is doing cannot be seen as a 'distorting influence'... In the case of oríkì, if you discount that there may be literally nothing left.
>
> Oríkì could therefore be dismissed by the oral historian as a non-historical or only unintentionally historical genre. But this would not solve the problem. The project of oríkì is not to chronicle events and indeed is not narrative at all. But there is a sense in which oríkì are intrinsically and profoundly historical,

both in terms of their genesis and in terms of their present-day function. They represent the 'past in the present', the way the knowledge of the past makes itself felt stubbornly and often contradictorily today.

Oríkì seem to be a genre pre-eminently belonging to 'oral tradition', yet they are impenetrable if one works from Vansina's perspective. Barber argues instead (with examples) that they are susceptible to analysis which starts from different presuppositions. These proceed from a different social theory, and a related textual theory. Comparable sociological points have been made by another critic, this time a historian, D. W. Cohen, who was also disturbed by the Vansinan model of transmission.

Vansina originally proposed that such oral traditions were messages which should be treated as codes in an information-theory sense, that is, as carrying more or less information and transmitted through human channels.[11] He has much modified this view, but has kept from it the notion of core data, and, while avoiding his old metaphor of a chain of transmission over time, seems still to be arguing that there is a kind of historical testimony, 'tradition', through which such transmission occurs. A theoretical objection to this view is that it presupposes a succession of 'steady states', enduring social relationships of the kind which, as I have described, were modelled in structural-functional theory. This theory permits us to see role occupants transmitting various genres of verbal account to their successors. I believe this is an asocial view, compared with a perspective in which one sees actors as agents, making society (and history) by acting out their lives, not simply fitting slots in a predetermined system. Part of their interaction includes using knowledge of the past as a resource, but rarely does the interaction continue in an unchanged pattern over time.

Cohen objected to Vansina's privileging of 'formal tradition and framed modes of transmission' and argued that

> the general processes of circulation of historical information in society ... are not orderly, are not predictable, and are not reconstructable. In this sense, there is no 'original tradition' and no 'discernible chain of witnesses'. While Vansina sees the 'original tradition' and the 'initial testimony' undergoing distortion through time until they are finally recorded by the historian as a historical testimony, this writer sees the historical testimony as the outcome of a variety of processes that essentially constitute the modes of communication of information in the society. The 'historical memory' is not taken here to be a specialised 'relay' either in content or mode of transmission.[12]

This important objection is overly general, and this has allowed Vansina to answer it by agreeing that 'historical gossip' is a valid source of information but categorically distinct from 'oral tradition'.[13] (Cohen himself, failing to find such traditions, nevertheless discovered that people recalled marriage transactions from the past which allowed him to reconstruct larger movements of people.) Vansina is right to stress that memorised performances exist, and court historians: we should see that these 'modes of communication of information', as Cohen calls them, are themselves societal features, as are memorised marriage accounts and family trees – and also informal reminiscence and gossip about the old days. We can distinguish in them different kinds of 'processes of historical information', that is, they are orderable and to some extent predictable. As Cohen says, however, they are not necessarily reconstructable to the point that earlier information conveyed could be recovered.

D. W. Cohen's arguments rest on an interactionist theory of the social, in which society, far from being a moulding set of institutions and norms, as a secondary outcome of ongoing social action, a set of emergent properties with institutions and norms created (and by some analysts this means rather unthinkingly assumed as being created) as a consequence of that interaction. Barber's arguments and instances add to the weight of Cohen's critique. To understand oríki, she says, you have to see them as

> a very specific, intense and heightened form of dialogue, in which the silent partner is as crucial as the speaker. The meaning of this dialogue only becomes clear through the structure of social relations in which it inheres and which it represents in dramatic form: relations between patrons and clients, 'big men' and their followers. The social context is not just useful background information, but the very stage upon which this drama is enacted and the supplier of the very dramatis personae themselves. Nor can we limit our enquiry to the immediate context of performance, as much performance theory in folklore has done: for it is clear that the dramatic communication of oríki chants is at the heart of very far-reaching processes of social action. In engaging in this action, the oríki chanter is reactivating the encoded past for a present purpose: in order to enhance the reputation of a subject, often a living subject sitting before her. The form, style, and organisation of her performance derive from this fact. She directs her attention not to the past as history, but to the present in which elements of the past are embedded and can be reactivated.

> Thus to grasp their historical intent we need to view oríki as literature; to grasp their literary mode we need to view them as part of social action; to grasp their role as social action we need to see their historical intent.

This delineation makes the point now familiar from my previous chapters that an oral genre cannot be understood without its constitutive social relationships. It also points to ways in which the term 'audience' will always need analysis. Oríkì, for instance, are directed at specific people, but part of their effect depends on other listeners as well being present to hear the praise – that is part of their power. Oríkì are resources, built up and used in several ways. Some are conventional epithets, other accumulated through life, still more are *oríkì orílè*, property of lineage or clan and the oríkì of big men of the past who are numbered among the subject's ancestors.

> Their accumulated symbolic capital is raided to heap attributive riches on the head of the subject *as an individual* and in competition with, almost at the expense of, other individuals.[14]

The 'talking book' fallacy

The first Africanist historians to use oral material significantly called it 'tradition', because, to quote the *Oxford English Dictionary*, this signified 'a communication which has been handed from generation to generation', so that it is authorised and authorising but not so authoritative as History, and its contents can accumulate over time, be contaminated by spurious additions, or can include cruces which are due to copyists' errors. In other words oral traditions are like, and have indeed been evaluated as if they were, the manuscript recensions which, in Europe, were their accepted medium of transmission.

This perception of oral tellers as 'talking books' is an easy one for literates, especially when the oral accounts themselves appear as literate productions by transposition onto the printed page. Vansina no longer ignores the social realities of performance, but he retains the notion of oral account as document which can be combed for evidence, backed by a fairly resolute empiricism.[15] The argument here is that steady attention to the orality of accounts, which is to say to their actual, empirical production, must modify these old assumptions about traditions, giving at the least a richer picture of their historical significance, at the most calling in question Vansina's – and other historians' – received characterisation of documentary evidence.

I do not wish to belittle Vansina's achievements, or to put off potential readers from reading his textbook *Oral Tradition as History*. He has marvellous skill at identifying historical clues in very different kinds of communication, and continues to ask new and pertinent questions, for instance about the ways memory works. Nor am I necessarily arguing that the rhetorical structuring of accounts totally determines the conditions

under which they may be judged as true or not.[16] There are also clear senses
in which a common message can be produced through different styles. 'The
King's life is drawing peacefully to its close' and 'Mistah Kurtz – he dead'
both attest the death of a specified person. But that is only one of the
responses which the statements evoke. The more one knows about the
circumstances in which the statements are made and by whom, the more
discrepant their connotations. Conrad wrote about Mistah Kurtz, and
perhaps many people know this who have not read or who have long
forgotten their reading of the novel *Heart of Darkness* in which he did so.
The phrase has resonances now which mean it can be quoted allusively and
without explanation, resonances which ultimately derive from its placing in
the book, but have now a life of their own, partly because the fictional
context has enormous ambiguities, referring to horrors that readers may
interpret – and feel – quite differently. As for 'the King's life . . .' quite a few
people have long known this sentence as the bulletin announcing the
imminent death of George V, but recently they could learn from their
newspaper (based on more 'academic' findings) that the doctors hastened
the King's death so that it could be announced in time for the evening Press.
The dignity of the phrasing, for those who know this new information, will
now be interpreted ironically, and may even have sinister connotations.

Continued reglossing, shift into an independent existence 'in quotes', the
human ability to transpose and re-apply language: these are just some of
the features which characterise references to the past, and they include the
turning of written material into oral, and vice versa. Different presuppositions, expectancies and knowledge can make the same phrase or
discourse understood quite differently. 'To the pure', ran a catch-phrase of
the Twenties, 'all things are pointless.' The indeterminacy of meaning,
which arises because meaning is always interpreted by people, never a static
given, is also an aspect of history-as-lived. As an example, I will look a little
further at Yoruba orientations to the past through ìtàn, and at the
connections between ìtàn and oríki, their 'intertextuality', to see how this
affects historical response, that is, the kind of significance which the
listeners and practitioners may find in different representations of past
events.

Yoruba verbal arts are categorised by purpose and occasion. Thus there
are *ekún ìyàwó*, sung by brides at their weddings, and *èfè*, chanted by
satirists at the *Gèlèdé* masquerades. To tell an ìtàn indicates the narrative's
authoritative veracity. Themes, expressions and tropes cross over from one
genre to another, and may therefore cross-refer too.[17] According to
Deirdre LaPin, the term ìtàn is used for performed narratives of different
shape and import, 'expressive behavior which recounts events in sequence'.
An informed audience recognises different kinds of ìtàn through generic
conventions of structure, content, performance style and so on. Historical

ìtàn generally imply the guarantee of precedent, the sequential chain of narrative is understood as a chain, linking each event described causally to those before and after it in a chronological sequence, and according to LaPin songs which break this sequence are held to heighten its realism, presumably because they evoke particular emotional responses to points in the narration.[18]

Barber adds to this interpretation the claim that ìtàn 'exist in a subtle symbiotic relationship with oríkì'. They have, generally, gender-distinguished performers and different degrees of 'licence' to perform. In the Yoruba town of Òkukù, she found that most people knew a few of their lineage oríkì, but the experts were selected women, while ìtàn were the province of elderly men. The women who know the oríkì often claim not to know the ìtàn behind them, while the elderly men who know the ìtàn know far less of the oríkì than the women. Nevertheless, the two traditions are interdependent. 'A performance of oríkì is a rapid passage from one allusion to another; each allusion is to a different narrative hinterland, sometimes quite extensive and detailed.' Ìtàn are also told to justify oríkì, while the condensed weight of oríkì metaphor and allusion enriches the evocatory power of the narrative ìtàn.

The argument of John Peel, who uses LaPin's findings in regard to the history of the Ijesha Yoruba, is that the performance of an ìtàn has a meaning for the audience 'now'; the expectations set up by the ìtàn can also be used to interpret or indeed to act upon new events. He claims that ìtàn offer 'stereotypic reproduction' which irons out the complexities of real pasts, but nevertheless encourages community members in the present to act so as to make the future conform to the stereotype. History does not repeat itself in an eternal 'presentism' however, because audience experience is much more diverse; 'an *opitan* [ìtàn teller] has to manage an 'unruly' present by means of precedents from the past; but first he has to justify the relevance of the past to the present, even to an audience which is disposed to believe that there are such precedents'.[19] In other words, the opitan's authority is contestable.

Barber describes the 'exemplary' historical significance of oríkì in terms similar to Peel. They are indeed valued partly because 'they represent a way not just of looking at the past, but of re-experiencing it and reintegrating it into the present'. We can add her point that they are believed to animate the present. 'They are concerned with the evocation of what is latent and potentially present in everybody, and with the opening of boundaries between entities, whether living, dead or supernatural.'[20]

From contextualised analyses such as Barber's, LaPin's and Peel's, which also themselves offer different interpretations, we can see how limited and misleading would be any meanings which result from deconstructing Yoruba texts as subjectless verbal compositions. 'Authorisation' – like 'audience' – also labels different sorts of authority and this in turn affects the participants' interpretation of the text. Yoruba insights about the creativity of words are extended to beliefs (not peculiar to them) that words can have efficacy which includes the power to cure sickness.[21] Authority can also be 'inspiration', 'word of God' or *ex cathedra*. Although it was only in the nineteenth century that Popes' words could in special circumstances be made infallible, it's interesting to note that it was a Pope who in 1124 said 'We put greater faith in the oral testimony of living witnesses than in the written word.' This view was common at the time, as Michael Clanchy has shown. It is quoted in a study of medieval ordeals (such as still exist today, for instance among Kru) in which the author addresses the question of changes in what is accepted as authoritative evidence.[22] The insistence on the criteria for accepting historical evidence which I discussed earlier in this chapter is, as is well known, a modern development. It's worth noting too that, insofar as the acceptance of evidence turns on the authority of a teller, such historians', and policemen's, criteria are still being contested, not least by believers in world religions.

The false dichotomy of subject and object

Earlier, I suggested that when historians started to use oral evidence in Africa, their criteria for admissible evidence led them to fear that orality is by definition subjective, produced as it is by individual subjects. It is the opposite of material evidences 'in spite of themselves', which are usably objective. Vansina, who accepted the background arguments for this dichotomy, nevertheless overcame it through a model of oral representations of pastness which enabled him to find usable, preserved evidences in them. One price was a new dichotomy, between the subjectivity of eyewitnesses and the irrelevance of this subjectivity in the material transmitted through later interlocutors when they were producing 'oral tradition'.

Vansina consciously articulated a methodology which was justified according to professional historians' demands for literate sources, and he has continued to modulate and develop it to take account of new findings and new approaches to the study of oracy, with a care and complexity which some might think is traduced by the bleak brevity of my last paragraph. This nevertheless summarises an issue at the heart of a debate which is really about the nature of the terms 'subjective' and 'objective', which are commonly used in relation to oral history. As the tracing of criticisms levelled against Vansina's position shows, argument must turn on the status allotted to tellers, which is different too within different theories, and to the power of genre in structuring interpretation.

The positivist separation of subject and object appeared to secure oral tradition as a source capable of producing objective evidence. Vansina's critics argue that focus on telling as social action, backed by a competing social theory, enables analysts to grasp oral telling better, if they also follow the perspectives of literary and linguistic analysis so as to include the structuring of language and the messages cued by its genre. To contextualise tellers, audiences and genres in their living culture with its webs of meaning should further enrich understanding of a telling's historical significance, but the cost of the interactionist viewpoint is confidence that a message of 'now' could be conserved from an earlier 'then'. If the structures of society and/or of genre have been fluid or changing over time, so must have been the occasion for delivery and the significance of the message; certainly one cannot extrapolate backwards from today's significance and apply it to a presumed rendition in the distant past.

The debate also calls in question the meaning of the word 'subject'. Much is assumed by users of the term 'subjectivity', while the very idea of historical transmission raises questions about the teller's control over material, which I have not yet addressed except in passing and from the perspective of authorisation. I therefore return to this topic in the next chapter, and there link to it the related topics of cognition and memory. In this final section, I return as promised to 'objectivity', by considering the relevance to students of oral history of actual objects, material evidences which are not necessarily verbal at all.

Material evidences and their interpretation

A good way for an interviewer to stimulate recall is to bring out old photographs, or even objects which were current in the interviewee's youth. This often brings a flood of recollections about people and events seemingly long forgotten. The capacity of memory to be so unlocked is curious and complex. Proust's famous example of it as he eats a madeleine makes the point that memories can be triggered by repeating an experience which had a strong emotional ambience. 'Evidences in spite of themselves' are in such cases often significant because of humans' past relations with them. This can extend to the present; the appeal of heritage and working museums to anyone over forty is their evocatory power: this is what we did every day, that's what my mum used! Mental pictures from the teller's own experience accompany the cry. Besides their practical value to a student of the past, which meant, for instance, that George Ewart Evans, talking to old farmworkers about some tool, suddenly realised that it evoked the unfaltering detail of a lifetime's skilled use which was also testimony to a disappearing agricultural world,[23] we can see that our sense of identity is bound up with objects. Such objects may be the means of production, through whose use a farmworker directly earned the means of life, the instruments of its sustenance – the kitchen ranges and mangles which women wrestled with, sometimes for money as well as family work – or mementoes, garments, books, old metro tickets, which reassure their owners by reminding them of what they have been.

'Proust's madeleine' is now a reference in quotes like 'Mistah Kurtz'. This is not just because people know more or less vaguely that he wrote a book about it, but because people understand the reference, that is, they know the evocatory power of small re-experiences. Hearing popular tunes from one's youth is a well-worn example – and a common, powerful one too. Material evidences have been as it were encoded in our lives. Historians take advantage of that fact to recover recall, which may include information that seemed tangential to the teller, but which, when put together with other information, can give a clearer picture of the pasts behind our lives.

Even after literacy was well developed in Europe, it was not always seen, or available, as the main means of record for future reference, and as Frances Yates fascinatingly described, there were elaborate 'arts of memory' in the Renaissance, whereby memorisers deliberately tied items to be memorised to different parts of a picture they could visualise. Examinees often have privately developed mnemonic aids of this kind, which are also appealed to by institutional logos, intended to evoke a 'corporate identity'.[24] Thinking about the structuring of Sieh Jeto's history has led me to wonder if some of the accounts he incorporated might not have been earlier 'tied' to specific sacred objects in the priest's house, the jiwon. The story of the kloba's belt, for instance (p. 36), was woven into the plot, but the belt had been held in the jiwon, and the story was that when Civilised men destroyed it, one who wanted to become kloba stole the belt for himself. Its story cannot now be recalled by seeing the object, which is lost, but it's possible that the story had once been etiological, that is, told to explain the significance of the object (the iron 'thing' in the belt). If so, Sieh had memorised the story, and his own telling entailed a change of its 'occasionality'. It may be then that the story's repetition, and survival, has occurred by placing it in a different genre, whose rhetorical structuring in the larger history allowed listeners to make new connections with other characters there, and new moral interpretations too; historical rethinking which is hardly addressed in Vansina's notion of survival.

Material evidences, then, have all sorts of uses to those who wish to reconstruct the past. Oral historians may take advantage of the conditions of human life, which can include the survival of buildings, earthworks and documents beyond the lives of those who made them, and the emotional ties of humans to the objects which help to make their identity. No historian would want to rely only on oral accounts without also making use of these other human features and I am not making any argument for their exclusion – quite the contrary. I have however argued in this chapter that what humans recall is strongly connected to their identities, which include their social roles. It is therefore appropriate and enlightening to start from the position that oral accounts are part of social action – which may itself be patterned, just as it uses genres that are recognised, repeated and modified. Theoretically and practically, it is less appropriate and enlightening to detach accounts from tellers as material objects and evidences in themselves.

6

MEMORY MAKES US, WE MAKE MEMORY

The status of the subject

So far, I have urged that oral narratives be seen as social actions, situated in particular times and places and directed by individual tellers to specific audiences. At the same time, they involve repetition and patterning. Genres evolve because successful tellings are imitated, and some performances become provinces of skilled personnel. Interactively, audiences and tellers develop conventions which cue 'a horizon of expectation'; these conventions include performers' delivery features, as well as presuppositions about appropriate time, occasion and purpose. The rules of grammar are further modulated through discourse, register and stylistic rules which limit and direct performers, but their creative work, even in and with the constraints of genre, can make it increasingly 'artful', aesthetically, emotionally and intellectually.

In the last chapter, I examined contentions that oral narrations encapsulate pieces of verbal repetition that can be treated as if they are objects, material 'evidences in spite of themselves'. I argued that this perception derives from assumptions about text-as-product and a congruent social theory which are opposed by the approaches that I am supporting here. In this chapter, I extend my theoretical perspective to cognition and memory. I argue that memory and cognition are partly constituted by social relations and thus are also constitutive of society. We are all simultaneously bearers and makers of history, with discursive representations of pastness as one element in this generation and reproduction of social life.

The 'subjectivist' and 'objectivist' positions I have contrasted are actually alike in assuming that the producer, the historian, is quite distinct from the product, the history. That, theoretically, is their common weakness. The assumption fits with a distinction between individual and society that – as many now realise – permeates Western thought. Social and literary theories assume, justify or attack this dichotomy, which is also presented in the so-called Cartesian division of mind and body. In arguing for a view of representing pastness that makes it active and socially constitutive, I necessarily attack theories which dichotomise individual and society.

The status of the subject is one issue on which this opposition is debated.

Theories of society, that is, have to show the degree to which individual members of society are agents of social forces, forces produced by society itself. How far are we 'active subjects', how far free to follow our will and alter the world? Just as different theories of history-as-lived give different answers, so do different theories about the status of history-as-written. In arguing that oral historians are acting socially through their telling, I have to explain how far they too are active subjects. To do so, I explain that there is a key mediating term between individual and society, and it is memory. Memory therefore is a crucial topic, theoretically as well as practically, for social analysts as well as historians; representations of pastness become their necessary meeting ground.

Vansina's claim that one can in certain circumstances disregard the social conditions of oral telling and its teller's subjectivity rested, as we have seen, on structural-functional social theory. This treats people as part unique individuals, and as such outside the theory, and part social persons, operant through institutionalised social relationships. The structuralism developed by Claude Lévi-Strauss goes further. He has argued, for instance, that to understand the oral narratives of pastness called 'myths' we should disregard the 'thinking subject'. Famously, he 'claim[ed] to show, not how men think in myths, but how myths operate in men's minds without their being aware of the fact'. For Lévi-Strauss, 'myths are anonymous: from the moment they are seen as myths, and whatever their real origins, they exist only as elements embodied in a tradition. When the myth is repeated, the individual listeners are receiving a message that, properly speaking, is coming from nowhere.' They are therefore, he argues, a coded product of the structuring human brain. 'The eye', for instance, does not merely photograph objects,

> it encodes their distinctive characteristics. These consist not of the qualities we attribute to the things that surround us, but of an ensemble of relationships... Each cell ... responds only to a stimulus of a certain type: contrast between motion and im- mobility; presence or absence of color; changes in light or dark ... direction of motion either straight or oblique, from right to left or the reverse, horizontal or vertical; and so on. Out of all this information, the mind reconstructs, so to speak, objects that have not actually been perceived as such.

Mythology interests Lévi-Strauss because he believes it exhibits this structuring power in all of its conditions and versions, including an analyst's, and offers a chance of success, 'if the final aim of anthropology is to contribute to a better knowledge of objectified thought and its mechanisms'.[1]

In this view, we cannot untwine our concepts from our perceptions. The structuring processes of our biology are also manifested in the patterning of oppositions which likewise constructs language (absence/presence, the recognition of contrasts which permits the 'phonemic inventory', that is, each language's choice of significant sounds, the paradigmatic contrasts from which one tense or another is chosen etc.) From early on, Lévi-Strauss has implied that 'to contribute to a better knowledge of objectified thought and its mechanisms is the final aim of anthropology'. He also argued that the variations in structure found when he surveyed versions of a myth regionally can be related to the different social structures and ecological concerns of the communities which supplied each variant.

To thus connect patterns of thought with patterns of society is to follow in the sociological footsteps of Durkheim and Mauss, who argued that the cognitive ability to make structuring contrasts, or in their terms to classify, was an outcome of the ability of humans to organise themselves in different social groupings.[2] Durkheim's grand-theoretical claim about the reality of religion was that we individually feel the force upon us of being in a collectivity, and label it as God, instead of Society. Society is a higher-order reality, it cannot be reduced to the aggregation of individual instances of the species *Homo sapiens*, and its orderings 'drive' the members to act collectively (for instance, we have to use existing languages) as the price for being human.

Lévi-Strauss is better known as an opponent of Durkheim's ideas, especially those taken up by the British structural-functionalists. For them, structure was a function of the relationships between the holders of social roles, and symbolic and cognitive elaborations were functional supports for the reproduction of social order. The 'structuralism' which Lévi-Strauss initiated is nevertheless a method which operates on and through society, and though it is 'objectified thought', not 'objectified social relations' which he identified as the primary phenomenon to explain, he shares with these other Durkheimians a focus on 'objects' rather than 'subjects'. It is not surprising, then, that Vansina's arguments should be so comparable, even though he now objects to structuralist explanations in historical research.

The great nineteenth-century social theorists all concurred in dismissing individual volition as the significant causal factor in society and history that it appears to be. What looks like individual choice is, in this view, social choice, and empirical support for the theoretical arguments comes from what are now the ordinary commercial practices of market researchers and opinion polls, which show that individuals' beliefs and choices are largely representative of what all the people in their occupational class/age-range/sex category believe and do.

In all these theories of society, then, interest groups, classes, even biological structures drive the world, and belief in autonomous selves has to be explained as ideological. Lévi-Strauss has said that he has no personal sense of identity himself. 'There is no choice, it is just a matter of chance.' 'A passive locus simply could not have this kind of perception about itself', counters Tim Ingold, who has argued at length that we are all active subjects, constituted and conscious through the activity of social relations.[3]

To discuss the status of individuals in society therefore entails arguments on the nature of cognition, consciousness and choice. These topics must also be the concern of historians, as they are part of historical explanation. Many historians accept that economic and social trends can be discerned by aggregating individual cases and subjecting them to statistical analysis. But even those who have learned from Marx to stress the economic underpinning of social relations in the periods and places they study may also wish to allot causative powers to human actors. In a well-known attack, E. P. Thompson struck back hard at the arguments of Louis Althusser, who, combining structuralism with Marxism, denied significance to the individual subject in the name of both –isms. 'History is an immense natural–human system in movement, and the motor of history is class struggle. History is a process and a process without a subject.'[4]

As a historian sympathetic to Marx, Thompson both denounces structuralist revisions of his ideas as heresies and argues instead for a modulated version of Marxist arguments on the nature of human action. His arguments are wide-ranging, many to do with the nature of the historical enterprise. He concludes that subjects do act in history.

> What we have found out (in my view) lies within a missing term: 'human experience'. This is, exactly, the term which Althusser and his followers wish to blackguard out of the club of thought under the name of 'empiricism'. Men and women also return as subjects, within this term – not as autonomous subjects, 'free individuals', but as persons experiencing their determinate productive situations and relationships, as needs and interests and antagonisms, and then 'handling' this experience within their consciousness and their culture (two others terms excluded by theoretical practice) in the most complex (yes, 'relatively autonomous') ways, and then (often but not always through the ensuing structures of class) acting upon their determinate situation in their turn.[5]

If choice is understood as a fundamental property of consciousness, a cognitive necessity, in fact, and a cultural one too, in that, as Lévi-Strauss himself argues, we have to choose a perspective every time we speak, it becomes possible to argue that we constitute ourselves and one another in society as active subjects even if we are powerless ones. We can also connect, as I have done in other ways, the status of subjects in history-as-lived with those making history-as-recounted. Even those analysts of oral accounts who argue that they can be plucked away from the temporal act of telling, do so from a social theory. The telling is still seen as a social action. Either this action is to use the narrative to maintain society, because its contents are structured so as to reproduce the social structure – but in an unconscious and indirectly realised way, as Lévi-Strauss has argued with immense detail and subtlety – or, as many historians and anthropologists have assumed or argued, the overt content of the narrative offers a moral precedent or warning. The contents may also be deployed to support one political faction against another.

In these perspectives, it is the account as resource which matters, and the significance of the tellers is that they lend their authority to the account, just as the moral of the account authorises the policy that the teller supports. Powerful as all these arguments are, and I will return to their use, they still do not explain fully how oral-historical accounts are produced by individual tellers, who have to remember, reconstruct, order and direct their own recollection and clearly sometimes do so with better or worse success. On the other hand, the mere recognition of choice does not account for the social constitution of persons, occasions and genres (which Thompson includes as 'culture'): an active subject is not simply a wilful one. Theories which construct subjects as social outcomes are at least consonant with sophisticated understanding of this process in literary production, and we must be particularly careful not to assume that agency means all individual human subjects equivalently effect actions of which they are the nominal subjects, especially given the sense in which the word 'individual' is usually understood.

Individualism

For us to understand the active subject properly, I believe we will have to analyse more fully socialisation, which I argue includes cognitive development. But first, it's very important to be clear what one means by the word 'individual'. Arguments about agency in history and society all turn on the use of this word, and because these issues touch many more people than the tiny minority who care about social theory (and may argue their views in an arcane way) they have been subjected to often vituperative debates which could not possibly be summarised here. Debaters are often at odds because their assumptions about human nature are different.

I commonly hear the word 'individual' as meaning 'unique', or as indicating a property of human beings to be individualistic and break through the social conventions set up by the many, even to fight against society, which exists as a control in itself. When there is talk about individuals, the meaning attached to the word often slips unnoticed from one to another of three senses. There is: (i) the meaning of individual as a separate body, all of us uniquely living our span of life on earth; (ii) the individual as an instance of the species *Homo sapiens*, a biological category of which we are all recognisably members; and (iii) the sense conveyed by arguments that individuals are unique personalities. As such, the individual may be said to fight against the pressures of society.

This last meaning is contentious, since it is part of a theory about what society is. It draws on a long intellectual and social history in the West, which has included religious claims about the nature of the soul that in turn have taken into account senses (i), (ii) and (iii). The notion of the unique personality is also confused, since, in a very obvious and banal sense, individuals are always social beings. If you try to describe someone you know, or yourself, under two headings, one 'individual characteristics' and the other 'social' ones, it will prove difficult to assign many features unambiguously to either column. That which makes me individually recognisable includes features understood by comparison with others – 'dark' contrasts with 'fair' – and which also identify me as coming from a period, class or place – as in accent and choice of slang; my profession, and address. Indicators of personality such as 'difficult', 'discreet' or 'feminine' indicate social expectations too. To distinguish the individual from the social in any human being's makeup is like trying to pull apart the two sides of a piece of paper.

Doctrines of individualism which give every person a unique but equivalent value and explain actions in personal terms are widely held. But insofar as they ignore the ways in which individuals are social beings, such doctrines are misleading. Sociologists have therefore criticised social explanations so predicated as 'methodological individualism'. Individuals are members of classes or groups which have different interests to defend and unequal economic power. These experienced and constitutive features of every individual's identity, including gender and varying with age, since that affects one's changing life experience, will generate what people genuinely wish and feel as personal conviction. The decisions they make (as the market researchers know) are not their own 'individual' decisions – if that means 'unaffected by social and cultural background'.

The development of individualism as a doctrine cannot be ignored, since it clearly has long been a powerful element of Western thought. There are critical debates about the degree to which it is an ideology, and how far individualism and the social/political/economic practices which promote it have been dialectically interactive. Since one version included the injunction that we must all work to save our unique souls, for instance, did this Protestant Ethic tie together work, profit and individualist soul-saving as a denominational imperative which encouraged the growth of capitalism? That was a theory put forward by Max Weber. As for Marx, the third member of the triumvirate of sociological founding fathers, he demonstrated the illusoriness of 'bourgeois liberalism', as an ideology in which individualism is an explanation of events that are really due to the economic practices of the bourgeoisie. Marx clearly argued that examples of personal action were less autonomic than the socio-economic processes that generated them, although as the example of Althusser's and Thompson's arguments shows, his words have aroused conflicting inter-pretations and re-interpretations. There is no way that this debate with its vast literature can be covered here.[6] I can but mention some of the issues so as to show how they affect our interpretation of oral-historical accounts, and, more strongly, the significance of such representations in the processes of social life.

Theories of society, therefore, themselves create definitions of agency and the individual. That socially reproduced role-holders can be such awkward customers, rejecting their upbringing, fighting one another and even appearing to change the course of events is a notorious problem for structuralism, functionalism and Marxism alike. Hard-line proponents of these theories have to have a notion of socialisation through which individuals (senses (i) and (ii)) are made into members of society. Some forms of functionalism actually created the opposition of individual to society that I have already mentioned as sense (iii), since deviants could be described as persons poorly socialised to accept society's norms. The notions of socialisation employed in this case derived from a psychological individualism, where individuals are made up of senses (i) and (ii) and socialisation is treated as an extraneous process on them.[7] Socialisation, therefore, is also a term of theory. I shall consider it as a constitutive process, through which we build ourselves as conscious social beings. There is no need for a theoretically supported dichotomisation of individual and society wherein oral accounts of pastness have to be either 'a strictly personal effort of intelligence', to apply Marc Bloch's words, or the subjectless messages of the human mind that Lévi-Strauss discovered in myths.

Memory, cognition and socialisation

Human actions can have results, but, as humans are not pure individuals, neither are their actions. What is interesting is to work out the implications of being social individuals. We must all be socialised, but this process can't result in clones, or individuals would indeed only be instances of an animal species. Instead we are all social actors, affecting others and being affected by them, differently as time goes on, in societies that are different from one another but not infinitely so – they have changed, and will change, and they are not isolated from one another. Other animal species beside humans can be called social,[8] but so far as we know humans are distinct in their use of language to permit reflection and their development of technology, which, in some social conditions at least, has become incredibly complex. These special developments are crucially important, but we mustn't forget that they rest on basic cognitive abilities, whose execution and development depends on memory.

Imagine yourself without a memory.

What can you achieve? Can you even imagine memory's absence? 'If a man has lost a leg or an eye, he knows he has lost a leg or an eye, but if he has lost a self – himself – he is no longer there to know it.'[9] The writer of these words, Oliver Sacks, was describing an amnesiac who could not carry out calculations or plans for more than a few seconds, because after that he could no longer grasp them. Our intentions for the future are grounded in the past and without remembering we cannot see, for how else would we know what we see?

Memory, when we look at it, dissolves its boundaries and cannot be wholly distinguished from imagination or from thought itself. These in turn cannot be understood without taking memory into account. That is why Maurice Halbwachs, a pioneer thinker about memory and history, effectively treated all these terms as one. For Halbwachs, memory in this larger sense is also not an individual property; it comes from outside. Everyone recalls, but we recall our responses to the outside world, and so it is the outside world which gives us our understanding of what we individually are.

Whereas people commonly think that every person's memories are unique to them, Halbwachs pointed out that memories are coded in language, which is a 'social fact' and not an individual's choice. The pictures of memory are of a world not made by that individual. Insofar as every individual occupies social roles, it is memory of others in those roles which guides each occupant. Even imitation requires memory, how else could you know how to behave? By acting out the appropriate behaviour, you repeat it, and others in turn use their memories of your actions. So memory helps to perpetuate tightly ritualised institutions like the law or the army.[10]

Halbwachs was a member of the Année Sociologique group, followers of Durkheim. The emphasis in *Les Cadres sociaux de la mémoire* is on the continuance and transmission of society, rather than on the evolution of the social.[11] Besides exploring this central Durkheimian theme, of society's transcendence over the succession of individuals who form it, many references in the book show that Halbwachs was also arguing against a climate of assumption that human nature is universally individualistic, and that individual wills of this kind are the irreducible cause of historical change.

Durkheim himself argued that society included 'social facts' which by definition are 'capable of exerting over the individual an external constraint', so that while theorising the priority of social reality he still counterposed individuals to it.[12] Halbwachs' arguments derive from this paradigm, which is why he cannot properly controvert psychological individualism? Memory for him mediates between the social world and the mind, but only so as to reproduce society? One difficulty with this view is that it seems to imply a *perpetuum mobile* of memory and institutions, continuously reproducing each other, not only indistinguishable but by definition unchangeable. Yet changes happen!

The missing term in Halbwachs' account is socialisation, which I would define as the ways and means by which we internalise the external world. Memory for him is like an album of photographs. He does not analyse it as a structuring and creative process. Socialisation is dealt with as education, and like many other earlier social analysts he unthinkingly subscribes to the receptacle theory, in which children are filled up with the correct facts by their elders and betters. The functionalist definition of socialisation as 'inculcating norms' perhaps modifies this into a Big Stick or Squeersian theory. For those of us who cannot square such theories with results, there are fortunately alternative ways of understanding socialisation. These make it into an active part of individual (senses (i) and (ii)) development.

Many psychologists today[13] are showing how active and interactive, how early and cumulative are the processes of learning. In this perspective, infants initiate: they do not just respond or copy, but they can only become human through interaction with other persons and the whole environment around them, which is to say that cognition, the ability to think, is developed interactively. The world outside is used to build the means of understanding that same outside world, and as we grow, we continue to process and internalise the outside to think with, as well as to think about. For social analysts, this psychological model usefully bypasses the chicken and egg question of whether innate cognition models social relations or social relations somehow instigate cognition. The question is not solved, but can be posed more fruitfully, since the two terms are no longer mutually exclusive.

The implications of this perspective on cognition and memory are of course manifold for the study of history. For instance, it suggests that nobody's ability to recall is independent of social milieu because it is through that milieu that the cognitive ability was forged. Equally, the social milieu is not independent of the cognitive operations of the persons in it. Insofar as the milieu exists as practices, these practices act dialectically, structuring the people who think and act them. As genres are themselves social practices, they are active mediators of structuring representations. They may thus be conducive both to stability and to change.

The model is not yet complete, however, since as it stands there are still questions about its power to explain change. By introducing modern views of social cognition, Halbwachs' insights about collective memory become usable. But the word 'collective' is misleading, because there is no single undifferentiated collectivity which is 'the social'. Human beings are born, mature and die, and not simply as cohorts but unevenly. Division of labour seems universal – everybody does not do all the same tasks in even the least specialised communities. In most, perhaps all communities, differently organised groups co-exist, recruiting their members according to different criteria. Human beings belong to more than one group simultaneously, and are excluded from others. They change their membership over the course of a life. Inequality is found universally, as well as being different in form and strength in different conditions. Rather than holism, the hallmark of 'the social' is discontinuity, and no two people will have identical lives. Cognitively, the recognition of dislocation and difference is built into us all, and we are all creatures of choice.

Homo sapiens developed as a social species, using language. We don't know the evolutionary stages of human cognitive development for sure, or their order. In humanity as we know it, and that is including past history, new members enter an already complex social world of cognising human beings. We can modify Halbwachs' picture when we accept that each baby starts from scratch, cognitively speaking, but that all babies develop very quickly their own active ability to direct reaction from others, and to organise and integrate their own responses.[14] They are not passive receptacles. With each step in cognitive grasp (and I let this mixed metaphor pass so as to stress that early perception involves direct body orientation) the child compounds cognitive ability, and the full command of language is a quantum leap.[15]

If cognition and memory are social in this sense, the model makes provision for the real, material pressures on individuals who as biological bodies have to appropriate and modify matter in order to survive. It also permits us to situate people in time and change, in history. They become subjects and agents in the different senses of these words, able in different degrees to achieve action, and to be acted on.[16] Sometimes they rise: circumstances and their own skills enable them to impose their will on others. Often they are in reality agents of more powerful and skilful wills, or of forces that cannot be reduced to individualist or mono-causal or even human terms. In fact, from moment to moment and in changing social situations, the multiplex and many-layered character of agency for every one of us shifts between all these kinds.

Habitus

We are all born into the practices of everyday, which we learn by doing, by living them, and by paying attention to explicit advice ('Don't eat with your mouth full!') and more pervasively to implicit advice, so that we pick up the attitudes and expectations of our *habitus*. That's the term of Pierre

Bourdieu,[17] who points out that much of everybody's life is taken for granted and unreflexive. Reflection and questionings are themselves guided by underlying expectations and already-provided channels of expression. Just as the language or languages we learn to think in are specific varieties, English, Swahili, so also are they grasped in their uses and therefore as having occasions of use. Many children, for instance, learn languages, not a single 'mother tongue', in a multilingual milieu and can be observed at two years old showing that English was used with white and Swahili with black, as I noted in colonial Kenya, or, a common case, children's relationships with parents, grandparents and their own friends may include three different language varieties.

Habitus is shorthand for a complex of features that help to constitute people. When Bushmen children pick berries they also 'pick up' the way to gather berries, including that adult men don't do this task. In the same way children in my culture learn by doing to be male or female, and this includes gender-specific bodily stances which convey cultural meaning unconsciously and sometimes against the will of the persons. For Bourdieu, habitus cannot fully explain itself, though it will contain explanations, ideologies, moralities, because it is 'driven' by material forces. Nevertheless, it is actively constructive, and not just a construction as in some structuralist thought. To Bourdieu, subjectivity is an illusion, created in and through the habitus.

My model of the creatively cognitive person alters this conclusion. As with other objectors to 'subjectivity', Bourdieu in my view regresses from the implications of his otherwise excellent stress on praxis to the old individual/social dichotomy. Nevertheless, so long as we ignore this regression and keep consistently in mind the cognitive and social dimensions of a truly praxis-focused model, I believe the notion of habitus is helpful in its breadth and diversity if one wishes to relate 'history', 'thought' and 'society' – terms which share the same subject matter, but which are often discussed in theoretically incompatible frames. Social theorists have problems in accounting systematically and comprehensively for change, as historians readily point out, but historians are often uninterested in the theoretical problems of explanation posed by the changes they describe. It is possible to see how human abilities to imagine and to deny, to persuade and to contradict others exist even in those seemingly closed worlds where habitus defines and legitimates life with the least reflexivity. I am suggesting here that the seeds of contradiction are cognitive and material, both because cognition is socially developed, and because social holism is an illusion. (It is however an illusion which is actively and really sustained.) To Bourdieu, habitus is:

> a system of lasting, transposable dispositions, which integrating past experiences, functions at every moment as *a matrix of*

perceptions, appreciations and actions and makes possible the achievement of infinitely diversified tasks, thanks to analogical transfers of schemes permitting the solution of similarly shaped problems and thanks to the unceasing corrections of the results obtained.

This makes the habitus dynamic, and since there is a dialectical movement between it and the environment (which, though experienced as nubbly fact, may equally be habitus), it will only *tend* to reproduce itself. It can therefore admit change, and, as it links memory and action, it is the product of history which also produces history.[18]

Genres, like languages, are a part of habitus. Clearly, the individual subject is not free to dispense with the rules of language and equally may have to obey the rules of a genre in order to be heard in it. Yet this necessity co-exists with freedom in that speakers have to choose: they must 'pivot' to orient themselves, for instance, and choose their point of view, temporal relationships with other subjects, including listeners, and so forth. Although the scope of choice is very variable, all verbal art entails both the expansion of practices which enable one to 'say it better' and skills in complying with and even transcending the limitations which the genre determines by its very existence, since what it is includes not doing or saying something outside the rules of the genre.

A commonly noted virtue of Bourdieu's approach is that he distinguishes external observers' codifications of 'rules', 'structures' and 'society' from the practices which people actually experience – though, as he says, these can include conscious rule-making too. With the possibilities for developing cognitive awareness of contradiction I have sketched out, it also becomes easier to explain two-facedness, perceptions of irony, and abilities to subvert the rules set out in one's habitus which some also feel Bourdieu does not take into account.[19] Theories of socialisation have to be able to explain these cognitive features of life, like the ability to imagine – and to lie – which are also so significantly developed in oracy, where they can be conveyed through the indeterminacies and complexities of reference that I have already described, and by other techniques which are recognised and appreciated by knowledgeable listeners.

So many features of closure and choice make up any oral communication that one can never say that it is a completely authorless message, any more than one can treat a teller as simply originating an individual statement. When speakers utter locally standard stereotypes, or their status is overridden by the 'licence' a genre is considered to have in itself, it may appear that their individuality is irrelevant, but their project has itself depended on memory and constructive cognitive powers. Social memory as a verbal representation is therefore a complex reality to explain, even before one tries to relate it to social action, a relationship which I will discuss through different illustrative examples.

Action and recall: the social dialectic

(a) Recall and social reproduction

The dialectical interlocking of recall and social nexus can be exemplified from the case of *Womunafu's Bunafu*, by D. W. Cohen, to which I referred in the last chapter. He found that past marriages were well remembered in Bunafu, and from their patterning he could reconstruct key past events, which must have structured the marriage sequences. Seen in the perspective of habitus, we can note Bourdieu's point that marriages result from strategies which tend to reproduce the conditions which have made the antecedent marriage possible.[20] In other words, there has been an enduring interlock of conditions encouraging certain marriage strategies, the strategies themselves, and recall of their results – the marriages contracted – both because these are practically important and because they seem so: for marriage strategies have economic and/or political ends in view, and because the marriages are contracted they have economic and/or political effects which constrain and affect, and of course may change, the strategies of successive marriage brokers.

Perhaps because Cohen realised that recall of marriages would be a historical clue, he referred to it as 'the intelligence of ordinary life' in contradistinction to the fixed traditions which Vansina had put forward as historical genres. However, what the historian picks up from 'gossip' – Vansina's term – is for local participants not casual information. There are occasions on which it is likely to be proffered. Neither Vansina nor Cohen in their debates refer to the types of discourse in which the information is carried, by whom, etc., and so there is a confusion between 'data for the exogenous historian and how he may acquire it' and 'indigenous knowledge for certain persons and how it is conveyed'.

I pointed out (pp. 94–5) that memory is triggered by material evidences with personally evocative significance, and that words, phrases and actions can have the same effect. Recall likewise need not be expressed in a fully fledged genre (p. 28). A variation of Vansina's argument which can be set against my perspective is that memories of marriage events are not histories, in the sense that they are not discursive accounts which would be, for instance, institutionalised chronological lists of alliances, together with an explanation of how the practice first occurred. But such distinctions are not in practice absolute. One can see in the example of Bunafu marriages that while there must have been at least modes of expressing in words what went on before, the cueing of occasions, all the practices of the actual marriage arrangements, the putting of these events to memory and the formulation of recall are intimately connected, and in ways that mean one can't confine 'oral history-as-recorded' to lengthy and generically defined accounts. Likewise, confining peoples' own history to 'tradition' or 'myth', even when the analyst (like myself!) relates this term to particular indigenous genres, will, if no other types of recall are recognised, create an over-narrow literate or textual category of 'usable past' for the historian, and this exclusion, as Cohen noted, blocks off real historical practice from notice or analysis.

Even if genealogies are examples of discursive chronological lists, they too cannot be understood without reference to practice. As anthropologists early learnt, they get successively readjusted so as to better explain contemporary conditions.[21] A genealogy is, after all, a selective representation of demography in the light of social rules about succession. There are people in many communities across the world who can recite a genealogy of their ancestors back ten generations or more, and yet others who can barely remember the names of their grandparents. This not because they have good or bad memories.

Anthropologists generally expect genealogical recall to be a function of practical social conditions. Rules of inheritance and dynastic succession are well-known instances of conditions which can require such recall. In his account of Nuer people of the Southern Sudan, E. E. Evans-Pritchard argued further that they, who apparently lacked institutions of authority – chiefs, jurists, a priesthood – organised themselves through a genealogical grid. Friendship and enmity were contingent and relative states because everyone Nuer was theoretically kin. The allies one could mobilise against an internal enemy were therefore those more closely related to oneself than to him. Socio-political identity and relative genealogical placing were aspects of each other.[22]

For the Jlao Kru, the measures of identity have been more economically settled. As explained in Chapter 1, every infant at birth is recognised as the member of a panton, normally the accepted father's. This membership in turn confers citizenship of the dako. Unlike Nuer, Jlao Kru social organisation is not segmentary (to use the conventional anthropologists' term). Although panten are subdivided, membership of a subdivision did not determine key rights and duties so much as panton membership, and also common settlement in a town of the dako. Some of the Jlao people I know proffered, with pride in their achievement, the name of a great-grandparent; most could manage their grandparents' names. No-one sought me out with genealogies! The Kru are like English people in their ignorance. As I write this, I realise I cannot call to mind all the surnames of my great-grandparents, let alone their Christian names.

In other words, rules of marriage, social identification and organisation are originally choices, which through their very operation tend to fixity. Nevertheless they will change as an aspect of other changes. The terminology and some of the rules are likely to stay though their meaning has really changed. The details I have given about Jlao social organisation suggest why there are currently no long genealogies – they are not needed. As we have seen, however, there have also been some repositories of genealogical knowledge in greater depth, like the praise singers, who seem principally to have identified heroic deeds, thus placing the doers in a tradition which simultaneously explains and authorises a belief in the pugnacity and courage which have made Jlao. Jlao is seen to be made up of its panten, and these are presented as having existed continuously over time. Before branding this an 'illusion of holism', which it partly is – as Sieh Jeto understood – one has to ask how far its principles are absent from any other history?

People do not need discursive accounts to represent themselves as historical entities. Insofar as their memorisations create the sense of a past – even where there is no coherent stream of narrative but only of disparate individual recollections – they contribute to the experience of group identity *now*. They help to constitute the social, which has communicative as well as institutional aspects. This is to say more than 'history is propagandist', which has always been well understood. It is to claim that people are thinking historically if they recognise themselves as part of a group and that this thought is action which helps them to be one. We are back with Halbwachs! And since 'the social' is not a seamless robe but even where least institutionalised a very complicated interaction of practices, it follows that these practices re-enact, modify, deny and conserve 'pastness' as both lived experience and mode of understanding, differently for individual members of any community.

Can there really be 'societies without history'? This expression is of course ambiguous, but the logic of my argument is that because social relations imply both continuity and discontinuity in time, everyone who practises them practises 'history', and their practice enters into memory which is required if the social practices are to endure and survive. Where 'practical consciousness' also becomes 'discursive consciousness' is a problem in many domains of enquiry,[23] but they are not mutually exclusive. I return to these points in the next chapter.

People's discursive consciousness can include the denial of historical change, so that they apparently misrecognise their own practices. To some theorists this exemplifies the dominance of the social over subjectivity, but one can also see it as an example of how complex subjectivity is. People create incorrect explanations (as found in most discursive accounts) *because* they can recognise and misrecognise. Sometimes their mis-recognitions have powerful consequences. Nor are their representations wholly wrong, again because social life is complex. To return to a simple example, Jlao talk of their panten as if they have endured unchanged over time. This is a belief which helps to maintain them: it is as real as the fissions and realignments which have occurred and will continue. The very notion of *panton* is a representation, part of reality, acting on reality, but not the whole of reality. This last point is crucial, and missed by many academic observers, anthropologists and historians, who have mistaken – misrecognised – the generated phenomenon and the descriptions people give of it for a constitutive reality-in-itself.[24] I repeat that eyewitness propositions are not necessarily true, that is correct in their conclusions. Misrepresentation complexly relates personal and social identity, so I look at it more closely in the next chapter.

Conclusion: Mnemosyne's message

In ancient Greek belief, memory, Mnemosyne, was one of the nine muses. Sometimes she was said to be their mother. Zeus was their father. In many patrilineal cosmologies, fathers are awarded the power to animate, to give life itself; mothers, who obviously bring life into existence, are in this ideology believed merely to be the bearers of life, who carry unborn babies as a pot carries water.[25] To me, memory is creative in all senses, so Mnemosyne would have to be androgynous!

If the imagery of parenthood also evokes the mental and physical support a baby needs after birth, 'Mnemosyne' is all the more powerful a representation. Memory is part of cognitive empowering and a means to being; it is developed through social interaction; it is medium as well as message. The contents or evoked messages of memory are also ineluctably social insofar as they are acquired in the social world and can be coded in symbol systems which are culturally familiar.[26] And so the processes of social reproduction, of keeping social relationships alive, and therefore patterned, and of maintaining human organisations, depend not only on members' knowledge and expectations, on their memories, in other words, but their very ability to know, to interpret and indeed to speak also depend on the cognitive skills which are developed in social interaction too. Memory is part and parcel of these skills as well. If we are to understand how people continually constitute themselves as social beings in the processes of social interaction and survival, these social aspects of cognition and memory are necessary components of our explanations.

7

TRUTHFULNESS, HISTORY AND IDENTITY

A theme of this book is *interconnection*, an aim to assert that the separate
approaches of different disciplines must be brought together if we are to
understand the actual unity of an oral representation of pastness. In such a
unified approach, we can also recognise key distinctions between genres
and see how these relate to the social formation in which they appear, and
which they help to reproduce.

In this concluding chapter, I argue that we must also make connections
between terms commonly distinguished: truth and falsehood, memory and
history. These connectivities are also imbricated in the final topics of
discussion – personal identity, social identity, and their relation to history-
as-recorded.

Truth, falsehood and forgetfulness

In the analyses I have presented of African narrations, I have not given
much time to their status as historical evidence, concentrating rather on
their constitutive features, because these must be understood before such
evaluative judgments can be made. Historians may object that I have
downplayed distinctions between true and false, given that their business is
to try to reconstruct the passage of the past, and for that it is crucial to test
for what in an account is true, or can be shown to be false. As with 'time',
'truth' is a term to which massive attention has been given, and this book
cannot rehearse all the arguments. Yet it is about the interpretation of
accounts, and I have argued that their construction must be understood if
one is to judge their veracity. Just as one learns how differently constructed
'facts' may be, so that one ceases to accept them as given, so truth, in this
perspective, is an assertion which may be falsified, but is not otherwise a
simple state any more than fact is. The point is obvious, but it bears
repeating.

Even professional historians may have been experientially convinced by
a narrator's account, and then dashed to find that it is inaccurate, despite
their also knowing, as part of their expertise, that sincere people need not be
telling the truth and that all accounts must be tested. Oral history is not
intrinsically more or less likely to be accurate than a written document –
though more than one historian has remarked that discovering the illusory
truthfulness of a convincing teller makes one realise that conventional

literary historians have taken documents over-literally; documents, after all, are often orality recorded.[1] I have argued that because it is presented through a social relationship, the researcher cannot treat an oral testimony purely as a thing. Within the language of positivist science, this would mean that the testimony must therefore be less objective. However, since no accounts, oral or written, exist without a point of view by the teller, no listener, or researcher, can avoid judging how authoritative the account, and therefore the teller, seems to be. The canons of judgment have to include likelihood, reasonableness; yet apart from the possibility of falsification, in the Popperian sense, that is, of proving that a claim is false, it is an enigmatic feature of our experience that there is no innate representational difference between plausibility and fact, which is one reason why history-as-lived includes people acting on history-as-reported which can be false. In different legal systems, therefore, truth is accepted as what a group of people judge is the most likely story – and that verdict is then enforced, irrespective of the uncertainties and judgmental faults that may have contributed to it.[2]

The finding of error in an account, whether written or oral, does not necessarily invalidate the account, or the medium through which it is purveyed. It may also be very revealing. In what purports to be reminiscence, it is well known that all sorts of errors, foreshortenings and forgettings occur which need not mean that key information is absent. This has been interestingly shown by a study of testimonies in the Watergate investigations, about the content of conversations which later were found to have been recorded, so that the different transcripts can be compared.[3] It turned out that a witness could mistakenly think he had photographic recall of what was said on specific occasions. But he still might have correctly registered and remembered the meaning of what was going on. It is also known that individuals may become traumatised into forgetting – or into remembering with great vividness what they could not have seen. The condensations and displacements which Freud described for dreams may also operate in memory.[4] Here we also see yet again the importance of genre, which provides a mode or code for people's transmission of experience, and, as well, by its own transmission, maintains a version of the past which people can use for their own ends.

Alessandro Portelli, whose analysis of conflicting dates by witnesses has already been discussed (p. 68), has also described his experiences with an old teller who gave what proved to be a fantasy version of events which had sadly tested his loyalty, along with many others. He had, without any conscious deception, come to present a 'what might have been' story, perhaps because he could not acknowledge to himself the contradiction in which he had been involved. In one sense, though, the incorrectness of the history is veracious, in that these 'uchronic dreams' bear witness to the depth of the conflicts involved, the problems which lay behind a final action which we have to call 'history' because that, ultimately, was the road chosen.[5]

Portelli commented in discussion on this example that comrades of the old man had similar tales. This also points to the originary cleavages and the social alignments which must have been at work. An obvious way in which recall is 'wrong' comes from the well-known presentation of self-in-the-best-light. Other reasons why a historical account may appear systematically deformed are proposed in case studies from Australia and Greece. Here we see the reproduction of cognitive structuring which codes events in ways apparently antithetical to historical reality.

(a) Ngalaka: the historical reproduction of social-structuring practices

Propaganda, that which must be propagated, as in the Catholic Church's missionary section *Propaganda Fide*, has come through poignant events in European history to mean (dis)information propagated for one's own ends. What are we to make of histories that apparently mis-recall to the tellers' *dis*advantage? Howard and Frances Morphy found that public reminiscence by aborigines in an area of North East Australia included no account of systematic European attempts to exterminate them in the 1900s. They do not accept this blanking out as due to current fears or collective trauma. Rather, they emphasise that 'it is through ... the integration of the past within the consciousness of the present that history enters, in an active way, the system of social reproduction'. In the Roper Valley, that process has occurred since the massacre period, and accounts became shaped through the tellers' characteristic cognitive structuring into 'a picture of the pre-contact and contact past that has the characteristic of a generalisation about what people and things were like rather than the form of a chronological sequence of events'. 'What people were like' included a sharp distinction between station blacks and wild blacks. Station blacks were originally brought to work on cattle stations and fed there, and then sent to persuade in wild blacks, represented by Europeans, and now by Ngalakan aborigines, as raw savages.

In the 1920s, these Aboriginal Australians enjoyed some stability and success and believed they and station owners were mutually dependent. Internal aborigine conflicts also increased and station blacks in police favour might use it to shoot down clan enemies. History has been shaped in the experience of these later events and, as the Morphys emphasise, through a cognitive practice which, by its structuring, 'prefers' social discontinuities over temporal ones, a practice which in turn survives because experience seems to ratify its validity – it has paid to present oneself as a station black. Fear and traumas no doubt mattered too, but they also provoked responses which invoked existent means of distinguishing others to set up contrasts between tame and wild that could accommodate the dominant white Australians' ideology.[6]

(b) Misremembering over time: Greeks and Turks

An important point in the case study of the Ngalaka is that between the collection of an oral testimony and the events it purports to describe, many presents have intervened. Society and the interpretation of an event's significance may have changed in the interval, but the survival of a story about that 'pre-past' can mean either a reconstitution in different forms or the retention of a single genre – which, however, may also have changed its occasion of use, its authority, or in other ways which affect the openness to interpretation that is always a feature of genre. Because Shakespeare's plays and Cervante's novel *Don Quixote* have survived in print along with commentaries on them, we know that readers and audiences for over three hundred years have responded to these works in different ways, and have interpreted them differently. They have also been able to engage with earlier commentaries. In orality, even orality which includes some literacy, it is as if the original texts and the intervening recensions have been lost and we have only their outcomes, recent performances, to go on.

'Mis-remembering' may be better understood as the outcome of such successive reconstitutions. It can also point to the ways in which people perceive that their pasts have had different phases, and they may use their understanding of the one phase to deal with another. Anna Collard has described how the members of a Greek village did not talk much in a historical way about their experiences thirty-five years earlier, though these were evidently central, given the desperate sequences of the Greek national and civil wars from 1940 to 1950. Nevertheless, they did describe, often in quite small detail, and as if they had been eyewitnesses, events from the Ottoman occupation which they could not have experienced, and which are also sometimes falsifiable by reference to documents. Collard argues that there are several reasons why the Ottoman period should be singled out, including that 'it provides a means of talking about some aspects of the early 1940s. It may be that one historical "story" has come to stand in for another one which, for a variety of reasons cannot be spoken of in any other way.' These reasons include the circumstances of civil war, though this in turn can be invoked to explain agrarian and family disputes which actually have more recent causes.

Collard also points out that the villagers' uses of history may include the handling of profound changes in their identity. In the civil war, all the local villagers were evacuated as refugees, and all their frames of reference were changed. 'Property ownership, kin status, social values and criteria for the judging of everyday events and social behaviour, were no longer appropriate.' Their well-defined community had disappeared; social relationships had unavoidable political dimensions of national scale. From this point onwards, the villagers were unable to maintain their sense of 'us' with everyone else as 'them', for they were evidently part of the State. She gives details of the ways in which they may be trying to reckon with these changes through emphasising, ignoring or transposing their personal memories through oral historical accounts.[7]

Connections between memory, cognition and history

(a) 'Memory makes us': a social model

⊘The principle that memory makes us is also the principle that we make memory. The representations of history are praxis, and are enacted as well as formulated with cumulative effect. Here of course is the old problem of sorting out, analytically, effect and commentary, a problem whose intractability is exemplified in the double meaning in English and French of history as what has happened and what people say has happened. These distinctions interact in practice where there is contemporary reflection on events. For example, 'in a historic meeting today...' may be just a media cliché, but it also categorises actions so that people may treat them or even act on them as the stuff of history.

In this book, distinctions between 'memory', 'history' and 'cognition' have deliberately been overridden. So long as we keep them separate their common social significance may be missed. Given that it is clearly proper to distinguish these terms for particular analytical purposes, and that they point to huge domains which are studied by specialists in diverse disciplines, I believe the basic model of their interconnection presented in the last chapter is a justifiable deduction from a range of different disciplinary arguments. The centrality of these topics to social and historical analysts means that, however humble we feel, we cannot creep ignorantly away from the bastions of psychology and biology.

⊘ The notion that we make ourselves and others, cumulatively, and build a directive consciousness as part of the socialisation which humans have to experience if they are to become cultural beings, fits with findings in several disciplines. It is a powerful model. It also makes many classical conundrums secondary. The dualisms of body and mind, individual and society, cease to be fundamental as do those paradoxically co-existent oppositions which mean, for instance, that one has to explain how individuals participate in a society superordinate to them, and can't comfortably relate the two terms in a single theory.[8]⊘

To some religious believers, this kind of developmental model can be called (kindly or not) 'humanist'. Although this is a washy term in view of its range of connotations, it is appropriate, in that human responsibility is demanded in the model. Active subjects thus become moral persons also,[9] and they can achieve a kind of immortality. In the Western tradition, artists gain posthumous fame because their products outlive them. A friend of mind, now dead, once commented rather sadly that instead of producing careers or masterpieces, much of women's time goes on producing people, so there is less to show for their labours. Yet, a little of her really does live on in that people-work, not only in her children but in her friends, and all those she came in contact with. All our consciousness and action includes the experience of others, living and long dead. 'We are not of today, or yesterday – we are people of an immense age.'[10]

That 'memory makes us', then, is a simple principle whose operation must be complex. It is not incompatible with evidences found in different theoretical perspectives, and in different cultural situations. Anyone who reads the theoretical literature from a background which includes such a variety of experience becomes quickly aware of how extraordinarily culture-specific is the modelling of 'family' – for instance – in Western psychology. A middle-brow, white nuclear group seems to be assumed, even though the empirical incidence of such groupings is small even in Britain or America.[11] The model allows for a much more diverse socialising input than this nuclear family, whose character in the literature of socialisation is really an ideological assumption generated in the habitus.

Such researchers' models are no different from non-academic representations. This does not mean they are worthless. Learning about others' perceptions, we can see both how our own are not universal and how they could be enriched. Collective representations of personhood and responsibility for social action vary the world over. Even so, they are likely to be patriarchal and to legitimate inequality. Scrutinising the differences helps us to spot the commonalities. To take one example: the fact that women are everywhere treated as important primary socialisers does not mean that this construction is wrong. But from the perspective of 'memory makes us' we can see a flaw in the common corollary acceptance that such work is purely domestic. Through their relationships with children, mothers affect the public political world in which those children may enter, and, equally, the social practices and symbols of this domain enter into the domestic one, so that mothers cannot be the only agents of socialisation.

(b) Memory versus history, a useful dichotomy?

In opposition to this view of interconnectedness are historians' arguments that history is a phenomenon different from and superior to memory. Memory is even sometimes treated as if it is pre-historical, a distinction which sits all too neatly with traditional versus modern, primitive versus civilised and oral versus literate – all dichotomies which, in practice, are balanced unequally in favour of 'us', not 'them'*'On the periphery, the independence of new nations has dragged societies already awakened by the colonial rape out of their ethnological slumber into history.' Thus Pierre Nora, manifesting his own historical ignorance and prejudice. But his claim is part of a bigger project, to assert that history and memory are totally opposed, and thereby to show the superiority of his own discipline.

> Mémoire, histoire: loin d'être synonymes, nous prenons conscience que tout les oppose. La mémoire est la vie, toujours portée par des groupes vivants et à ce titre, elle est en evolution permanente, ouvert à la dialectique du souvenir et de l'amnésie, inconscient de ses deformations successives ... L'histoire est la reconstruction toujours problématique et incomplète de ce qui n'est plus. La mémoire est un phenomène toujours actuel ... Parce qu'elle est affective et magique, la mémoire ne s'accommode que des détails qui la confortent ... L'histoire, parce que operation intellectuelle et laicisante, appelle analyse et discours critique.

In this moving piece of intellectual's rhetoric, oppositions are asserted which replace the obvious experience that history (if that means the practice of professional historians) continues to 'accommodate itself only to the details that comfort it', since, however carefully and critically they reconstruct, the historians also have been formed by memory.[12] This means also that their choice of topic is unlikely to be independent of social identity, a historical construction rich in the imaginary, which claims us all, as I later discuss.

It could be argued that the three examples of 'misremembering' earlier discussed all conform to Nora's criteria of memory as opposed to history, and it is true that the commentators have been able to critique the 'false truths' offered to them because written sources were part of the available historical material. In all three cases this material would also include other examples of oral evidence, but it could have been difficult in a totally oral world to establish the chronological distance of Turkish occupation, for instance, without using broad comparative sources, which are of course infinitely easier to find in print or manuscript. I myself stressed the historian's limitations faced with such data by my analogy of Shakespeare and Cervantes. Yet the point that the analogy included the transmission of commentary, and not simply the corruption of a text, is important, is exemplified by the Morphys, Portelli and Collard, and shows that Nora's account of memory is reductionist. People use available representations for new ends and these may effectively be critical, even if they are not explicit, verbally rational disquisitions.

Equally untenable, and more misleading, is the synonymy which Nora makes of memory and the inconscient. As I have noted (p. 111), there are well-known difficulties in distinguishing between the operations of discursive and practical reason. We can of course properly distinguish extremes of practice. The 'unconscious' knowledge we have of our arms and legs, which lets us use them, can for most practical purposes be ignored if we want to understand the knowledge encoded in a critical historiography. Nora later conflates 'history' with this sort of historiography and its conflictual explanations – a real shift of ground. But the mental registration of an event is itself an event. These registrations are so many and so hard to pin down, as Nora says, that it is tempting to set them apart from critical analysis. But it is misleading to do so, since they are formative of history in all its senses – action and report. There are strong arguments that the flux of life is not in itself demarcated into 'events'; it is the subject who registers them as structured and discrete.[13] And so much of the inconscient can be brought to consciousness, including awareness of the body's action, as Mauss found when he had to dig trenches in World War I with another nation's spade. He then realised that 'techniques of the body' are learned in culturally different manners.[14] The analysis of practical reason has exercised many, including Bourdieu, whose notion of habitus draws attention to its power without the need to separate out the conscious from the non-conscious.

Because we learn by doing, we often make our knowledge tacit, no longer thought out but a matter of habit, though as with Mauss, the knowledge can sometimes be recovered. Neat distinctions between different cognitive effects are challenged by this manifold indeterminacy, in which people's explanations of why they have acted are also often evidently incomplete.[15] The complexity of our cognitive movements from conscious to non-conscious is exemplified by the difficulties of interpreting the differences in cognitive ability between literates and non-literates, which have been discovered by comparative experiment. The experimenters concluded that the difference is due to the acquisition of literacy. This word actually labels a process of considerable complexity, as is outlined in the Introduction. Does the process include the new relations of subordination that pupils enter into, and through which they learn that school is a place where you have to answer questions that are absented from any practical context and to solve similarly absurd problems, thus making cognitive leaps which are frowned on in the practice of their own non-literate lives? If cognition is seen as partly social practice, such possibilities can be seriously entertained. A properly historical view of cognitive change will also take into account the cumulative material, social and creative practices which over time have led to different worlds for literates and illiterates, so that it is reductionist to treat the differences between the two states as a unitary, still less a purely cognitive phenomenon.[16]

I have moved from memory versus history to oracy versus literacy because a lot of debate has subsumed memory to oracy, and history to literacy. The argument presented here is that such identifications are misled. We understand the actual differences better if we look closely at the social construction and production of historical discourses, written as well as oral, while being careful not to overrate the power of either to effect social action: there is practical history as there is practical reason and through it the past informs the present. Trying to reconstruct 'what really happened' in the distant past is a tiny proportion of historical action and discourse in any community.

Pasts in the present: practices and interpretations

Even if intellectuals' efforts to reconstruct accounts of the past are a specialised activity, they can still affect the expectations of others about the significance of present events. In proportion to the degree of differentiation and hierarchisation of a community, such specialist interpretations may continue on their way with little impact or limited but significant impact, or their message may be understood much more broadly. In these different conditions, oral and literate genres can be kept separate, while at the same time non-literates may be affected by literates' representations and vice versa. The purposes of historical references are likewise multiple, as are expectations of its nature. The processes of interaction between memory, social praxis and structure of oral representation can only be suggested here; many of them deserve a book to themselves.

(a) Contradictions in co-existence: Mormonism

In Chapter 2, I argued that personal reminiscence is not an order of knowledge different from other forms of memory. An important practical point is that such oral history can be constructed and told by literates. In Europe and America nowadays of course it generally is. The complexity of relationships between history and memory and their crucial third term society in the common context of habitus can be nicely illustrated through an example from the advanced, developed United States, of the Mormons, the Church of Latter Day Saints.

Douglas Davies points out that 'Mormons possess such an explicit and self-conscious concern with history that some have seen history as replacing theology in Mormon religion. Paradoxically, yet others have suggested that Latter Day Saints exhibit a form of memorylessness, an inability to outline in detail aspects of the factual past.'[17] He explains that if 'there is no history without archives'[18] Mormons certainly have history.

Mormonism arose in the nineteenth century in a climate of millenarian expectation, and their sacred *Book of Mormon* explicates a historical succession of events leading to a providential emigration. In this periodising scheme, 'time in the sense of *chronos* is replaced by time in the sense of *kairos*, mere duration is endowned with intention and revelation discloses its pattern. All history becomes the history of the church and as such the history of the Mormon community.' Much of this history is known to be relatively recent, and Mormon historians have been valuable in confirming it. Indeed, since there are no professionally trained theologians some think that the professionally trained historians have a similar authority role in the church.

Davies shows how Mormon practice supports in members a theory of history which is commonly called mythic, but which can actually be supported by conventional historians' means, except for some crucial points which have to be taken on faith. Mormons are consciously social in that salvation is a communal activity. Distinct from (secular) time is eternity, in which family members are 'sealed to' one another, and this includes ancestors, who once identified by genealogical research can, by rites undergone on their behalf, be transposed to the eternal realm. That is why Mormons are the most earnest and sophisticated genealogists. Yet being 'unable to speak coherently about the past they had lived through themselves . . . they have also been accused of memorylessness: which in this case expresses a disinterestedness in bare facts and a concern over the faith element in life events'.

In Mormonism, social practice and representations of pastness continue tightly to support each other. Davies has asked himself how Mormons believe and act as they do and argues that authority and faith are felt, experienced through the literal embodiments of Mormon rites. I would further note that their concern with past events is likewise directed to becoming; in other words, it is strongly present-and-future oriented. Philosophically, a sense of history can be said to depend on recognising that consequences cannot precede causes, nor oaks turn into acorns. A Mormon paradox is to deny such temporality in the very practice of a common temporal reckoning, by family trees.

To Africanists, genealogies have been important evidences of a sense of history. As I have pointed out (p. 110), there will be a relationship between politico-economic needs and genealogical span, but one cannot talk of 'direct reflection': the relationship is dialectical and cannot be reduced to a 'vulgar Marxist' equation. As the Mormon case warns us, relations between remembering and material conditions must be more subtle and complex than this. The model of creative cognition and social habitus is a better guide to explanation. For one thing, there is intellectual space in the model for a differentiated exercise of remembrance. Here, for instance, there are not only differences between Mormon and non-Mormon beliefs. Intellectual Mormons were also much more involved in learning about the history of the church than the rank and file, who only discussed and repeated some of their findings. Emotional interest centred on genealogies and not on mundane personal memories. This interest is intense, and within the Mormon belief system and general habitus, it is practical and material.

Mormonism is also an example of how huge nation states encapsulate distinct sub-cultures which can be elaborated socially and culturally by their members to set themselves off from the hegemony of the centre or from the dominance of its mass culture. Historical genres in such cases can be subversive as well as supportive. It is important to note the potential creativity of any genre, which can be developed through its performance by an author with an audience, because at first sight the argument whereby 'memory makes us' suggests that histories will support the status quo. Thus John Peel's view of the Yoruba ìtàn (discussed on p. 92) is, essentially, that they work to reproduce the past in the present.

Peel's argument is mainly directed to the issues I raised in Chapter 3, since he is proposing that the 'stereotypifying' characteristics of ìtàn, in which reflexivity on past events is simultaneously shaped as a guide to future action, are common to a particular kind of political culture and that this type of culture must be generated by a particular type of social structure. He does not enlarge much on this observation, but is concerned to show that, for all its limitations, 'stereotypic reproduction' is reflexive, that is, it is an aspect of a quite complexly dynamic society which needs, and produces, a self-representation to achieve that dynamism which – nevertheless – transcends its own stereotype.

This apparent contradiction is the tender nub of all questions about the relationship of collectivities and their historical accounts of themselves. Peel begins his article with the intention to show how this 'society's sense of its past is integral to its self-production through time', and says that the means are a twofold (dialectical?) process: first, the present is organised by 'structures of significance', taken to be of the past, second, representation of the past 'derives from present practice working mainly upon present evidences of that past, including memory'.[19] This is an unexceptionable account, but ìtàn are only one example of the way Yoruba people's sense of the past is structured, and for a complexly differentiated set of peoples like 'the Yoruba' – over 10 million of them in Nigeria alone – we must expect multiple representations and more than one past, just as the 'unruliness' of their past and present lives has included sequential events too diverse to be assimilated into one guiding habitus. Ìtàn are today – and were yesterday – guides, but not the only prescriptions to political conduct.

(b) No history, no society?

A friendly archivist in Liberia once asked me confidentially, as I bent over the files, 'Why you doing this, Lizzie?' Liberians seemed, generally speaking, uninterested in conserved history, that is written documentation, except for the deeds that record their title to land and house. Many were however passionately interested in the 'contemporary history' accompanying political argument, and as we have seen, some also have thought deeply about the history of their community orally. The same archivist gave me an understandably vivid account of how the policeman friend with whom he was walking to church was shot at the beginning of the military coup in 1980. This eyewitness evidence will undoubtedly have been repeated over the years, and I too could use it (to show police/army relations, for instance) were I to write a history of those times.

In other words, the intellectual disassociation of a Liberian archivist from the archives he is employed to guard is neither an index of an ahistorical mind nor a perverse individual quirk. Liberians in the mid 1970s often gave more credence to personal testimony than to writing, and when one considers the country's history of education and bureaucracy, this attitude can be compared to that in medieval Europe when literacy was only slowly gaining ground (see p. 93).

What people do not remember, and what they think is historically insignificant, can nevertheless be a pointer to their community's social practices, but as with recall, the connections are not direct and simple. Many Jlao Kru, as I have illustrated, had had experiences, history-as-lived, which made their lives discontinuous and sharply contrastive: such deconstruction of previous life trajectories may have encouraged that sense of a staged, individual chronology and interest in the worlds preceding and impinging on it which is often described as 'a sense of history'. I shall return to this point. They also had – for how long, we cannot tell – a tradition of narrative history developed by performance and discussion which made history a subject of intellectual interest and imaginative attention.

Jlao tended to identify their town as the subject of events, along with the larger dako. I was never offered any panton histories, and this is consonant with a hypothesis that the social organisation of exogamous patriclans is a specific outcome of recent coastal history for what were more generally 'spider's webs' of small cultivating groups in the high forest. When they became more involved with external trade, and their towns more densely populated, clan corporateness and a degree of over-rule (by kloba) also developed.[20] Weddings were not key Jlao social events (unlike death ceremonies), and this is not altogether surprising, because neither land nor, usually, internal political alliances were secured by marriage. Any earlier time when this could have happened would of course be the harder to recover, in the absence of a dialectic of marriage strategies and recall such as has been described (p. 109) for Bunafu.

One of the reasons why Africanists first described 'oral traditions' was that they found it easiest to write the histories of states. African kingdoms and emirates, like those in other continents, were units asserting their centredness, with leaders who were in the business of enveloping and engrossing others, and power was legitimated in accounts of great leaders who were recognised as temporally discontinuous. Citizens experienced successive changes and caused them. They often explained this consciousness of life by reference to a constitutive founder or event that set time in motion for them.[21] In other words, there were histories of a kind recognisable to investigators who were heirs of the same processes, and these 'traditions' were also accessible because they were promulgated as knowledge resources by court officials or other important men.

The so-called stateless societies of Africa had no such central drive. The segmenting pattern analysed by Evans-Pritchard (and found elsewhere including the Middle East) meant contingent boundaries and relational identities. He did not enquire systematically about Nuer sense(s) of history. Nor did Meyer Fortes, an influential propagator of the segmentary lineage model. He also created a unity, 'The Tallensi', through his writings, even while explaining that it did not exist – there was no finite field of control of the peoples he called Tale; nor a Tale identity expressing it. He claimed that a unity existed because component groups participated in a single annual ritual festival, but we are not told what sort of historical consciousness these recurrent, solidary efflorescences promoted.[22]

More recently, John Tosh, who constructed a political history of the stateless Langi people in Uganda, found, as my readers might now expect, that there was no overall oral history of Lango. 'Those traditions which do purport to be valid for the entire society are much the least reliable and informative.' Better knowledge of the past is found at the 'clan section' level, the nodal point of Lango identity and action. It is neither restricted knowledge nor organised into one consecutive narrative.

> Almost every elder has absorbed something of his clan section's history; how much he remembers or cares to communicate depends on personal qualities, such as interest or intelligence, rather than on social factors like genealogy or ritual status. Traditions are transmitted piecemeal in any domestic setting which brings people together round a beerpot or hearth. It is conceived of in an episodic way and when recounted to an audience is less like a recitation than a response to questions and promptings.

Tosh wrongly assumes that all this informality is, like its protagonists' intelligence, 'strictly personal'. This is an account of active subjects, who tend to reproduce Langi social relations – and independent-mindedness – through their apparently informal tellings.[23]

For Ngalakans of the Roper Valley, the dialectic of historical represen- tation and social action had included the coding of differences, but not as a 'we' maintaining a bounded existence through a temporal sequence of encounters with 'others'. Two students of Melanesia, Marilyn Strathern and James Carrier, go further to suggest that the latter sense depends on the former order: that is, if people's identity and organisation do not include a Durkheimian sense of a finite, organic 'society', they will not need history – I would say instead that they will not themselves elaborate a version of the past which Westerners call historical. Strathern and Carrier give examples from Mt Hagen, Papua New Guinea, and Ponam Island respectively. In both cases they nevertheless note elements counter to their main picture: seances in which 'a community' confronts a spirit, via a medium, to divine what happenings in their collective past will affect their future, and on Ponam, recall of genealogies to establish family land-holding rights.

According to Carrier, Ponams share Durkheim's view of society, but with a secular confidence that Durkheim did not envisage they believe that they made it, can remake it, and have in fact often done so. We should remember, too, that even the simplest social orders are rarely homogenous, for that term implies a self-contained finitude which hardly ever exists. Migration to an island separated Ponams (currently numbering only 500) from mainland customs, but also gave them room to experiment. Hageners' senses of personal/social identity arise partly from the com- plexities of their exchange relationships, so that one may suppose the sense of bounded community sustained in seance is only a limited part or strand of it.[24]

(c) Symbolic effects and the uses of history

People do not need discursive accounts to communicate to one another their sense of being in a community with a past (see p. 111). To emphasise as I have done the organisation of long and sustained narratives is of course misleading if the historical power of brief and oblique references and symbols is thereby ignored. As we have seen (p. 63), audiences can make connections between assertions or images which are not set out in a narrative argument, and such connections may contribute to the historical import of component representations.[25]

Even a brief image – one given by Anna Collard is of a beautiful Turkish woman 'recalled' on her swing in the centre of the village – may have a concentrated richness, for such images are both picture and metonym, evoking clusters of connotation that may be used as comment or contrast (consider here the images of femininity, play, foreignness and centrality in relation to the villagers' very different experiences, which have included civil war). Tiny things can be immensely potent and evocatory in any individual's life: Eternity is seen in a grain of sand, madeleines when eaten take Proust back into a forgotten childhood, for a child in one of Virginia Woolf's novels, a lighthouse is fringed with joy. Such instances may also become public symbols, and have to be considered along with more obviously historical narratives if we are to understand how people relate to the past. They can work independently of sustained recall, and they may also occur in such recall and be modified there by other symbols and by the higher-order structurations of discourse and genre.

Apart from considering how 'time' works in discourse, I have given only a few examples of the different ways in which people represent the nature of the past's operations to themselves, for instance as motored by Destiny. The Western Apache and Cumbales representations that follow are cases in point; I present them particularly to show how symbolic resonances can have powerful pragmatic uses in the deployment of historical accounts. The ways in which time and place operate as metaphors of one another has already been noted as a very common feature of language (p.78).

(d) Placement and displacement

People tie time and place together for different purposes and in ways which show how culture-bound any one interpretation of their relationship would be. To Andean peoples, for instance, 'history is in front of the observer, and moves backward toward the observer'. Joanne Rappaport, who made this observation, suggests that the monolingual Spanish-speaking Cumbal Indians of Colombia 'have retained what was probably a feature of their ancestral Pasto language and have translated the same distinction into Spanish: in Cumbal, when one wants to refer to a past action, one says "*adelante*" ("further on" or "ahead")'. Cumbales explain this usage by arguing that 'although events occurred in the past, we live their consequences today and must act upon them now. For this reason, what already occurred is in front of the observer, because that is where it can be corrected. History is, therefore, most relevant to the present and is *of the present*.' With this perception, they categorise land repossessed after long dispute in ways 'they should have been, had the lands been occupied continuously by Indians' and such practice 'does not simply *reconfirm* history but *re-establishes* historical process in lands that have been outside of the flow or resguardo [local administrative unit] time, so to speak, because they were usurped by non-Indians'.[26]

In an entirely different linkage of time, persons and land, Keith Basso brilliantly shows how it is that Western Apache can say 'the land is always stalking people', 'the land still looks after us' and 'stories make you replace yourself'. Since his account is itself a well-turned story it seems a shame to reveal the plot, but he moves from these remarks to a demonstration of how 'oral narratives have the power to establish enduring bonds between individuals and features of the natural landscape, and that as a direct consequence of such bonds, persons who have acted improperly will be moved to reflect critically on their misconduct and resolve to improve it'. What happens is that features to the Apache landscape are 'chronotypes' (a term borrowed from Bakhtin), 'points in the geography of a community where time and space interfuse' and, since they are associated with moral stories, they make the Apaches who are told such a story apply it internally, as if they had been arrow-shot, and the place will remain a powerful reminder. 'In short, [Apache] historical tales have the power to change people's ideas about themselves.'[27]

Social identity, personal identity

(a) Making history work

On 14 February 1986, the President of France, François Mitterrand, had a day in Nièvre, a department with which he has a long political association. He inaugurated a new railway station at Nevers, for instance, and spoke of his railway-worker father. Marc Abélès has analysed the events of this day, also an annual 'Pentecostal ritual', on which Mitterrand ascends Mt Solutré 'to relive in memory the war years when, newly escaped from Germany, he went into hiding nearby'. He later married a daughter of the family who sheltered him. Unlike his public functions, when local personages feel obliged to be present, the ascent is performed as an informal, family event, though of course the press and photographers are there too.

Abélès focuses on the way these often apparently empty and banal occasions work as ritual: ritual, that is, which is politically powerful and includes 'the acting out of performances that mobilise public support'. Every occasion of asserting the politician's devoted and *shared* history of service to the region is used. Abélès' discussion focuses on the nature of ritual, but one can also note Mitterrand's practice of history, which both validates the ritual and is validated by it. A selection of supposedly shared memories is invoked and the choice of occasion also implies that they have powerful but uncontroversial moral status – from the heroism of the Resistance to the solidarity of labour. These evocations are richly evoked in many cross-references, teased out in too much detail to be presented here, but their very detail is significant and obviously part of their power. Mitterrand has had 'a rendezvous with history' at the Panthéon as well as on Mt Solutré, and all these events create different sorts of identification, with the region, with the Republic, with France.

Abélès notes that Mitterrand's methods have been different from those of de Gaulle, 'who had discovered in television the ideal medium to embody the relationship uniting him with the nation'. It's instructive to extend the comparison: when Mrs Thatcher was the British Prime Minister, she did not make symbolic pilgrimages to her constituency, Finchley, a suburb of North London, or to her birthplace, the provincial town of Grantham. To the outsider, Finchley lacks sacred spots, but Grantham has several buildings with what are called 'proud historical associations'. Since Mrs Thatcher was adept at evoking popular solidarity, these absences were not necessarily political weaknesses; they attest to her personal formation and skills, as with de Gaulle. They also point to different sorts of social formation and political structure. British politicians are not necessarily dependent on a regional identification with their constituents, though some certainly do have such an identification and use it. Prime Ministers are not yet Presidents, and some of the affirmation of continuity and of sacred support which Mitterrand enacts is in Britain done by Royalty.

Anthropologists who discussed Abélès' analysis noted also the different political conditions in which leaders need to legitimate themselves in ritual ways. One noted that Mitterrand's ritual acts were all profoundly involved with ageing, death and regeneration, themes which are far older than the Presidency. So the appeal of 'photo-opportunities' and the like, which are commonly criticised as set up for TV's requirements and the packaging plans of admen, may still answer to the metaphysical and material concerns of viewers, who are not going to find them convincing unless these concerns are satisfied, and even if so convinced, are still capable of political criticism. The power of the political rituals lies more in the way that their banality forbids open defiance, and so subjects legitimate the leader simply by acceding, by being there, and by accepting the TV pictures as an everyday practice, whether they are sceptical or not.[28]

The symbolic powers of place evoked by Mitterrand in his different engagements are of course not specific to modern society, though the particular ways they are invoked and work attest to different levels of political control, including control of communication. There are many other examples of politico-sacred pilgrimage that could be mentioned.[29] After all, it is a condition both of language and of social practices that temporal reference must imply also personal identification and orientation, and 'person' likewise implies social reference. In other words, time, place and identity are so constituted that reference to one of them has to include some reference to the other two. Time and place are again and again metaphoric stand-ins for each other, while human productive needs have to be met by forms of social co-operation in space, on land, which societies also claim as territory. Given these mutually defining relations, people have to use historical accounts when they work to construct social identities which will support and legitimate their claims to resources and land. These constructions in turn succeed when individuals internalise the social identities and thus really become members of the asserted social group.[30]

Mitterrand uses history as a political resource, and the process also exemplifies the complex transpositions that occur between constitutive memory and discursive explanation. The efficacy of his appeals to solidarity rests on individuals' identification with larger groups and in turn intensifies it. The Western Apache's uses of place show a perhaps less common means of identifying 'homeland' with morality, but the connecting of the two is common.

It's well known that minorities are likely to have a sharper sense of their special identity than do the majorities with whom they have to share a country. Majority identities are constructed in just the same way, but insofar as they are uncontested, they can become naturalised as reality. If they lack such grounds of confidence, majority identities too will become more self-conscious. Germans are an instance: where there was a powerful ideology that asserted a nation should become a state, defeat and partition broke that identification (but did not destroy the belief) and put into question what it means to be German; for, as social identity is supported by myths of a noble past, how are Germans to cope with a past that is suppressed or clearly infamous? Powerfully 'supportive' histories which claim that a people's history is God-given may likewise arise from insecurity and awareness of the contradictions on which a ruling community's legitimacy is actually founded.[31]

Delineating and supporting social identities or ethnicities requires innovative and active work by many people which then often has to be repeated over and over; it is not an automatic consequence of living or working together. Indeed in 'nation building', as in all historically oriented legitimations, massive political effort which includes 'intentional rhetorics' and symbolic evocation is undertaken to convince people of a social identity which they may not otherwise experience as such. My point is that such action, which can include all sorts of conscious, argued representations of pastness, also involves the processes which link individual and social identity in the consciousness of active subjects, and which operate toward reproducing even those kinds of groups which Strathern and Carrier argue do not need history (as-recorded).

To recognise these constitutive processes, then, does not imply that one ignores the active and manipulative practices of history users or the consciousness which enables tellers to look critically at the make-up of groups, explain their demise, etc. This book has drawn on diverse sources to show that oral accounts no less than written ones can be means of comment and reflection, in which different pasts are conceptualised, and, often, contradiction and failure are admitted. Historical narratives are also not just historical in the identity-forming sense; they can serve many ends, and be aesthetic elaborations, philosophical or religious discourses; by the same token ways of representing pastness include genres that can be indigenously distinguished from 'history'.[32]

(b) The multiplicity of subjects

The notion of genre carries with it, necessarily, the implication of a social public. Even if it is esoteric, there will be selected initiates to which it can be interpreted. When, as in the Australian and Greek examples, there is as it were a collective delusion apparently at work, and hence a seemingly undifferentiated public, it is easy to treat a number of testimonies as one, and certainly to discount authorial subjectivity when this proves to be illusory, as when a claimed memory could not actually be a personal experience. But what is a personal experience? That has been an issue throughout this book. I have argued that historians are mistaken to argue that testimony comes from an individual as a 'singular universal' whose 'limitation ... is precisely that it is the historical experience from one consciousness and however informative it may be it remains singular'.[33] Human beings are not only individuals in this limited sense: to be singular experiencers, their individual consciousnessness must be socially formed. It is for these reasons that they may lie, forget, or misremember as singular individuals and also socially, as part of a pattern.

I think that the only legitimate use of 'collective' for such patterns is as a question mark: why should a number of people proffer the same, or the same sort of account? The practices of discussion and recall over time lead to preferred versions, obviously, but there is no way that some collective memory can be tapped by asking one informant. What then is heard is that person's production, which may prove to be standard for those of a particular social background. Not all of Collard's informants, for instance, gave her the same information, and the differences were related to their relative wealth and standing, and of course to their age. I have already discussed the reasons why 'social memory' will not produce 'collective memory', and the reason for taking genre into account is precisely that the term points to the specificities of available styles, authority and distinctions between public and private, which are all occluded by the label 'collective' memory or history.

In the oral history movement, the strong impulse to give a voice to the voiceless has been supported by a claim that such effort will raise true consciousness. Marxism also argues that conventional literary history is a bourgeois product, which propagates not only a bourgeois value to the individual 'I', but an intrinsically false consciousness, of which such claims of agency are a part. In a softer version, the term 'popular memory' – instead of collective memory – implies (not necessarily deliberately) that the people's representations are especially authentic.[34] Yet, of course, theories of ideology and hegemony suggest that 'the people' may be the subjects of ideological representations which work so as to delude them, and many students of the popular (capitalist) media fear that this is happening. How far they are right is a matter which needs investigation. So far, the findings of oral historians suggest that the voiceless very often can voice an opposition, but they are not immune to the structuring plausibilities which the genres of modern media can offer, and, as the examples in this book repeatedly show, to all the processes of self-construction in particular social circumstances.

It is not easy or even always possible to say how far tellers are authors or authored by their telling. I have argued that the single word 'subject' misleads if it is understood as a simple and unitary initiator of action, and it is misunderstood just as much when it is used as equivalent either to 'the singular universal' or 'the collective'.

(c) Constructing a self

Comparable difficulties arise over analysing processes of self-construction. As with 'subject', the analyst's connotations for 'self' can slip between personhood and personality, and include all the ambiguous meanings of subject as well. Anthropologists have increasingly become interested in how selves are constructed and what social conditions support or constitute what kind of self, but according to their sense of the word, their approaches and conclusions are often very different.[35] Nevertheless, as personal identity, social identity, processes of identification and historical representations are so intertwined, self-awareness is an important connecting point of anthropology, history and literary analysis. In what is only a very brief discussion, I start by considering a contrary instance that shakes common assumptions.

I generally found Kru people of all ages and experience to be willing and able to give a sequential account of their lives, often tied at some points to Western dates. A few hundred miles to the north west, in Sierra Leone, Michael Jackson found that 'spontaneous biographies are almost impossible to elicit from Kuranko individuals'. He argues that this is because Kuranko give 'little conventional significance' to 'an inner personal dimension' of existence. The Kru examples suggest that Jackson's explanation is insufficient, since Kru can give autobiographies without 'inner dimensions'. I can readily suppose that a longish tradition of Western education, substantial and sustained migration which included wage labour on time-contracts and varied cultural displacement, and continued economic and political changes which culminated in seven years' conflict with the Liberian government, are features which socialise those who are affected by them towards a sense of personal discreteness and periodisation. Such tellers represent their lives and others' lives as a sequential career, and one which can be redirected and reshaped by events. Yet the autobiographically reticent Kuranko are like the Kru in that they have also had chances to travel, have had Western types of periodicity imposed on them, and have experienced successively very different political controls. They also represent pastness in a variety of genres.[36] They can be equally categorised as small-scale upland rice cultivators, though this definition conceals important differences, since Kuranko are part of the great Mande tradition, and organised into ranks and secret societies that are not found in Jlao. Since the evidence is that the differences between Kru and Kuranko tellers is not due to 'personal intelligence' or 'singular experience', the answer may lie in features of social organisation, religious belief, the development of genre, or elements of all these in the ways that memory makes them.

I cannot claim to have explained these differences between Kuranko and Kru satisfactorily. The comparative presence or absence of 'spontaneous biography' have not been systematically examined; in Europe and the United States, its existence is presumed, although the articulacy and informativeness of tellers is found to vary. Much anthropological work elsewhere focused until recently on 'texts' collected from informants but not about them, though autobiographical detail might be added to support a point. Remembering that written autobiography is not universal and critics are developing a social history of its forms and appearances (see p. 56), supports the argument that oral genres which present a 'self' – and which are equally capable of variations in structure and connotation – must likewise be socially situated and developed over time. Although there will rarely be sufficient evidence of such spoken counterparts in the past, there must also have been a relationship between the emergence and development of spoken and written presentations.

Much more scrutiny will be needed before one can really specify the social conditions which promote self-awareness, or clarify the sort of 'individual' (or subject) which this self is, at any moment. But the development of oral genre, in the broad sense advocated in this book, is an important component of self-awareness as the articulate representation of oneself.

An inarticulate interviewee may be so through having had so little authority over the life described that actions and events can only be rendered blurrily and inconsequentially. This 'poor informant' may, however, have a respected skill like cooking, or a private passion for gardening, and in these domains have developed a confident if still not verbally confident self. In such cases, there may be no culturally recognised genre of discourse through which this passion can be expressed: it is after all a form of action, not words.

In contrast, Jua Sieh was only a dispossessed youth during a long, bitter 'little' colonial fracas, but that very experience promoted a social identity which could in turn unify and give status to distinct sorts of experience. He was not atomised or alienated and he had genres of discourse to use (that is why 'consciousness raising' must include a means of discourse). He became a locally important person. He was helped by the conditions of Kru knowledge transmission which mean that verbal skills are acquirable cumulatively; these also advantage men over women, since men have the right to practise them publicly.

Since inarticulacy and articulacy are social conditions, the practice of oral history is an interactive process in which a sympathetic interviewer may be able to give a speaker the awareness of agency, and therefore of developing into an author, through listening – which grants the right to be heard. Obviously, fluency in some ways is a gift like other aesthetic skills, but I am arguing that conditions which inhibit authorial competence, including where no recognised genre is appropriate to a would-be author, must as a consequence limit the narrative ability of a speaker. This is not at all to say that the downtrodden are always inarticulate, but to draw attention to the different kinds of condition which may foster both a sense of identity and the production of genres. What we perceive as 'awareness' or 'confidence' (and the features are not necessarily accompanied by verbal agility) develop from complicated but specific roots.[37]

(d) The 'I''s continuity: survival and loss

For all the differences between them, Cumbales and Apaches are alike in retaining a place, quite literally, through which they can continue to be: and when the connection between place and people is severed, the successors will in certain senses be different people. It was hardly by chance that an East German novelist, Christa Wolf, sombrely explored the connections between memory and action, place and identity. In her novel *A Model Childhood*, the narrator speaks in the second person, 'you remember', of the third-person child Nelly who was herself; the 'estrangement from ourselves' which the novel investigates includes the fact that the town in which Nelly grew up is no longer inhabited by anyone she knew and it has a new name: it is now in Poland and Polish speakers live there. It also means that this childhood in the 1930s and 1940s is both forbidden and necessary to remember. Christa Wolf is addressing memory and forgetfulness, the narrator's difficulty in conveying to her teenaged daughter what life in Nazi

Germany meant – 'She does not wish – not yet – to hear how one could be there and not there at the same time, the ghastly secret of human beings in this century' – and also the moral necessity of knowing, and of recovering the presences and the absences, the good, the bad, and the in-between.

It is hardly surprising that so much history is an assertion of social identity, when we consider the ways in which it is formative of personal identity too. That's why sophisticated and sceptical deconstructers of other peoples' legitimating histories can be very upset when someone tries to deconstruct their own social identity! Any representation of pastness is identity-constitutive, and can be elaborated into an identity-support as well. Even when a teller or writer is interested in the past for its own sake – or more correctly, for the author's sake? – there is an audience to be gratified if the author's version is to succeed. It is in these circumstances that so often the construction of a 'we' who suffered and achieves incorporates the 'you' who read or listen as well. As the story of Jua Sieh exemplifies, 'we' incorporates 'I', but without necessarily clarifying which 'we' can be meant. And such tellings are active social identifications, though on occasion only retrospectively so!

If one considers that 'I' is a complex construction, then it may not be false of oral tellers to use 'I' for events they could not have witnessed, like the Greek villagers who had 'seen' Turkish occupiers. Many such usages have been noted. An anthropologist explains of one such in Central Africa, 'In the story of Chisamba, which is related as given by him, 'I' is not only the man who is speaking but also the first Chisamba and all those who have held the post in succession.' Researchers have tended to see these instances as a puzzle which requires an analysis of how timelessness and structures of repetition inform social structure and in turn construct the self.[38] Certainly, an ideological projection of society as a bounded unit in time is made, but it may be we both underestimate the sublety of skilled tellers (whose own explanatory commentaries are rarely recorded) and ignore the ideological character of the Western belief in an autonomous bounded self, unique and coterminous with a body's life.

If I'm asked the question 'Where is your home?' the answer depends on where we are when I'm asked, for 'home' is a relative and relational term. Likewise with 'I'. I am a construction partaking of other Is. My own gender may encourage me to see this point: Isabelle Bertaux-Wiame found when she examined French life stories that men structured their accounts as a quest for goals sought, in which the 'I' was the subject of action. Women talked of a network of relationships in which 'I' was one pole of a relation; *nous* or *on* were often used as subject pronoun instead of *je*.[39]

The problem addressed by Christa Wolf in fiction has been a real one to all too many people: the problem of finding a secure identity when history-as-lived has destroyed the literal place of one's social identity, the familiar connections (in all senses) through which a positive and recognised 'I' can be brought together with 'we', and the goal of an expected life trajectory has disappeared. The future continuity of the self can then perhaps only be envisaged in a representative sense, as T. S. Eliot imagined the continuity of Tiresias:

> (And I Tiresias have foreshadowed all
> Enacted on this same divan or bed,
> I who have sat by Thebes below the wall
> And walked among the lowest of the dead.)

But Eliot's lines can have different interpretations, and, as in other examples quoted in this book, his art permits creative openness to his audience.[40]

After considering how different are the ways in which people can recognise, order and re-order representations of pastness, ways for which we have to consider the nature of perception, agency and the sociology of knowledge as well as of genre if they are to be understood, the construction of 'I' remains central and always open to question. It's not an inappropriate topic, then, on which to end this study, and it reminds us of the open and potential character of all identity. That one's self is both variable and vulnerable may be disconcerting to consider, but it does not follow that selves are non-existent. We really have consciousness, we are really agents, till death, of past-into-future. For it is a banal but terrifying conclusion that knowledge and social life itself have to be passed on if they are to survive. If humans annihilate what's present, they annihilate what's past as well, and so prevent a future.

NOTES

Introduction

1 Bielenberg 1984. For 'the past as another country', see Lowenthal 1985.
2 Cf. the work of Tzevtan Todorov, a structuralist arch-enemy of literary appeals to an author's intentions, who nevertheless said 'We too often forget an elementary truth regarding all activities of knowledge: that the point of view chosen by the observer delimits and redefines his object' (1976: 161).
3 Adapted from Barber 1989: 15; cf. the discussion on pp. 89–90 where the original is cited in context.
4 Portelli 1981b: 162.
5 L. White 1989: 35.
6 The approach to structure as conveying meaning is consonant with Hayden White's, though his particular model is not used. Most of what White argues is the basic premise of literary criticism. 'The meaning of meaning' is the focus of much philosophical (and other theoretical) debate. I do not expatiate on these debates here, though I have tried to take them into account.
7 John Gumperz and his collaborators (1982) give many examples of how subtle differences in syntax, topic, orientation and representations of time can cause misunderstandings between speakers who are all apparently fluent in English but some of whose language use is actually structured according to different rules. In unequal situations, e.g. job interviews, this registers as 'stupidity' and reinforces ethnic stereotypes.
8 Genette 1976: 4.
9 Culler 1978: 608. In his sense the structure of discourse generates these events; we could also say discourse itself forms 'persuasion', and 'revelation'.
10 Kermode 1979. See especially his Chapter 5 for the terms of historical truth. It briefly lists the types of authority which make us believe that an account is authentic. 'There is an agreed way of registering reality; and it has authority over us. There is also authority in the person making the report or maintaining its veracity; part, but not all, of this is the mere authority of the printed word. There is also the authority of the institution or the person' (113–14).
11 There are a great many studies of reminiscence which show how people misremember, or omit events in their own lives, and of group versions of history which are equally inaccurate in suggestive ways. Examples of all these processes are discussed in this book. It is assumed in such discussions that the 'events' at issue are significant for the tellers, or writers, and that absences of reference indicate absence of significance for them – or that there are interesting reasons for the absence. In the case of our general knowledge, or memories of school lessons, there are obviously many degrees of significance entailed. We are rarely

tested on such knowledge after our formal education is ended! Michael Frisch, however, tested each new batch of freshmen history students in his university class by asking an immediate 'free-association' response to the prompt 'American history'. He found (1987) a virtually identical list, over the years, of mythic or near-mythic figures, which effectively created an iconography of American identity.

12 Burke 1969: 2. Not all medievalists would agree with him. It is possible for people to understand that times past were different though they have not developed genres that afford means of representing changes systematically (and cf. note 13 below). To Burke (19) 'secular' and 'temporal' are words reminding us that duration and time were once thought to belong to the world, not to the monastery, whose monks had relinquished time (*saeculum*) – though they were its only literate chroniclers (and see my Chapter 4).

13 Lowenthal 1985: xvi, 232, etc. Panofsky argues that Renaissance Italy established 'a *locus standi* from which it could look back at the art of classical antiquity (alien in time but related in style) as well as at the art of the Middle Ages (related in time but alien in style): each of these two could be measured, as it were, by and against each other' (1970: 227). They were in advance of European Northerners. The perspectives analysed are of course those of specialists, e.g. Vasari.

14 For sources and arguments on this issue in relation to Britain and British identity see e.g. the studies in Johnson (ed.) 1982.

15 Davis 1989: 110. His argument is supported by broader evidence as well.

16 See e.g. Olson et al. (eds.) 1985.

17 Street 1984: 46, 14–15. Street introduces comparatively the complexities of literacy/illiteracy. Estimates of British illiteracy continued to rise through the 1980s.

18 You can test your reverence for print by your responses to the following lines, reproduced from a nineteenth-century source on the walls of the Blists Hill print shop which has been set up in the Ironbridge Gorge Museum:

> This is a printing office
> Crossroads of civilization
> Refuge of all the arts
> Against the ravages of time
> Armoury of fearless truth
> Against whispering rumour
> Incessant trumpet of trade
> From this place words may fly abroad
> Not to perish on waves of sound
> Not to vary with the writer's hand
> But fixed in time having been verified in proof
> Friend you stand on sacred ground
> This is a printing office

19 'The Canadian economic historian, H. A. Innis, considered that empires developed according to the efficiency of their communications. They developed with literacy, and their structure depended on the tensions between the

limitations and potentialities of the media and the struggle for control of (them)'
(Tonkin 1971: 145).
20 Gellner 1983. For the rise of literacy in 'the West', see Cipolla 1969.
21 For a rich review of literate and oral interconnections, see Goody 1987.
22 Ong 1977: 413, 1982: e.g. 40, 47. Note too that the general argument that orality
is social-context-dependent is here exemplified by (1) a dependent secondary
code, (2) an esoteric social context which is not at all universal. It is like arguing
that the Morse Code is the epitome of speech in 'literate cultures'. In complete
contrast, Finnegan 1988 demonstrates the great variability and versatility of
oral communication.
23 This very professionalisation of African literate genres supports Euramerican
distinctions in the investigation of oral genres, so that African graduates are
encouraged to study oral genres within an academic discipline, and as an
appropriate work of cultural nationalism. This can perpetuate the divisions
which make an 'oral historian' look for 'oral traditions' while a student of
'literature' looks for genres which testify to performers' art and seem to match
the concerns of 'literature' – that is, originally, of *written* literature.
24 Finnegan 1970: 15ff., Chapter 17 etc.
25 The reasons why Western legal proceedings nevertheless largely remain oral
have been little studied, but see Portelli 1985.
26 For 'time and the other' cf. Fabian 1983. Some structuralist interpretations are
noted in the text, for instance Miller (ed.) 1980 and Willis 1981.

1 Jlao: an introductory case study

1 The material on Jlao summarised here has been set out in more detail in Tonkin
1978/9, 1981, 1982a, 1985 and 1989.
2 The name Kru has labelled many different spans of people and areas of territory
at different times; these uses are examined in Tonkin 1985. Linguists, however,
have agreed that there is a Kru-group language cluster, whose speakers use
cognate varieties, and whose relationship with other West African language
'families' is still uncertain.
3 In the 1940s, there was a mini gold rush in the interior of Sinoe County, and the
gold was brought, sometimes illegally, for sale in Sasstown. But it was short
lived, as the returns from panning grew less.
4 Sullivan 1985 and 1989 describes the events leading to the Fishmen's war.
5 The Tribes of Liberia are official designations, as is the word Tribe which
connotes different administration from that given to Civilised people; see
Tonkin 1981.
6 Bellman 1975, 1984, and Murphy 1980 describe the culture of secrecy among
Kpelle; Smith 1982 explains the channelling of knowledge through different Vai
scripts.
7 Tonkin 1988a gives summaries of Sieh Jeto's first narrative, as well as much
fuller commentary.
8 At one point, when discussing what he had told me, Sieh listed names of towns,
almost (though not quite) as he had given them in his history of how Jlao
reached the sea.
9 See also Davis 1976, for guesses as to this early history.

10 See Massing 1980: 44–8: his figures and findings are suggestive, though they need careful interpretation.

11 Goody (ed.) 1966: Introduction.

12 Several other men related histories to me, often substantial ones, in Kru and sometimes English. They came from the different Jlao towns. I was also given accounts by tellers in neighbouring Kru polities.

2 The teller of the tale: authors and their authorisations

1 Schrager 1983: 78.

2 The Journal *Oral History* has always been weighted towards reminiscence, and publishes a companion volume devoted to *Life Stories*. Paul Thompson, who has done much to foster the study of oral history in Britain, and elsewhere, is a sociologist whose interest came from collecting life histories. For general methodology and defence, with many further references, see the revised version of his textbook, 1988, also Thompson (ed.) 1982, and Lummis 1987. For some recent critical awareness of the processes that may shape these histories, see Samuel and Thompson (eds.) 1990. Africanist historians in contrast looked for data preceding the narrators' lives. Some of their approaches, and relevant references, are discussed in Chapter 5.

3 Besides the checking of specifically oral reminiscence, as proposed in the works cited in the previous footnote, Vansina 1985 provides a clearly referenced introduction to standard historical approaches to eyewitnesses.

4 Beer 1981: 22. Besides the issues discussed here, many of the other medieval criteria she discusses remain scholarly assumptions today.

5 Bloch 1954: 49.

6 Schrager 1983: 80. Bloch 1954: 49. See also e.g. Tonkin's 'participant observation' and other contributors to Ellen (ed.) 1984. A journalist who was asked to recall in court how he had correctly pieced together 'sensitive' information comments: 'Why should the details of how I pieced it together still be in my mind a year and a half later? Only if it had been wrong would they have stuck ... Who recalls a normal day's work after 16 months? For the prosecution there had to be "a source" because lawyers are used to examining "a witness". It seems beyond the power of the legal system to grasp the rambling erratic, untidy process by which this sort of information is culled. Even less as the cross-examination demonstrated, can it believe that such a shambolic method can produce accurate results.' Harold Jackson, 'Sources of Confusion', *Guardian*, 9 December 1986.

7 Jua Sieh was the oldest man of Sakrapo panton and therefore its 'big man' or head. My landlord, an elementary school teacher, was allowed to build on Sakrapo land because his mother had been a Sakrapo woman. My Kru and Jua Sieh's English were equally poor. His talk was translated at intervals into Liberian English by my landlord.

8 If this was the apogee of Jua Sieh's official career, it was also succeeded by a fall, and it looks as if his narrative, with its incidents accumulated, honed and repeated through the years, has taken on a new orientation through his chagrin at this event. Certainly he, like several others, reviewed the miseries of enforced

road building as the new road came to be made, and felt the new motor road at least rewarded those earlier pains: it was believed that the (decayed) existence of the old road had influenced the authorities, so they decided to extend it. The new road was completed between 1972, when I first collected Kru narratives, and 1975 when I went back: it is noticeable that in the 1975–6 collections, but not before, narrators 'foregrounded' the road building with this justification. These examples show how changed experiences led tellers to redirect recensions of their histories.

9 Tonkin 1982a.
10 Kofa says he paid three pounds (sterling) and a towel for this protection. Before World War II, when Liberia went over to the US dollar, the currency of Britain's West African colonies was used. In Kru, the terms for money are English loan words, coming from the old pounds, shillings, halfpenny – *epni* – and they stand now for dollars and cents at the original conversion rate of four dollars to the pound. Kofa paid quite a large fee in local terms.
11 For a lively account of how Mande griots in Mali embarrass nobles into recompensing their praises, see Kendall 1982.
12 These details were collected for me by Agatha T. Kofa: she participated also in the recording session and helped with later commentary, along with translator David Nagbe.
13 Cosentino 1982: 10, 96.
14 Bauman 1986: see especially Chapter 2 on lying, but throughout for the ways in which orientation and claims are managed in negotiation with audiences.
15 Presentations of the self, implicit understandings of personality, and practices which effectively bound and define the person are topics widely discussed by anthropologists who both try to delineate them and to cope with their theoretical implications, as I discuss briefly in Chapter 7. One well-known perspective is Mary Douglas', on the social understanding of the body (1966, 1972). For African notions of the person see e.g. *La Notion de personne* 1981 and cf. Gell's elucidation of the reproduction of bodily practices (1970). Other relevant works are referred to in Chapter 5.

3 Structuring an account: the work of genre

1 Finnegan has shown in different publications how diverse may be the indigenous expectancies, as well as the preparation and composition conditions of oral art. Her 1988 volume reviews many of these sources.
2 Critiques of genre in folklore studies suggest that they fail through being derived from untenable theory, ignoring real practices which lead to changes in use and significance, and because they ignore indigenous aims and contexts – see Ben-Amos 1976. The view of genre taken here is consonant with these points, since it treats oracy as practice rather than frozen text, and stresses its occasionality.
3 Hirsch 1967: 13.
4 Bakhtin 1986a and b. The first two quotations are from M. Holmquist's Introduction to 1986a: xviii; the last quotation is from Bakhtin's own chapter 'The problem of the text' in the collection.

5 Barber 1989: 13. I accept this view of written material, but cannot pursue its implications here.

6 Landeg White argues that 'in Southern Africa at least, it is not the *poet* who is licensed by literary convention; it is the *poem* ... It is not the performer that is licensed but the performance' (1989: 34). Composers of satirical *èfè* poems for the Gèlèdé masquerades of W. Yoruba are equally licensed to hit out at the audience (Bóláji 1984).

7 For 'secret' cues, see Bellman 1975. Tonkin 1988b discusses the means by which people can shift into 'play', ritual, drama or other activities which are thereby made special, or comment on 'ordinary life'.

8 Finnegan has commented on the world-wide variety of oral transmission, which can vary from fixed and memorised forms to considered reflections, such as were made by Sieh Jeto – see e.g. 1988: Chapter 5.

9 British radio listeners can easily test that delivery cues generic expectation by asking how they know, merely from listening to the announcer, which channel they have switched on. Relevant approaches to understanding the specifically oral features of oracy are now being addressed in ways very useful to students of oral history, as are ideas about how to represent oracy in print. See Sherzer and Woodbury (eds.) 1987 and Tedlock 1983.

10 Samuel 1980: all the quotations are from this unpublished paper.

11 In 'Zik's Story', I discuss the phenomenon of exemplary autobiography through the example of Nnamdi Azikiwe, a Nigerian leader who has used parts of his life in this way (Tonkin 1990b).

12 Nigel Dennis's novel *Cards of Identity* portrays a world in which identities are not stable as we like to think but built up of bureaucratic fragments: so if the instructions on the noticeboard change, you change with them.

13 For introduction to autobiography as genre see e.g. Olney 1972 and Olney (ed.) 1980, which includes articles referred to in the text.

14 Interesting commercial entertainment formats for the presentation of self are the TV 'This is Your Life' programme and an even more extraordinarily long-running series on British radio called 'Desert Island Discs', on which a 'guest' chooses eight discs for companionship on an imaginary desert island. It survives no doubt because this is a successful formula for autobiography. It personalises public figures, it licenses anecdote, and it creates a tiny tension – what would *you* miss if taken out of your daily world? How well could you cope with loneliness? – that listeners can also feel in themselves.

15 Mandel 1980: 62, Spender 1980: 170.

16 Cox 1980: 121–37.

17 Some of the patterns through which tellers constitute their lives are illustrated in Samuel and Thompson (eds.) *The Myths We Live By*, 1990.

18 Thus, for instance, Goody's work on orality and literacy virtually ignores delivery features, as in Goody 1987. For discussions of oracy, with some new attempts to look at African oral genres, including praise poems, in a historically situated and aesthetically responsive way, see in addition to other citations for this chapter, the whole collection of Barber and Farias (eds.) 1989.

19 Tonkin 1989 discusses the delivery features of Nimine Gbei, and refers to other African examples where the chanter/singer can counterpoint meaning or intensify emotional effects through prosodic structuring.

20 Deakin 1971. For Balkan epics, see for instance the work of the Chadwicks, Parry and Lord, cited in the notes below. Note also the comments of S. Kolyevic, *The Epic in the Making*, Oxford University Press, 1980: 'Oral epic singing at its best was both a way of coming to terms with history and a means of getting out of it. That is why its ultimate significance cannot be grasped in the analysis either of the technique of its composition or of the diverse historical sources of its social concepts, motifs and themes. For a song about fighting is not the same thing as fighting or even as the recording of an actual response to it. Similarly, songs about great defeats, vassalage, outlawry or rebellions attempt to grasp in language not only their historical but also their moral significance. They interpret the actual in terms of what it means as a challenge to the human spirit and to the whole tradition of oral poetic language in which it expresses itself' (in L. White 1989: 35).

21 Most people who refer to Lord (1960), a student of Parry (1930, 1932), appear to think that oral literature is composed of heroic formulae!

22 H. M. and N. K. Chadwick 1932, 1936, 1940; H. M. Chadwick 1912; note his comment that 'the comparative study of heroic poetry ... involves the comparative study of "heroic ages" and the problems which it presents are essentially problems of anthropology' (1912: viii).

23 Gunner 1989: 49.

24 Tonkin Daybook II: 22. For the cognate Grebo language, Innes and his informant, J. Y. Dennis, give as one meaning of *be, be no* 'he is a warrior, he is the leader of a gang' (Innes 1967).

25 Meeker 1979: 18, 120.

26 M. White 1965: 4. Important accounts of historical narrative include Hayden White, 1973, Canary and Kozicki (eds.) 1978 as well as Porter 1981.

27 Barber 1989: 17, 15, 18, *ibid.*

28 Agatha T. Kofa, letter, 13 January 1988.

4 Temporality: narrators and their times

1 Portelli 1981a: 175 quoting W. Benjamin.

2 Portelli 1981b: 104. Portelli also sums up succinctly in one paragraph (103) many issues which are more familiarly dealt with as the tendency to bias or subjectivity of oral testimony.

3 Portelli 1981a: 171. The idea that different periods have different characteristics is an old one – the Christian era which began with the birth of Christ (from Latin *aera*, number expressed in figures, pl. of *aes*, money), is one such epoch (from Greek *epokhe*, stoppage), Many such periodisations are cyclical. Others are sequential, but, as in Marxism, the sequences have no absolute temporal reference: instead they are considered to be inevitable stages through which a given community must pass over time. If we compare all these periodisations they show patterned similarities – so that, for instance tripartite schemes are common. (See e.g. Gombrich 1969, for an intellectual history of periodisation.) We can see therefore that they are collective representations, ideological constructions, and not reflections of natural truth.

4 Portelli 1981a. Apparently the worker's death is correctly marked on a plaque that tellers saw every day, but they still give the wrong date themselves.

(Comment by Portelli when delivering another paper [now Portelli 1988] to the 1987 International Oral History Conference on 'Myth and History'.)

5 Trevelyan 1949: 13.

6 Vansina 1978: 29.

7 McCaskie 1980 and Prins 1980 also treat cosmological ideas as historical data in their own right, as *mentalités* (to use the term popularised by the French scholars whose views have been put forward in their journal *Annales*).

8 This very limited sketch of the development of Western chronology is a summary of Denys Hay (1977, cited: 40–1) who himself summarises a very complex literature.

9 The historical development and uses of Islamic calendars are as complex as the Christians'. The Latin *Anno Hegirae* is modelled on 'AD': Arabic sources sometimes refer simply to the Hejira in dating events.

10 Islam is not always so progressivist, but Street notes (1984: 145) that Iranian villagers he knew in the 1970s argued that the succession of prophets was progressive, so that Hazrat Mohammed superseded Hazrat Esan (Jesus Christ) and it was therefore puzzling to them that Western Christians could be 'ahead' in technological development when they were 'behind' in historical–moral development – and indeed abused their technical knowledge.

11 Pepys' *Diary* Vol. III, 1970: 131. Pepys continued to get up at 4 am to learn his multiplication tables. Seventeen months later he was in turn teaching his wife (married at 15) 'and she is come to do Addition, Subtraction and Multiplication very well – and so I propose not to trouble her yet with Division, but to begin with the globes to her now'. Pepys also designed an improved slide rule for his work in measuring ship's timber. Rupert Hall's contribution 'Science' to R. Latham (ed.) *Companion to the Diary* suggests he would have used an abacus before he learnt multiplication. It is interesting to see that Pepys learned his arithmetic from a practical seaman, not a school teacher. Sea navigation in Micronesia and Europe has long been cognitively complex; see Frake's account of tidal reckoning by use of the compass rose, 'a very abstract model, a cognitive schema, of the relations of direction to time, of solar time to lunar time, and of time to tide' (1985: 266).

12 Sceptics and critics of such computers are also vociferous. To take just one example, computing has provided very powerful models for linguistics, but one can also argue that language is not just produced by 'information processing devices which operate on fixed elements according to fixed rules' Tyler (1978: 45), who points out the weakness of the computer model for understanding language. Most of us are ready to join in arguments as to whether computers can/will be able to think, however little we know about computing. It may be harder, however, to wonder if watches and chronologies are only a means of classifying reality and not of disclosing its real nature, because it is hard for people today, all over the world, to imagine life without chronological and calendrical time.

13 Even before schools or waged labour enforced new timing on Africans, conversion to Islam or Christianity entailed the marking of a seven-day sequence in order correctly to carry out rituals. Indigenous religions also had periodic rituals, of course, but these were generally tied to seasonal change.

When the Liberian prophet Harris converted Dida people in today's Ivory Coast (distantly related to Jlao Kru), they apparently had a six-day week, not geared to markets but including a day of worship with no farming. Harris preached that they should keep a seven-day week, with rest and worship on the seventh. People recalled filling a bottle with seven stones, taking out one a day, and marking off the house wall daily with charcoal as mnemonics for this new system (Krabill 1989: 118, 223–4).

14 Faris 1973 develops an account of how a community's weighting of 'occasions' may vary, structuring a habitus for members, and socialising children who make the terms key concepts for themselves.

15 'In calling his original jottings "epiphanies", Joyce underscored the ironic contrast between the manifestation that dazzled the Magi and the apparitions that manifest themselves on the streets of Dublin; he also suggested that those pathetic and sordid glimpses, to the sentient observer, offer a kind of revelation. As the part, significantly chosen, reveals the whole, a word or detail may be enough to exhibit a character or convey a situation' (Harry Levin, introduction to *Dubliners*, 1963).

16 Vansina 1978: 10–11.

17 Proposals for detecting superficially invisible 'structural changes' are made (principally by 'structuralist' means) in e.g. Miller (ed.) 1980 and Willis 1981.

18 Ricoeur explained 'the eclipse of the event' in a joint conference of historians and philosophers of history (1982).

19 Portelli 1981a.

20 Tedlock 1983.

21 The work of Brazil (1985) on British intonation is suggestive for the students of oral genres.

22 Russell 1985. All quotations are from this article, which also usefully refers to the work of other linguists who have studied the relations between linguistic structure and oral genre.

23 There is a large literature on this subject. Greenberg (1963) was the major innovator; Ardener 1971 comments on the theoretical issues.

24 See e.g. Welmers 1973, Bennett and Sterk 1977.

25 Vansina 1985.

26 Comrie 1985: vii, 1976: 1–2; 1985: 6 and these two books passim.

27 Singler 1979: 27. He also reviews the evidence for the development of verb-attaching temporal suffixes derived from an adverb, e.g. *poblaka*.

28 Singler 1979: 26.

29 Banfield 1985: 4, 5.

30 For these and other examples of discourse effects, see Grimes (ed.) 1978 (for Syuwa, see Höhlig therein, for Kham, see Watters).

31 Wolfson 1978: 236.

32 Fowles 1976.

33 Kru may also use CHP, as passages quoted suggest, but I have not yet a full enough analysis to be sure of its effects.

34 Schrager 1983: 82. The symbolic potential of language orientation may, to some audiences, become fixed, as when some members of Yoruba audiences may believe that the teller *becomes* his tale and makes known its knowledge (LaPin 1977).

5 Subjective or objective? Debates on the nature of oral history

1 I could not have read a history of an English landscape when I was a child, before W. G. Hoskins' books. He and his followers have produced work that seems the epitome of unpretentious factuality. Here are the results of painstaking practical research, untainted by ideological speculation and references to theory. They are of course highly ideological accounts simply by choice of topic. They are *presented* as being distinctive in openness to information from different disciplines and especially in their recourse to legwork, away from the muniment room to personal observation. See e.g. W. G. Hoskins' introduction to Norman Scarfe, *The Suffolk Landscape*, 1972. The diverse sources for this volume include a 'founding father' of the British oral history movement, George Ewart Evans, the great pioneer in the oral recording of agricultural skills.

2 Bloch 1954: 59, 61, 54.

3 Bloch 1954: 62.

4 Vansina 1985: 3. My comments and references are to this book unless I specify otherwise, e.g. to his *Oral Tradition*, which was first published in French in 1961, and in an (unauthorised) English version in 1965, and to the article of 1971 which summarises but already modifies the book.

5 Leach 1957: 120. Malinowski in fact also used others' observations, as all fieldworkers do.

6 Paul Thompson, as a sociologist, at first (1978) justified oral enquiry in empiricist terms (2nd edition, 1988). See the critique by Centre for Contemporary Cultural Studies, Johnson (ed.) 1982: 241 ff.

7 Anthropological interest in narrative is a developing field (see e.g. Clifford and Marcus (eds.) 1986, Marcus and Fischer 1986). Strathern 1987 includes references, as do Marcus and Cushman 1982.

8 Vansina 1985: 32 and passim.

9 In Tonkin 1982a, I argued from the case study of Jua Sieh that 'reminiscence' may be formally indistinguishable from 'tradition'. See also Tonkin 1986, for a review of changes in oral historians' assumptions, complementary to this chapter.

10 Vansina 1985: 4ff.

11 Vansina 1965: 79 and passim.

12 Cohen 1977: 9; cf. also 1980: 20.

13 Vansina 1985: 17–18, 96.

14 Barber 1989: 15, 19.

15 The tightness of Vansina's methodological excursions is in contrast to the greater openness of his methods in practice, in his empirical historical studies. Here, for instance, he has made a sensibly opportunist use of structuralist explanation (cf. Vansina 1978), but more recently he has vehemently attacked their use by others (Vansina 1983, 1985: 162–5).

16 For a philosopher's critique of 'rhetorical relativists' on historical truth, see Pompa 1982.

17 See examples in Bóláji 1984; Barber 1984.

18 LaPin 1977.

19 Peel 1984: 118.

20 Quotations from Barber 1989: 14–15, 16–17 and 20.
21 See Buckley 1985 for an account with examples of Yoruba medical beliefs in the power of words.
22 Bartlett 1986: 28. Relevant parts of Clanchy's argument are reproduced in Clanchy 1981.
23 George Ewart Evans describes in his autobiography (1983) how talking to old fellow villagers in Suffolk opened his eyes to their knowledge and skills, revealed as soon as they explained their old tools. He began to realise that there had been a very recent revolution in agricultural practice that was obliterating our understanding of how rural life had been, but 'asking the fellows that mowed the hay' would reveal a history that no documentary search on its own could recover.
24 Yates 1966. Such practices are also helpfully identified and summarised by Ong 1982 (although the arguments of this book challenge his dichotomising of orality and literacy, as indeed do the new iconographic practices of modern capitalism such as logos).

6 Memory makes us, we make memory

1 Lévi-Strauss 1970: 12, 18; 1985: 116.
2 Durkheim and Mauss 1963. The quotation is from Lévi-Strauss 1970: 13. His debt to Durkheim was celebrated in his intellectual autobiography *Tristes tropiques* (1973: 59). A useful entrée to theories of society-as-object is Frisby and Sayer 1986.
3 Ingold 1986: 197. Ingold's study of 'evolution and social life' argues that humans are constitutively social beings, and brings substantial arguments to bear, with references from both the social and the biological literature.
4 Althusser (*Essays in Self-Criticism*), cited by E. P. Thompson 1978: 297. Althusser can be simply functionalist, e.g. 'the structure of the relations of production determines the places and functions occupied and adopted by the agents of production, who are never anything more than the occupants of these places' (ibid.: 339). Insofar as Althusser argues that individual wills are causative (see his appendix to 'contradiction and overdetermination' 1969: 117–28), I accept his points, as my text shows.
5 E. P. Thompson 1978: 356.
6 So huge is the literature from which the arguments on agency are derived, that my references are confined to very specific quotations and allusions. A powerful account of how economics became theoretically 'individualist', rather than the social science it purports to be is provided by Dumont 1977. Dumont presents this work as part of his great study of how the notion has developed that individuals are, as such, equal and equally valued, that is, how sense (iii) has come to be united with senses (i) and (ii), arguing that this view has been specific to modern Europe.
7 Some of the relevant literature on theories of socialisation is discussed in Tonkin 1982b.
8 Ingold 1986 distinguishes the sociality of human and other animals; I do not deal with his and others' arguments here.

9 Sacks 1984.

10 Halbwachs 1975 (1st edition 1925).

11 Durkheim and Mauss put forward their account of the social origins of cognition in 1903. In the preface to his 1963 translation, Needham objects to the proposition that social relations precede and form cognitive ones, for how could people recognise and create social relationships without the perceptual ability to distinguish and to group? Such objections also underlie Godelier's objections to neo-Marxist theories on the causative dominance of modes of production in pre-capitalist societies (see e.g. 1978).

12 Cited in Frisby and Sayer 1986.

13 A good popular introduction to recent psychology is Jonathan Miller's published TV interviews with some of them (1983). See also Forgas (ed.) 1981. The work of Jerome Bruner and his associates is particularly notable in the field, see e.g. Bruner et al. 1966.

14 We have to explain ontogenetic development in an environment which is so to speak already phylogenetically developed. The cognitive and perceptual focus of psychologists is so far much more elemental and fine-grained than my examples, but is not I think inconsistent with them, and I am attempting here to sketch only short-hand, readily recognisable linkages which can let us see how change and the perception of change are alike possible, in humanity as we know and have known it.

15 See Halliday, e.g. 1975, 1978, for a theory of the social acquisition of language.

16 As Anderson has pointed out in a sympathetic critique of Thompson (1980), no individual subjects have full control. The words 'subject' and 'agent' connote opposed power relations in themselves. For a programmatic explanation within a theory congruent with arguments put forward here, see Giddens' work, e.g. 1979.

17 Bourdieu 1977.

18 Bourdieu 1977: 82–3.

19 See e.g. Herzfeld 1987 for a criticism that Bourdieu does not always obey his own directives against formalisation. One can also note that, as with many theorists who argue that the 'appearances' of society are but realisations of forces which the members of society do not understand, one is left to wonder how the analyst has managed to surmount habitus himself.

20 Bourdieu 1977: 70; 'every marriage *tends* to reproduce the conditions which have made it possible'.

21 Bohannan 1952 is an early demonstration of how recall can become 'telescoped' and connections between groups differently stressed over time.

22 Evans-Pritchard 1940.

23 See, for example, the brief discussion and definitions of these terms by Giddens 1984. The point is raised again in Chapter 7.

24 The status of kin-defined ordering remains a major debate in social anthropology. In the context of this chapter, an analysis of social organisation and its representation which I have found helpful is Kahn 1978.

25 The analogy of woman as a pan occurred in a Kru funny story – which was taken as very apt. The subtlety and socially indicative power of such images in kinship reference are well reviewed by Delaney 1986.

26 Against psychoanalytical arguments that certain symbolism is universal but individually manifested, social anthropologists have argued that symbol systems are wholly cultural (e.g. Leach 1958). Hook (1979) usefully reviews the different notions of symbolism involved. A more satisfying argument that cultures differentially develop symbol systems with psychological resonance and power was put forward by Hershman 1974. Dreams may also be seen as culture-bound, since, as with memory, one envisages a known world, including its symbols and these operate through cultural practice (cf. Sperber 1975).

7 Truthfulness, history and identity

1 Both P. Thompson 1988 and Lummis 1987 make good critiques of literate historians' over-reliance on the truthfulness of documents which are at base oral.

2 In English law, innocence and guilt are legal statuses, and not necessarily actual states. For a discussion of the legal concept of the 'reasonable man', applied in a non-literate legal system, see Gluckman 1955. It is important to note that not all legal systems are geared to finding 'the truth', or to making an 'impartial' decision. They may focus rather on social solutions to perceived social breakdowns, and support therefore the litigant who has mobilised the strongest support, which may be an equally rational (and honourably considered) decision. See e.g. Gulliver 1963.

3 Neisser 1982 – a rare study by a psychologist of how substantial accounts in natural contexts are remembered.

4 The structuring of memory is addressed by Vansina (1985, which also cites many relevant works by others and by him). In Freudian analysis, of course, the patient is asked to be an oral historian, and Ronald Fraser has interestingly combined and contrasted the differently collected and theorised remembrances involved in his autobiographically centred *In Search of a Past*, 1984. The intrinsically impossible testing of 'true' or 'false' in such testimony is of course exemplified in the work of Freud himself, see for instance his change of mind about the reality of sexual abuse reported by patients, which some later commentators are again arguing was not fantasy (Masson 1984).

5 Portelli 1988. See also Chapman et al., Introduction to Tonkin, et al. (eds.) 1989: 5–8.

6 H. and F. Morphy 1984: 460, 461.

7 Collard 1989: 96, 93. A very sharply realised and painful account of what some Greek villagers went through from 1940 to 1950 is Nicholas Gage's *Eleni* 1983, which is itself a thought-provoking use of oral sources (including his own memories) into a form derived from the relatively new genre of investigative reporting.

8 It is interesting that sociologists who have become interested in life history have typically become dissatisfied with positivistic constructions of the individual, cf. Plummer 1983, and contributions to Bertaux (ed.) 1981.

9 To accept that we are members of one another is morally demanding and ideologies which suppress, rather than cope with the consequences of such a belief, are commonplace. To take one example, debates about the nature of

intelligence polarise into inheritance versus environment and it is well understood that Rightists tend to believe that ability is genetically transmitted, whereas Leftists demand the ending of class and material inequalities which block children's potential. Neither side seems keen to accept that 'intelligence' may label an unevenly developing bunch of abilities which, whether or not genetic triggers are involved, can really be stunted by physical and by social malnutrition. Views which seem more clear-cut, and which are also more comfortable for their holders, get preferred.

10 Carl Jung, speaking in a 1959 'Face To Face' TV interview with John Freeman, repeated on BBC 16 October 1988. This seems a true account of social individuation (rather than 'collective unconscious'). 'What are you conscious of in yourself? . . . However far back you go in your memory, it is always in some external, active manifestation of yourself that you come across your identity – in the work of your hands, in your family, in other people . . . You in others are yourself, your soul. This is what you are. This is what your consciousness has breathed and lived on and enjoyed throughout your life . . . And what now? You have always been in others and you will remain in others. And what does it matter to you if later on it is called your memory? This will be you – the you that enters the future and becomes a part of it.' These quotations from *Doctor Zhivago* come from a passage which has been cited as giving Pasternak's own views (Pasternak, 1966: 68, Ivinskaya, 1978: 87).

11 A critique of methodological individualism is made by Urwin (1984) and her psychologist fellow-contributors. Ferrarotti argues that as a consequence of the standard psychological perspective, 'We know nothing about the individual of which Marx spoke as "an ensemble of social relations" ' (1981: 25).

12 Nora 1984: xviii, my translation of 'A la péripherie, l'indépendance des nouvelles nations a entrainé dans l'historicité les sociétés déjà reveillées par le viol colonial de leur sommeil ethnologique'; xix. Note too the suggestion by Peter Burke that 'Nora should replace his simple story of a shift from memory to history over the past few years with a more subtle account of the interaction of oral and written accounts of the past in France over the long term' (1989: 165, fn 26).

13 For the argument that events are cognitive constructions, not experiental givens, see Mink, 1978. Ardener's even more radical, but incomplete, version of registration (1989) elaborates arguments in his earlier publications. Such registrations are of course social, not simply subjective, as I argue in Chapter 6.

14 Mauss 1954 (tr. 1979). Lévi-Strauss has also cogently demonstrated (1966) that the basic cultural discoveries of humankind, like agriculture and pottery, could not have occurred without systematic testing and critical reflexion, although they can be 'practically' rather than discursively produced, while so-called primitive languages are frequently full of abstractions. Languages indeed are all rationally structured but cannot be successfully spoken without a large part of unreflective action.

15 See Polanyi 1967.

16 The Russian Luriya first raised these possibilities (1979), which his American student Michael Cole later adapted for studies in Liberia. Cole has come to suggest that innate cultural logics are not neatly matchable to the

illiterate:literate distinction (which itself has received much more critical attention recently). See e.g. Scribner 1979 – and the perceptive comments on the importance of social situation by Fernandez 1980, e.g. 45–8.

17 Davies 1989: 168, 169, 170, 181.

18 Davies here cites Goody 1977: 148.

19 Peel 1984: 118.

20 The model of a web is Emmanuel Terray's: for initial discussion of this history, see e.g. Brown 1984 and Tonkin 1985 (where Terray is cited). Kru-group peoples do not seem to have been segmentary societies in the formal meaning of this term.

21 Henige 1974 pointed out that such motifs of African traditions are common to traditions of many other times and regions.

22 See Fortes 1970 (first published 1936) and 1940.

23 Tosh 1978: 6. Obviously transmission, and hence social reproduction, is the more fragile in such situations. I discuss Tosh's assumption that informality = realism, in Tonkin 1990a. Kenny 1977 shows how segmented peoples code history in terms of opposed structures.

24 Carrier 1987 and Strathern 1984. M. and A. Strathern have written very considerably on Hagen life, and M. Strathern especially has developed contrasts between Western and Melanesian senses of identity.

25 In addition to the disjunctive devices of oríkì, parallelism can be studied as another almost world-wide means of setting up connections by contrast (see e.g. Fox 1974).

26 Rappaport 1988: 721, 732. This is a richly worked out account of how '"historical" interpretation . . . is expressed through ritual, in political oratory, and in judicial arguments . . . the negotiation of historical knowledge does not necessarily conclude in an overtly historical representation': 719. The Cumbal view of past and future are also compared with Maori description of the past as 'the days in front' and the future as 'behind' (she cites the work of Metge).

27 Basso 1984: 23, 44–5, 43n.

28 Abélès 1988. The citations are from 396, 393, 397. Abélès in his reply to commentators noted that historians have been more interested than anthropologists in 'the symbolic bases of legitimacy' and their continuing power in what are apparently secular contemporary environments (403). Maurice Bloch in various publications (e.g. 1986) has analysed how ritual action in its very emptiness, politically speaking, may nevertheless block political action.

29 Whenever visiting Heads of State are taken to historical sites – the Great Wall of China is an obvious example – one can look for politico-sacred messages. These can be complex and elaborate, as in the African examples analysed by McCaskie 1980 and Prins 1980.

30 Since people commonly identify with several, sometimes overlapping groups, identity is not a single or uniform entity (see Southall 1970). Nor are ethnic identities, for instance, explicable simply as reflexes of social relations; this point is brought out in Tonkin et al. (eds.) 1989 – see e.g. Peel therein.

31 The conditions in which social identity is constructed by versions of history are illustrated in Tonkin et al. (eds.) 1989. Forsythe looks at contemporary constructions of what it is to be German, while Schutte and Buckley show how

Afrikaaners and Northern Irish Protestants assert their God-given legitimacy in face of threats to this construction and to their controlling power. Buckley 1985/6 also shows how this 'sacred history' is evoked in secret society rituals, which use biblical stories to show that his chosen people will overcome when in a land that hitherto belonged to somebody else.

32 Brian Crow has used the work of Franco Moretti (1983) to argue 'that Elizabethan and Jacobean tragedy and tragi-comedy can only be usefully considered as culturally *structural* concepts, that is, as particular forms of representing history – in this case the history of absolutism as the ruling class's political stratagem for shoring up a crumbling feudal system – rather than as genres expressive of the "tragic" or the "tragicomic" as historical permanencies' (1988).

33 Lummis 1987: 136.

34 In this respect, I am unsatisfied with the arguments of the Centre for Contemporary Cultural Studies' delineation of 'popular memory' in Johnson (ed.) 1982, although in many other respects this is a forceful and valuable attempt to see how histories are made.

35 The self is also discussed in anthropology along with the person. See e.g. Carrithers et al. (eds.) 1985. I do not go into these distinctions here, but note that Charles Taylor's contribution to that volume offers a philosophical justification of the person consonant with this book, arguing that 'I become a person and remain one only as an interlocutor' (277).

36 For Jackson's discussion of Kuranko expressions of self, see 1982 (e.g. Introduction, the citation is 31). He gives examples of Kuranko history in his ethnographic novel, *Barawa*, 1986.

37 For the 'muting' of subordinate groups, such as women, see S. Ardener (ed.) 1975. Hoggart later (1970) recorded his difficulties in representing working class life for his *Uses of Literacy* (1957) since literary genres only used standard language.

38 Besides the report by Cunnison, cited by Willis 1986: 251, see e.g. James 1979: 197ff. Sahlins 1981 argues that Fijian 'stereotypic reproduction' structurally reproduces society.

39 Bertaux-Wiame 1979: 32, also in Bertaux (ed.) 1981.

40 There are many wider identifications which a use of 'I' can make, and they have fuzzy edges. Take, for instance, reincarnation. This is not, supposedly, an English belief, but the English assert (unclearly) that people 'take after' an older relative, and call their children 'after' others too.

BIBLIOGRAPHY

Abélès, Marc 1988. Modern political ritual: ethnography of an inauguration and a pilgrimage by President Mitterand. *Current Anthropology* 29.3: 391–404.

Althusser, Louis 1969. *For Marx* (tr. B. Brewster). Harmondsworth: Penguin.

Anderson, Perry 1980. *Arguments within English Marxism*. London. NLB & Verso Editions.

Ardener, Edwin 1971. Social anthropology and the historicity of historical linguistics, in Edwin Ardener (ed.) *Social Anthropology and Language*, ASA Monograph 10: 209–41. London: Tavistock.

  1989. The construction of history: 'vestiges of creation', in E. Tonkin, M. McDonald and M. Chapman (eds.) *History and Ethnicity*, ASA Monograph 27: 22–33. London: Routledge.

Ardener, Shirley (ed.) 1975. *Perceiving Women*. London: Malaby Press.

Bakhtin, M. M. 1986a. *Speech Genres and Other Late Essays* (tr. Vern W. McGeo). Caryl Emerson and Michael Holmquist (eds.). Austin: University of Texas Press.

  1986b. *The Dialogic Imagination* (tr. C. Emerson and M. Holmquist) M. Holmquist (ed.) Austin: University of Texas Press.

Banfield, Ann 1985. Ecriture, narration and the grammar of French, in Jeremy Hawthorn (ed.) *Narrative: from Malory to Motion Pictures*: 1–22. London: Edward Arnold Ltd.

Barber, Karin 1984. Yoruba *oríkì* and deconstructive criticism. *Research in African Literatures* 15.4: 497–518.

  1989. Interpreting oríkì as history and as literature, in K. Barber and P. F. de Moraes Farias (eds.) *Discourse and its Disguises*: 13–23. Birmingham: Centre of West African Studies.

Barber, Karin and Farias de Moraes, Paulo (eds.) 1989. *Discourse and its Disguises: The Interpretation of African Oral Texts*. Birmingham University African Studies Series 1. Birmingham: Centre of West African Studies.

Bartlett, Robert 1986. *Trial by Fire and Water*. Oxford: Clarendon Press.

Basso, Keith H. 1984. Stalking with stories, in Edward Bruner (ed.) *Text, Play and Story*: 21–55. Washington DC: American Ethnological Society.

Bauman, Richard 1986. *Story, Performance and Event*. Cambridge University Press.

Beer, Jeanette M. A. 1981. *Narrative Conventions of Truth in the Middle Ages*. (Etudes de Philosophie et d'Histoire 38). Geneva: Librairie Druz SA.

Bellman, Beryl L. 1975. *Village of Curers and Assassins: On the Production of Fala Kpelle Cosmological Categories*. The Hague, Paris: Mouton.

  1984. *The Language of Secrecy*. New Brunswick NJ: Rutgers University Press.

153

Ben-Amos, Dan 1976. Analytical categories and ethnic genres, in D. Ben-Amos (ed.) *Folklore Genres*: 215–42. Austin: University of Texas Press.

Bennett, Patrick R. and Sterk, Jan P. 1977. South Central Niger-Congo: a reclassification. *Studies in African Linguistics* 8.3: 241–65.

Bertaux, Daniel (ed.) 1981. *Biography and Society: The Life History Approach in the Social Sciences*. Beverly Hills: Sage.

Bertaux-Wiame, Isabelle 1981. The life history approach to the study of internal migration. *Oral History* 7.1: 1979: 26–32, repr. in D. Bertaux (ed.) *Biography and Society*. Beverley Hills: Sage.

Bielenberg, Christabel 1984. *The Past is Myself*. (Chatto & Windus 1968), Ealing: Corgi Books.

Bloch, Marc 1954. *The Historian's Craft* (tr. P. Putnam). Manchester University Press.

Bloch, Maurice 1986. *From Blessing to Violence*. Cambridge University Press.

Bohannan, Laura 1952. A genealogical charter. *Africa* 22: 301–15.

Bóláji, Bámidélé Emmanuel 1984. The dynamics and the manifestations of Èfè: the satirical poetry of the Yoruba Gèlèdé groups of Nigeria. Ph.D, University of Birmingham.

Bourdieu, Pierre 1977. *Outline of a theory of practice* (tr. Richard Nice of revised version of *Esquisse d'une théorie de la pratique* 1972). Cambridge University Press.

Brazil, David 1985. *The Communicative Value of Intonation in English*. Birmingham: Bleak House.

Brown, David 1984. Warfare, oracles and iron: a case study of production among the pre-colonial Klowe, in the light of some recent Marxist examples. *Africa* 54.2: 29–47.

Bruner, J. S. (et al.) 1966. *Studies in cognitive growth*. New York: Wiley.

Buckley, A. D. 1985. *Yoruba Medicine*. London: Oxford University Press.

1985/6. The chosen few: Biblical texts in the regalia of an Ulster secret society. *Folk Life* 24: 5–24.

1989. We're trying to find an identity: uses of history among Ulster Protestants, in E. Tonkin, M. McDonald and M. Chapman (eds.) *History and Ethnicity*, ASA Monograph 27: 183–97. London: Routledge.

Burke, Peter 1969. *The Renaissance Sense of the Past*. London: Edward Arnold.

1989. French historians and their cultural identities, in E. Tonkin, M. McDonald and M. Chapman (eds.) *History and Ethnicity*, ASA Monograph 27: 157–67. London: Routledge.

Canary, Robert H. and Kozicki, Henry (eds.) 1978. *The Writing of History: Literary Form and Historical Understanding*. Madison: University of Wisconsin Press.

Carrier, James G. 1987. History and self-conception in Ponam society. *Man* 22: 111–31.

Carrithers, Michael, Collins, Steven and Lukes, Steven (eds.) 1985. *The Category of the Person*. Cambridge University Press.

Chadwick, H. Munro 1912. *The Heroic Age* (repr. 1926). Cambridge University Press.

Chadwick, H. Munro and Chadwick, N. Kershaw 1932, 1936, 1940. *The Growth of Literature*, Vols. I (repr. 1968), II and III. Cambridge University Press.

Cipolla, Carlo 1969. *Literacy and Development in the West*. Harmondsworth: Penguin.

Clanchy, Michael T. 1981. Literate and illiterate; hearing and seeing. England 1066–1307, in H. J. Graff (ed.) *Literacy and Social Development in the West*: 14–45. Cambridge University Press.

Clifford, James and Marcus, George E. (eds.) 1986. *Writing Culture*. Berkeley: University of California Press.

Cohen, David William 1977. *Womunafu's Bunafu: A Study of Authority in a Nineteenth-Century African Community*. Princeton University Press.

1980. Reconstructing a conflict in Bunafu's past: seeking evidence outside the narrative tradition, in Joseph C. Miller (ed.), *The African Past Speaks*: 201–20. Folkestone and Hamden: Dawson and Archon.

Collard, Anna 1989. Investigating 'social memory' in a Greek context, in E. Tonkin, M. McDonald and M. Chapman (eds.), *History and Ethnicity*, ASA Monograph 27: 89–103, London: Routledge.

Comrie, Bernard 1976. *Aspect*. Cambridge University Press.

1985. *Tense*. Cambridge University Press.

Cosentino, Donald 1982. *Defiant Maids and Stubborn Farmers*. Cambridge University Press.

Cox, James M. 1980. Recovering literature's lost ground through autobiography, in James Olney (ed.) *Autobiography*: 123–45. Princeton University Press.

Crow, Brian 1988. Tragedy and beyond: Soyinka and the problem of power. Paper delivered to the African Studies Association of the UK Conference, Cambridge.

Culler, Jonathan 1978. On trope and persuasion. *New Literary History* 8.3: 607–18.

Davies, Douglas 1989. Mormon history, identity and faith community, in E. Tonkin, M. McDonald and M. Chapman (eds.) *History and Ethnicity*, ASA Monograph 27: 168–82. London: Routledge.

Davis, John 1989. The social relations of the production of history, in E. Tonkin, M. McDonald and M. Chapman (eds.) *History and Ethnicity*, ASA Monograph 27: 104–20. London: Routledge.

Davis, Ronald W. 1976. *Ethnohistorical Studies of the Kru Coast*. Liberian Studies. Newark, Delaware.

Deakin, F. W. D. 1971. *The Embattled Mountain*. London: Oxford University Press.

Delaney, Carol 1986. The meaning of paternity and the virgin birth debate. *Man* 21.3: 494–513.

Dennis, Nigel 1960. *Cards of Identity*. Harmondsworth: Penguin.

Douglas, Mary 1966. *Purity and Danger*. London: Routledge & Kegan Paul.

1973. *Natural Symbols* (2nd edition). Harmondsworth: Penguin.

Dumont, Louis 1977. *From Mandeville to Marx*. University of Chicago Press.

Durkheim, Emile and Mauss, Marcel 1963. *Primitive Classification* (1903) (tr. and introduction R. Needham). London: Cohen & West.

Eliot, T. S. 1958. *Collected Poems 1909–1935*. London: Faber & Faber

Ellen, R. F. (ed.) 1984. *Ethnographic Research: A Guide to General Conduct*, ASA Research Methods in Social Anthropology I. London: Academic Press.

Evans, George Ewart 1983. *The Strength of the Hills*. London and Boston: Faber & Faber.

Evans-Pritchard, E. E. 1940. *The Nuer*. London: Oxford University Press.
Fabian, Johannes 1983. *Time and the Other: How Anthropology makes its Object*. New York: Columbia University Press.
Faris, J. C. 1973. Occasions and non-occasions. *Man* 3.1, 1968: 112–24, repr. in M. Douglas (ed.) *Rules and Meanings*. Harmondsworth: Penguin.
Fernandez, James 1980. Edification by puzzlement, in I. Karp and C. S. Bird (eds.) *Explorations in African Thought*: 44–59. Bloomington: Indiana University Press.
Ferrarotti, Franco 1981. On the autonomy of the historical method, in D. Bertaux (ed.) *Biography and Society*: 19–27. Beverly Hills: Sage.
Finnegan, Ruth 1970. *Oral Literature in Africa*. Oxford: Clarendon Press.
  1988. *Literacy and Orality*. Oxford: Basil Blackwell.
Forgas, Joseph P. (ed.) 1981. *Social Cognition*. London: Academic Press.
Forsythe, Diana E. 1989. German identity and the problem of history, in E. Tonkin, M. McDonald and M. Chapman (eds.) *History and Ethnicity*, ASA Monograph 27: 137–56. London: Routledge.
Fortes, M. 1940. The political system of the Tallensi of the Northern Territories of the Gold Coast, in M. Fortes and E. E. Evans-Pritchard (eds.) *African Political Systems*: 239–71. London: IAI by Oxford University Press.
  1970. Ritual festivals and social cohesion in the hinterland of the Gold Coast (1936) repr. in M. Fortes *Time and Social Structure*: 147–63. London: Athlone Press.
Fowles, John 1976. *The Ebony Tower* (Cape 1974). St Albans: Panther.
Fox, James J. 1974. Our ancestors spoke in pairs: Rotinese views of language, dialect and code, in Richard Bauman and Joel Sherzer (eds.) *Explorations in the Ethnography of Speaking*: 65–85. Cambridge University Press.
Frake, Charles O. 1985. Cognitive maps of time and tide among medieval seafarers. *Man* 20.2: 254–70.
Fraser, Ronald 1984. *In Search of a Past*. London: Verso Editions & NLB.
Frisby, David and Sayer, Derek 1986. *Society*. London: Ellis Horwood and Tavistock.
Frisch, Michael 1987. American history and the structures of collective memory. Paper presented at 6th International Oral History Conference. Oxford.
Gage, Nicholas 1983. *Eleni*. London: Collins.
Gell, Alfred. 1979. Reflections on a cut finger: taboo in the Umeda conception of the self, in R. H. Hook (ed.) *Fantasy and Symbol*: 133–48. London and New York: Academic Press.
Gellner, Ernest 1983. *Nations and Nationalism*. Oxford: Basil Blackwell.
Genette, Gérard 1976. Boundaries of narrative. *New Literary History* 8.1: 1–13.
Giddens, Anthony 1979. *Central Problems in Social Theory*. London: Macmillan.
  1984. *The Constitution of Society*. Cambridge and Oxford: Polity Press with Basil Blackwell.
Gluckman, Max 1955. *The Judicial Process among the Barotse of Northern Rhodesia*. Manchester University Press.
Godelier, Maurice 1978. Infrastructures, societies and history. *Current Anthropology* 19.4: 763–71.
Gombrich, E. H. 1960. *Art and Illusion*. London: Phaidon.
  1969. *In Search of Cultural History*. Oxford: Clarendon Press.

Goody, Jack 1977. *The Domestication of the Savage Mind*. Cambridge University Press.
   1987. *The Interface between the Written and the Oral*. Cambridge University Press.
Goody, Jack (ed.) 1966. *Succession to High Office*. Cambridge University Press.
Greenberg, J. H. 1963. *The Languages of Africa*. Mouton: The Hague.
Grimes, Joseph E. (ed.) 1978. *Papers on Discourse*. Dallas: Summer Institute of Linguistics Inc.
Gulliver, P. H. 1963. *Social Control in an African Society*. London: Routledge & Kegan Paul.
Gumperz, John J. (ed.) 1982. *Language and Social Identity: Studies in International Linguistics 2*. Cambridge University Press.
Gunner, Elizabeth 1989. Orality and literacy: dialogue and silence, in K. Barber and P. F. de Moraes Farias (eds.) *Discourse and its Disguises*: 49–56. Birmingham: Centre of West African Studies.
Halbwachs, Maurice 1975. *Les Cadres sociaux de la mémoire* (1925) (preface by François Châtelet). Paris, La Haye: Mouton.
Halliday, M. A. K. 1975. *Learning How to Mean*. London: Edward Arnold.
   1978. *Language as social semiotic*. London: Edward Arnold.
Hay, Denys 1977. *Annalists and Historians: Western Historiography from the VIIth to the XVIIth century*. London: Methuen & Co. Ltd.
Henige, David 1974. *The Chronology of Oral Tradition: Quest for a Chimera*. Oxford: Clarendon Press.
Hershman, P. 1974. Hair, sex and dirt. *Man* 9.2: 274–98.
Herzfeld, Michael 1987. *Anthropology Through the Looking-Glass*. Cambridge University Press.
Hirsch, E.D. 1967. *Validity in Interpretation*. New Haven and London: Yale University Press.
Hoggart, Richard 1957. *The Uses of Literacy*. London: Chatto & Windus.
   1970. *Speaking to Each Other* (2 vols). London: Chatto & Windus.
Höhlig, Monika 1978. Speaker orientation in Syuwa (Kagate), in Joseph E. Grimes (ed.) *Papers on Discourse*: 19–24. Dallas: Summer Institute of Linguistics Inc.
Hook, R. H. 1979. Phantasy and symbol: a psychoanalytic view, in R. H. Hook (ed.) *Fantasy and Symbol*: 267–91, London: Academic Press.
Ingold, Tim 1986. *Evolution and Social Life*. Cambridge University Press.
Innes, Gordon 1967. *A Grebo–English Dictionary*. West African Language Monographs 6. Cambridge University Press.
Ivinskaya, Olga 1978. *A Captive of Time: My Years with Pasternak* (tr. M. Hayward). London: Collins & Harvill Press.
Jackson, Michael 1982. *Allegories of the Wilderness: Ethics and Ambiguity in Kuranko Narratives*. Bloomington: Indiana University Press.
   1986. *Barawa and the Ways Birds Fly in the Sky*. Washington and London: Smithsonian Institution Press.
James, Wendy 1979. *Kwanim Pa*. Oxford: Clarendon Press.
Johnson, Richard (ed.) 1982. *Making Histories*. London, Birmingham: Hutchinson/CCCS.
Joyce, James 1963. *The Essential James Joyce*. Harry Levin (ed.) Harmondsworth: Penguin Books in association with Jonathan Cape.

Kahn, Joel S. 1978. Ideology and social structures in Indonesia. *Comparative Studies in Society and History* 20.1: 103–23.

Kendall, Martha 1982. Getting to know you, in D. Parkin (ed.) *Semantic Anthropology*, ASA Monograph 22: 197–209 London: Academic Press.

Kenny, Michael G. 1977. The relation of oral history to social structure in South Nyanza. *Africa* 47.3: 276–88.

Kermode, Frank 1979. *The Genesis of Secrecy*. Cambridge MA: Harvard University Press.

Krabill, James 1989. The hymnody of the Harrist church among the Dida of south-central Ivory Coast (1913–1949): an historico-religious study. Ph.D, Birmingham University.

LaPin, Deirdre 1977. Story, medium and masque: the idea and art of Yoruba storytelling. Ph.D, University of Wisconsin-Madison (University Microfilms).

Latham, Robert (ed.) 1983. *The Diary of Samuel Pepys* Vol. 10, Companion. London: Bell & Hyman.

Leach, Edmund R. 1957. The epistemological background to Malinowski's empiricism, in R. Firth (ed.) *Man and Culture*: 119–37. London: Routledge & Kegan Paul.

1958. Magical hair. *Journal of the Royal Anthropological Institute* 88.2: 147–69.

Lévi-Strauss, Claude 1966. *The Savage Mind*. London: Weidenfeld & Nicolson.

1970. *The Raw and the Cooked* (*Mythologiques I*) (1964) (tr. J. and D. Weightman). New York: Harper Torchbooks.

1973 *Tristes tropiques* (tr. J. Weightman). London: Jonathan Cape.

1985. *The View from Afar* (1983) (tr. J. Neugroschel and P. Hoss). Oxford, New York: Blackwell.

Lord, Albert B. 1960. *The Singer of Tales*. Cambridge MA: Harvard University Press.

Lowenthal, David 1985. *The Past is Another Country*. Cambridge University Press.

Lummis, Trevor 1987. *Listening to History*. London: Hutchinson.

Luriya, A. R. 1979. *The Making of Mind* (ed. and tr. M. and S. Cole). Cambridge MA: Harvard University Press.

McCaskie, T. C. 1980. Time and the calendar in nineteenth-century Asante: an exploratory essay. *History in Africa* 7: 179–200.

Mandel, Barrett J. 1980. Full of life now, in James Olney (ed.) *Autobiography*: 49–72. Princeton University Press.

Marcus, George E. and Cushman, Dick 1982. Ethnographies as texts. *Annual Review of Anthropology* 11: 25–69.

Marcus, George E. and Fischer, Michael M. J. 1986. *Anthropology as Cultural Critique*. University of Chicago Press.

Massing, Andreas 1980. *The Economic Anthropology of the Kru (West Africa)*. Wiesbaden: Franz Steiner Verlag.

Masson, Jeffrey M. 1984. *Freud, The Assault on Truth*. London: Faber.

Mauss, Marcel 1979. *Sociology and Psychology* (1950) (tr. Ben Brewster). London: Routledge and Kegan Paul.

Meeker, Michael E. 1979. *Literature and Violence in North Arabia*. Cambridge University Press.

Miller, Jonathan 1983. *States of Mind*. London: BBC Publications.

Miller, Joseph C. (ed.) 1980. *The African Past Speaks: Essays on Oral Tradition as History*. Folkestone and Hamden: Dawson and Archon.

Milton, John 1958. *Paradise Lost* (1674) in *The Poetical Works of John Milton*, Helen Darbishire (ed.) London: Oxford University Press.

Mink, Louis O. 1978. Narrative form as a cognitive instrument, in R. H. Canary and H. Kozicki (eds.) *The Writing of History*: 129–49. Madison, London: University of Wisconsin Press.

Moretti, Franco 1983. *Signs Taken for Wonders* (tr. S. Fischer, D. Forgaes and D. Miller). 2nd edition. London: Verso.

Morphy, Howard and Morphy, Frances 1984. The 'myths' of Ngalakan history: ideology and images of the past in Northern Australia. *Man* 193: 459–78.

Murphy, William P. 1980. Secret knowledge in Kpelle society. *Africa* 50.2: 193–207.

Neisser, Ulric 1982. *Memory Observed: Remembering in Natural Contexts*. (USA): W. H. Freeman & Coy.

Nora, Pierre 1984. Entre mémoire et histoire: la problématique des lieux. Introduction: Pierre Nora et al. (eds.), *Les Lieux de mémoire Vol. I: La République*. Paris: NRF, Editions Gallimard.

1981. *La Notion de personne en Afrique Noire*. Colloques Internationaux du CNRS no. 544, Paris, 11–17 October 1971 (1973), repr. Paris eds. du CNRS.

Olney, James 1972. *Metaphors of Self: the Meaning of Autobiography*. Princeton University Press.

Olney, James (ed.) 1980. *Autobiography: Essays Theoretical and Critical*. Princeton University Press.

Olson, David R., Torrance, N. and Hildyard, A. (eds.) 1985. *Literacy, Language and Learning*. Cambridge University Press.

Ong, Walter J. 1977. African talking drums and oral noetics. *New Literary History* 8.3: 411–29.

1982. *Orality and Literacy*. London and New York: Methuen.

Panofsky, Erwin 1970. *Meaning in the Visual Arts* (Doubleday 1955). Harmondsworth: Peregrine Books.

Parry, Milman 1930, 1932. Studies in the epic techniques of oral text making. (i) Homer and Homeric style, (ii) The Homeric language as the language of an oral poetry, *Harvard Studies in Classical Philosophy*. 41, 43: 73–147, 1–50.

Pasternak, Boris 1966. *Doctor Zhivago* (tr. Max Hayward and Manya Harari 1958). 3rd edition. London: Collins & Harvill Press.

Peel, J. D. Y. 1984. Making history: the past in the Ijesha present. *Man* 19.1: 111–32.

1989. The cultural work of Yoruba ethnogenesis, in E. Tonkin, M. McDonald and M. Chapman (eds.) *History and Ethnicity*, ASA Monograph 27: 198–215. London: Routledge.

Pepys, Samuel 1970. *Diary* Vol. III. Robert Latham and William Matthews (eds.) London: G. Bell & Son Ltd.

Plummer, Ken 1983. *Documents of Life*. London: George Allen & Unwin.

Polanyi, Michael 1967. *The Tacit Dimension*. Routledge & Kegan Paul.

Pompa, Leon 1982. Narrative form, significance and historical knowledge, in D. Carr et al. (eds.) *Philosophy of History and Contemporary Historiography* (*Philosophica* 23): 143–57. University of Ottawa Press.

Portelli, Alessandro 1981a. The peculiarities of oral history. *History Workshop* 12: 96–107.

1981b. The time of my life: functions of time in oral history. *International Journal of Oral History* 2.3: 162–80.

1985. Oral history, the law and the making of history. *History Workshop* 20: 5–35.

1988. Uchronic dreams: working class memory and possible worlds. *Oral History Journal* 16.2: 46–56.

Porter, Dale H. 1981. *The Emergence of the Past: A Theory of Historical Explanation*. Chicago and London: University of Chicago Press.

Prins, Gwyn 1980. *The Hidden Hippopotamus*. Cambridge University Press.

Rappaport, Joanne 1988. History and everyday life in the Colombian Andes. *Man* 23.4: 718–39.

Ricoeur, Paul 1982. L'Eclipse de l'événement, in *Philosophy of History and contemporary Historiography*, David Carr et al. (eds.) (*Philosophica* 23): 159–77. Ottawa University Press.

Russell, Joan 1985. Women's narration: performance and the marking of verbal aspect, in *Swahili Language and Society*, J. Maw and D. Parkin (eds.): 89–105. Vienna: Afro Pub.

Sacks, Oliver 1984. The lost mariner, in *New York Review of Books* Vol. 31.2, 16 February 1984.

Sahlins, Marshall 1981. *Historical Metaphor and Mythical Realities*. Ann Arbor: University of Michigan Press.

Samuel, Raphael 1980. Life histories. Paper delivered at the International Oral History Conference, Amsterdam.

Samuel, Raphael and Thompson, Paul (eds.) 1990. *The Myths We Live By*. London: Routledge.

Scarfe, Norman 1972. *The Suffolk Landscape*. London: Hodder & Stoughton.

Schrager, Samuel 1983. What is social in oral history? *International Journal of Oral History* 4: 76–98.

Schutte, Gerhard 1989. Afrikaner historiography and the decline of apartheid: ethnic self-reconstruction in times of crisis, in E. Tonkin, M. McDonald and M. Chapman (eds.) *History and Ethnicity*, ASA Monograph 27: 216–31. London: Routledge.

Scribner, Sylvia 1979. Modes of thinking and ways of speaking: culture and logic reconsidered, in Roy J. Freedle (ed.) *New Directions in Discourse Processing*, Vol. II: 223–43. Norwood NJ: Ablex.

Sherzer, Joel and Woodbury, Anthony C. (eds.) 1987. *Native American Discourse*. Cambridge University Press.

Singler, John V. 1979. Verb suffixes in Klao. *Cahiers Ivoriens de Recherche Linguistique* 6: 9–32. Abidjan: Institut de Linguistique Appliquée.

Smith, Michael R. 1982. An ethnographic account of literacy in a Vai town. Ph.D, Cambridge University.

Southall, A. 1970. The illusion of tribe, in P. Gutkind (ed.) *The Passing of Tribal Man in Africa*: 28–50. Leiden: Brill.

Spender, Stephen 1980. Confessions and autobiography, in James Olney (ed.) *Autobiography: Essays Theoretical and Critical*: 115–22. Princeton University Press.

Sperber, Dan 1975. *Rethinking Symbolism* (1974) (tr. and ed. Alice L. Morton). Cambridge University Press.

Strathern, M. 1984. No culture, no history. Paper for Perception in History and Anthropology: the problem of otherness: workshop at the German Historical Institute, London.

1987. Out of context: the persuasive fictions of Anthropology. *Current Anthropology* 28.3: 251–81.

Street, Brian V. 1984. *Literacy in Theory and Practice.* Cambridge University Press.

Sullivan, Jo M. 1985. Fishers, traders and rebels: the role of the Kabor/Gbeta in the 1915 Kru Coast (Liberia) Revolt, in J. C. Stone (ed.) *Africa and the Sea*: 48–63. Aberdeen: African Studies Group

1989. The Kru coast revolt of 1915–1916. *Liberian Studies Journal* 14.1: 51–71.

Taylor, Charles 1985. The person, in M. Carrithers et al. (eds.) *The Category of the Person*: 257–81. Cambridge University Press.

Tedlock, Dennis 1983. *The Spoken Word and the Work of Interpretation.* Philadelphia: University of Pennsylvania Press.

Thompson, E. P. 1978. *The Poverty of Theory and Other Essays.* London: Merlin Press.

Thompson, Paul 1988. *The Voice of the Past.* (1978) 2nd edition. Oxford, New York: Oxford University Press.

Thompson, Paul (ed.) with Burchardt, Natasha 1982. *Our Common History: The Transformation of Europe.* London: Pluto Press.

Todorov, Tzevtan 1976. The origin of genres. *New Literary History.* 8.1: 159–70.

Tonkin, Elizabeth 1971. Some aspects of language from the viewpoint of social anthropology with particular reference to multilingual situations in Nigeria. D. Phil, Oxford University.

1978–9. Sasstown's transformation: the Jlao Kru c1888–1918. *Liberian Studies Journal* 8.1: 1–34.

1981. Model and ideology: dimensions of being civilised in Liberia, in L. Holy and M. Stuchlik (eds.) *The Structure of Folk Models*, ASA Monograph 20: 307–30. London: Academic Press.

1982a. The boundaries of history in oral performance. *History in Africa* 9: 273–84.

1982b. Rethinking socialization. *Journal of the Anthropological Society of Oxford* 13.3: 243–56.

1985. Creating Kroomen: ethnic diversity, economic specialism and changing demand, in *Africa and the Sea*: 27–47. Proceedings of a Colloquium at the University of Aberdeen, March 1984. Aberdeen University: African Studies Group.

1986. Investigating oral tradition. *Journal of African History* 27.2: 203–13.

1988a. Historical discourse: the achievement of Sieh Jeto. *History in Africa* 15: 469–91.

1988b. Cunning mysteries, in Sidney L. Kasfir (ed.) *West African Masks and Cultural Systems.* Musée Royale de l'Afrique Centrale, *Annales,* Vol. 126: Sciences Humaines: 241–52. Terveuren: Belgium.

1989. Oracy and the disguises of literacy, in Karin Barber and P. De Moraes Farias (eds.) *Discourse and its Disguises*: 39–48. Birmingham: Centre of West African Studies.

1990a. History and the myth of realism, in R. Samuel and P. Thompson (eds.) *The Myths We Live By*. Routledge. History Workshop Series.

1990b. Zik's story: autobiography as political exemplar, in P. F. de Moraes Farias and Karin Barber (eds.) *Self Assertion and Brokerage: Early Cultural Nationalism in West Africa*: 35–54. Birmingham University African Studies Series 2. West African Studies.

Tonkin, Elizabeth, McDonald, Maryon and Chapman, Malcolm (eds.) 1989. *History and Ethnicity*, ASA Monograph 27. London (and New York): Routledge.

Tosh, John 1978. *Clan Leaders and Colonial Chiefs in Lango*. Oxford: Clarendon Press.

Trevelyan, G. M. 1949. *An Autobiography and other Essays*. London: Longman.

Tyler, Stephen A. 1978. *The Said and the Unsaid*. New York, San Francisco, London: Academic Press.

Urwin, Cathy 1984. Power relations and the emergence of language, in Julian Henriques et al. *Changing the Subject*: 264–322. London and New York: Methuen.

Vansina, Jan 1965. *Oral Tradition* (1961) (tr. H. M. Wright). Harmondsworth: Penguin Books.

1971. Once upon a time: oral traditions as history in Africa. *Dedalus* 100.2: 442–68.

1978. *The Children of Woot*. Madison and Folkestone: University of Wisconsin Press and Dawson.

1983. Is elegance proof?, *History in Africa* 10: 307–48.

1985. *Oral Tradition as History*. London and Nairobi: James Currey and Heinemann.

Watters, David 1978. Speaker–hearer involvement in Kham, in J. E. Grimes (ed.) *Papers on Discourse*: 1–18. Dallas: Summer Institute of Linguistics Inc.

Welmers, William E. 1973. *African Language Structures*. Berkeley: University of California Press.

White, Hayden 1973. *Metahistory*. Baltimore: Johns Hopkins University Press.

White, Landeg 1989. Poetic licence: oral poetry and history, in K. Barber and P. F. de Moraes Farias (eds.) *Discourse and its Disguises*: 34–8. Birmingham: Centre of West African Studies.

White, Morton 1965. *The Foundations of Historical Knowledge*. New York and London: Harper & Row.

Willis, Roy 1981. *A State in the Making*. Bloomington: Indiana University Press.

1986. On being one's own grandpa: the contemporary ancestor revisited. *Journal of the Anthropological Society of Oxford* 17.3: 245–53.

Wojroh, G. T. and Broh, P. S. 1970. *A Short History of the Sasstown 'Jaoh' Tribe*. Mimeo: Jekwikpo.

Wolf, Christa 1983. *A Model Childhood* (tr. Ursula Molindro and Hedwig Rapbolt). London: Virago Press.

Wolfson, Nessa 1978. A feature of performed narrative: the conversational historic present. *Language in Society* 7: 215–37.

Yates, Francis A. 1966. *The Art of Memory*. London: Routledge & Kegan Paul.

GENERAL INDEX

aesthetics, 5, 15, 97, 131, 134, 142n
Africa, 5, 6, 13, 15, 21–2, 31, 53, 59, 63–4,
  71, 73–4, 76–7, 84–5, 93, 113, 125,
  135, 139–142n, 144n, 151–2n
Africanist historians, 15, 69, 83, 90, 122,
  125, 140n
agency, 4, 17, 34, 50, 85, 88, 98, 101, 103,
  106, 131, 134, 136, 147–148n
America, USA, and Americans, 5, 10, 13,
  21–3, 47–8, 49, 69, 73, 80, 118, 121,
  133, 138–9n, 141n, 150n
Annales writers, 73–4, 144n
anthropologists, anthropology, 1, 4, 11,
  16, 30, 32, 41–2, 54–5, 66, 74, 85–6,
  132–3, 141n, 143n, 146n, 148–9n,
  151–2n
Apache, Western, 127–8, 130, 134
Arabia, Northern, 61
Arabic, 28, 144n
art, 6, 12, 13–16, 18, 29, 37, 46–7, 49, 53,
  55, 68, 75 6, 81–2, 91, 97, 108, 136,
  138–9n, 141n
  arts of memory, 95
  artists, 27–8, 48–50, 59, 118
aspect (*see also* tense), 6, 67, 76–9
audiences, 2–4, 7, 8, 18, 28, 31, 37–8, 46–7,
  49–56, 58, 60, 62–3, 66 67, 78, 83, 87,
  90–4, 97, 116, 123, 125–6, 135–6,
  141–2n, 145n 152n
Australia and Australians, 13, 115–6, 126,
  131
authors, 4, 8–9, 17, 38–9, 49–58, 84, 93,
  108, 123, 131–2, 134–5, 137n
authorisation, 7–8, 38–9, 55, 74, 91–2, 94,
  101, 111
authority, 8, 10, 39–40, 42–3, 50, 55, 69,
  71, 90–3, 101, 114, 116, 122, 131, 133,
  137n
autobiography, 1, 43–4, 49, 55–8, 60, 66–7,
  80, 84, 132–4, 142n, 147n, 149n

Balkans, 14, 60, 143n
beliefs, 23, 34, 93, 99, 111–12, 117, 122–3,
  126, 130, 133, 135, 145n, 147n, 149n,
  152n
Benin, 5
bias, 7, 143n

Britain and the British, 5, 13, 15, 22–3, 38,
  54, 56, 63, 75, 84, 99, 118, 129, 138n,
  140–2n, 146n
British language use, 7, 13, 39, 55, 69,
  79, 180, 149n, 152n
Bunafu, 109–10
Burkina Faso, vi (map 1), 77

Catholic missions, 22, 31, 43, 71, 115
change, 4, 8, 10–12, 14, 16, 18, 22, 24–5,
  34, 47, 56, 65, 68, 72–7, 83–4, 95, 98,
  104–8, 111, 116–17, 120, 125, 133,
  138n, 141n, 144–6n, 148n
chanting, 29, 46, 51, 59, 76, 89, 142n
children, 12, 24, 28, 31–3, 70, 83, 107, 118,
  134, 145–6n, 150n, 152n
choice, 9, 28, 50, 58, 66, 68–70, 75, 86,
  99–101, 104, 106, 108, 111, 119, 128,
  137, 145n, 146n
Christianity, 22, 31–2, 43, 70–1, 102, 115,
  130, 143n, 144–5n, 152n
chronology, 30, 68–72, 76, 84, 92, 109–10,
  115, 119, 122, 144
  geochronology, 33–4, 72
civilisation and the Civilised (in Liberia),
  24–6, 29, 42, 47, 95, 139n
claim, 7–8, 38–9, 40–2, 50, 55, 58, 67, 69,
  114, 119, 130–2, 141n; *see also*
  orientation
class, 4, 12, 48, 81, 100, 102, 150n, 152n
classifications, 16, 44, 50–2, 69–70, 72, 77,
  99, 102, 110, 117, 144n
cognition, 1, 3, 11–14, 69, 75–6, 94, 97,
  99–101, 103–8, 112, 115, 117, 120,
  122, 144n, 148n, 150n
Colombia and Cumbales, 127, 134, 151n
communication, 2–3, 7, 12—13, 39, 55–6,
  67, 75—6, 78, 87—90, 108, 111,
  125–6, 129, 138–9n
conditions, material, 4–5, 12, 34, 38, 62,
  72, 95, 103, 122
  social, 11, 14–15, 47, 58–9, 61–2, 76, 87,
  98, 101, 104, 109–10, 129, 132–4, 148n
consciousness, 9–11, 26–7, 49–50, 57, 100,
  111, 115, 117–20, 125, 130–2, 134,
  136, 150n

163

INDEX OF NAMES